Readings for Writers

English 111
New Mexico State University

Bedford/St. Martin's   BOSTON ◆ NEW YORK

Contents

CONTENTS

How to Tame a Wild Tongue

Gloria Anzaldúa was born in 1942 in the Rio Grande Valley of South Texas. At age eleven she began working in the fields as a migrant worker and later worked on her family's land after the death of her father. Working her way through school, she eventually became a school-teacher and then an academic, speaking and writing about femi-nist, lesbian, and Chicana issues and about autobiography. She is best known for *This Bridge Called My Back: Writings by Radical Women of Color* (1981), which she edited with Cherríe Moraga, and *Borderlands/La Frontera: The New Mestiza* (1987).

"How to Tame a Wild Tongue" is from *Borderlands/La Frontera.* In it, Anzaldúa is concerned with many kinds of borders—between nations, cultures, classes, genders, languages. When she writes, "So, if you want to really hurt me, talk badly about my language" (par. 27), Anzaldúa is arguing for the ways in which identity is intertwined with the way we speak and for the ways in which people can be made to feel ashamed of their own tongues. Keeping hers wild—ignoring the clos-ing of linguistic borders—is Anzaldúa's way of asserting her identity.

"We're going to have to control your tongue," the dentist says, pulling out all the metal from my mouth. Silver bits plop and tinkle into the basin. My mouth is a motherlode.

The dentist is cleaning out my roots. I get a whiff of the stench when I gasp. "I can't cap that tooth yet, you're still draining," he says.

"We're going to have to do something about your tongue," I hear the anger rising in his voice. My tongue keeps pushing out the wads of cotton, pushing back the drills, the long thin needles. "I've never seen anything as strong or as stubborn," he says. And I think, how do you tame a wild tongue, train it to be quiet, how do you bridle and saddle it? How do you make it lie down?

"Who is to say that robbing a people of its language is less violent than war?" —RAY GWYN SMITH[1]

I remember being caught speaking Spanish at recess — that was good for three licks on the knuckles with a sharp ruler. I remember being sent to the corner of the classroom for "talking back" to the Anglo teacher when all I was trying to do was tell her how to pronounce my name. "If you want to be American, speak 'American.' If you don't like it, go back to Mexico where you belong."

"I want you to speak English. *Pa' hallar buen trabajo tienes que saber hablar el inglés bien. Qué vale toda tu educación si todavía hablas inglés con un 'accent,'*" my mother would say, mortified that I spoke English like a Mexican. At Pan American University, I and all Chicano students were required to take two speech classes. Their purpose: to get rid of our accents.   5

Attacks on one's form of expression with the intent to censor are a violation of the First Amendment. *El Anglo con cara de inocente nos arrancó la lengua.* Wild tongues can't be tamed, they can only be cut out.

OVERCOMING THE TRADITION OF SILENCE

> *Ahogadas, escupimos el oscuro.*
> *Peleando con nuestra propia sombra*
> *el silencio nos sepulta.*

En boca cerrada no entran moscas. "Flies don't enter a closed mouth" is a saying I kept hearing when I was a child. *Ser habladora* was to be a gossip and a liar, to talk too much. *Muchachitas bien criadas,* well-bred girls don't answer back. *Es una falta de respeto* to talk back to one's mother or father. I remember one of the sins I'd recite to the priest in the confession box the few times I went to confession: talking back to my mother, *hablar pa' 'tras, repelar. Hocicona, repelona, chismosa,* having a big mouth, questioning, carrying tales are all signs of being *mal criada.* In my culture they are all words that are derogatory if applied to women — I've never heard them applied to men.

The first time I heard two women, a Puerto Rican and a Cuban, say the word *"nosotras,"* I was shocked. I had not known the word existed. Chicanas use *nosotros* whether we're male or female. We are robbed of our female being by the masculine plural. Language is a male discourse.

> *And our tongues have become*
> *dry   the wilderness has*
> *dried out our tongues   and*
> *we have forgotten speech.*
> — IRENA KLEPFISZ[2]

2

Even our own people, other Spanish speakers *nos quieren poner can-
dados en la boca.* They would hold us back with their bag of *reglas de
academia.*

Oyé como ladra: el lenguaje de la frontera

Quien tiene boca se equivoca.
— MEXICAN SAYING

"*Pocho,* cultural traitor, you're speaking the oppressor's language by 10
speaking English, you're ruining the Spanish language," I have been accused by various Latinos and Latinas. Chicano Spanish is considered by
the purist and by most Latinos deficient, a mutilation of Spanish.

But Chicano Spanish is a border tongue which developed naturally.
Change, *evolución, enriquecimiento de palabras nuevas por invención o
adopción* have created variants of Chicano Spanish, *un nuevo lenguaje.
Un lenguaje que corresponde a un modo de vivir.* Chicano Spanish is not
incorrect, it is a living language.

For a people who are neither Spanish nor live in a country in which
Spanish is the first language; for a people who live in a country in which
English is the reigning tongue but who are not Anglo; for a people who
cannot entirely identify with either standard (formal, Castillian) Spanish
nor standard English, what recourse is left to them but to create their
own language? A language which they can connect their identity to, one
capable of communicating the realities and values true to themselves—
a language with terms that are neither *español ni inglés,* but both. We
speak a patois, a forked tongue, a variation of two languages.

Chicano Spanish sprang out of the Chicanos' need to identify ourselves as a distinct people. We needed a language with which we could
communicate with ourselves, a secret language. For some of us, language is a homeland closer than the Southwest—for many Chicanos
today live in the Midwest and the East. And because we are a complex,
heterogeneous people, we speak many languages. Some of the languages
we speak are:

1. Standard English
2. Working class and slang English
3. Standard Spanish
4. Standard Mexican Spanish
5. North Mexican Spanish dialect
6. Chicano Spanish (Texas, New Mexico, Arizona, and California
   have regional variations)
7. Tex-Mex
8. *Pachuco* (called *caló*)

My "home" tongues are the languages I speak with my sister and brothers, with my friends. They are the last five listed, with 6 and 7 being closest to my heart. From school, the media, and job situations, I've picked up standard and working class English. From Mamagrande Locha and from reading Spanish and Mexican literature, I've picked up Standard Spanish and Standard Mexican Spanish. From *los recién llegados*, Mexican immigrants, and *braceros*, I learned the North Mexican dialect. With Mexicans I'll try to speak either Standard Mexican Spanish or the North Mexican dialect. From my parents and Chicanos living in the Valley, I picked up Chicano Texas Spanish, and I speak it with my mom, younger brother (who married a Mexican and who rarely mixes Spanish with English), aunts, and older relatives.

With Chicanas from *Nuevo México* or *Arizona* I will speak Chicano 15 Spanish a little, but often they don't understand what I'm saying. With most California Chicanas I speak entirely in English (unless I forget). When I first moved to San Francisco, I'd rattle off something in Spanish, unintentionally embarrassing them. Often it is only with another Chicana *tejana* that I can talk freely.

Words distorted by English are known as anglicisms or *pochismos*. The *pocho* is an anglicized Mexican or American of Mexican origin who speaks Spanish with an accent characteristic of North Americans and who distorts and reconstructs the language according to the influence of English.[3] Tex-Mex, or Spanglish, comes most naturally to me. I may switch back and forth from English to Spanish in the same sentence or in the same word. With my sister and my brother Nune and with Chicano *tejano* contemporaries I speak in Tex-Mex.

From kids and people my own age I picked up *Pachuco. Pachuco* (the language of the zoot suiters) is a language of rebellion, both against Standard Spanish and Standard English. It is a secret language. Adults of the culture and outsiders cannot understand it. It is made up of slang words from both English and Spanish. *Ruca* means girl or woman, *vato* means guy or dude, *chale* means no, *simón* means yes, *churro* is sure, talk is *periquiar, pigionear* means petting, *que gacho* means how nerdy, *ponte águila* means watch out, death is called *la pelona*. Through lack of practice and not having others who can speak it, I've lost most of the *Pachuco* tongue.

CHICANO SPANISH

Chicanos, after 250 years of Spanish/Anglo colonization, have developed significant differences in the Spanish we speak. We collapse two adja-

4

cent vowels into a single syllable and sometimes shift the stress in certain words such as *maíz/maiz, cohete/cuete.* We leave out certain consonants when they appear between vowels: *lado/ lao, mojado/mojao.* Chicanos from South Texas pronounce *f* as *j* as in *jue (fue).* Chicanos use "archaisms," words that are no longer in the Spanish language, words that have been evolved out. We say *semos, truje, haiga, ansina,* and *naiden.* We retain the "archaic" *j,* as in *jalar,* that derives from an earlier *h,* (the French *halar* or the Germanic *halon* which was lost to standard Spanish in the 16th century), but which is still found in several regional dialects such as the one spoken in South Texas. (Due to geography, Chicanos from the Valley of South Texas were cut off linguistically from other Spanish speakers. We tend to use words that the Spaniards brought over from Medieval Spain. The majority of the Spanish colonizers in Mexico and the Southwest came from Extremadura—Hernán Cortés was one of them—and Andalucía. Andalucians pronounce *ll* like a *y,* and their *d*'s tend to be absorbed by adjacent vowels: *tirado* becomes *tirao.* They brought *el lenguaje popular, dialectos y regionalismos.*[4])

Chicanos and other Spanish speakers also shift *ll* to *y* and *z* to *s.*[5] We leave out initial syllables, saying *tar* for *estar, toy* for *estoy, hora* for *ahora* (*cubanos* and *puertorriqueños* also leave out initial letters of some words). We also leave out the final syllable such as *pa* for *para.* The intervocalic *y,* the *ll* as in *tortilla, ella, botella,* gets replaced by *tortia* or *tortiya, ea, botea.* We add an additional syllable at the beginning of certain words: *atocar* for *tocar, agastar* for *gastar.* Sometimes we'll say *lavaste las vacijas,* other times *lavates* (substituting the *ates* verb endings for the *aste*).

We use anglicisms, words borrowed from English: *bola* from ball, *car-* 20 *peta* from carpet, *máchina de lavar* (instead of *lavadora*) from washing machine. Tex-Mex argot, created by adding a Spanish sound at the beginning or end of an English word such as *cookiar* for cook, *watchar* for watch, *parkiar* for park, and *rapiar* for rape, is the result of the pressures on Spanish speakers to adapt to English.

We don't use the word *vosotros/as* or its accompanying verb form. We don't say *claro* (to mean yes), *imagínate,* or *me emociona,* unless we picked up Spanish from Latinas, out of a book, or in a classroom. Other Spanish-speaking groups are going through the same, or similar, development in their Spanish.

LINGUISTIC TERRORISM

Deslenguadas. Somos los del español deficiente. We are your linguistic nightmare, your linguistic aberration, your linguistic *mestisaje,* the subject of your *burla.* Because we speak with tongues of fire we are culturally

5

crucified. Racially, culturally, and linguistically *somos huérfanos* — we speak an orphan tongue.

Chicanas who grew up speaking Chicano Spanish have internalized the belief that we speak poor Spanish. It is illegitimate, a bastard language. And because we internalize how our language has been used against us by the dominant culture, we use our language differences against each other.

Chicana feminists often skirt around each other with suspicion and hesitation. For the longest time I couldn't figure it out. Then it dawned on me. To be close to another Chicana is like looking into the mirror. We are afraid of what we'll see there. *Pena.* Shame. Low estimation of self. In childhood we are told that our language is wrong. Repeated attacks on our native tongue diminish our sense of self. The attacks continue throughout our lives.

Chicanas feel uncomfortable talking in Spanish to Latinas, afraid of their censure. Their language was not outlawed in their countries. They had a whole lifetime of being immersed in their native tongue; generations, centuries in which Spanish was a first language, taught in school, heard on radio and TV, and read in the newspaper.

If a person, Chicana or Latina, has a low estimation of my native tongue, she also has a low estimation of me. Often with *mexicanas y latinas* we'll speak English as a neutral language. Even among Chicanas we tend to speak English at parties or conferences. Yet, at the same time, we're afraid the other will think we're *agringadas* because we don't speak Chicano Spanish. We oppress each other trying to out-Chicano each other, vying to be the "real" Chicanas, to speak like Chicanos. There is no one Chicano language just as there is no one Chicano experience. A monolingual Chicana whose first language is English or Spanish is just as much a Chicana as one who speaks several variants of Spanish. A Chicana from Michigan or Chicago or Detroit is just as much a Chicana as one from the Southwest. Chicano Spanish is as diverse linguistically as it is regionally.

By the end of this century, Spanish speakers will comprise the biggest minority group in the U.S., a country where students in high schools and colleges are encouraged to take French classes because French is considered more "cultured." But for a language to remain alive it must be used.[6] By the end of this century English, and not Spanish, will be the mother tongue of most Chicanos and Latinos.

So, if you want to really hurt me, talk badly about my language. Ethnic identity is twin skin to linguistic identity — I am my language. Until I can take pride in my language, I cannot take pride in myself.

6

Until I can accept as legitimate Chicano Texas Spanish, Tex-Mex, and all the other languages I speak, I cannot accept the legitimacy of myself. Until I am free to write bilingually and to switch codes without having always to translate, while I still have to speak English or Spanish when I would rather speak Spanglish, and as long as I have to accommodate the English speakers rather than having them accommodate me, my tongue will be illegitimate.

I will no longer be made to feel ashamed of existing. I will have my voice: Indian, Spanish, white. I will have my serpent's tongue—my woman's voice, my sexual voice, my poet's voice. I will overcome the tradition of silence.

> *My fingers*
> *move sly against your palm*
> *Like women everywhere, we speak in code. . . .*
> —MELANIE KAYE/KANTROWITZ[7]

"Vistas," corridos, y comida: My Native Tongue

In the 1960s, I read my first Chicano novel. It was *City of Night* by John Rechy, a gay Texan, son of a Scottish father and a Mexican mother. For days I walked around in stunned amazement that a Chicano could write and could get published. When I read *I Am Joaquín*[8] I was surprised to see a bilingual book by a Chicano in print. When I saw poetry written in Tex-Mex for the first time, a feeling of pure joy flashed through me. I felt like we really existed as a people. In 1971, when I started teaching High School English to Chicano students, I tried to supplement the required texts with works by Chicanos, only to be reprimanded and forbidden to do so by the principal. He claimed that I was supposed to teach "American" and English literature. At the risk of being fired, I swore my students to secrecy and slipped in Chicano short stories, poems, a play. In graduate school, while working toward a Ph.D., I had to "argue" with one advisor after the other, semester after semester, before I was allowed to make Chicano literature an area of focus.

Even before I read books by Chicanos or Mexicans, it was the Mexican 30 movies I saw at the drive-in—the Thursday night special of $1.00 a carload—that gave me a sense of belonging. *"Vámonos a las vistas,"* my mother would call out and we'd all—grandmother, brothers, sister, and cousins—squeeze into the car. We'd wolf down cheese and bologna white bread sandwiches while watching Pedro Infante in melodramatic tearjerkers like *Nosotros los pobres*, the first "real" Mexican movie (that was not an imitation of European movies). I remember seeing *Cuando los hijos se van* and surmising that all Mexican movies played up the love a mother has for her children and what ungrateful sons and daughters suffer when they are not devoted to their mothers. I remember the singing-type "westerns" of Jorge Negrete and Miguel Aceves Mejía. When watching Mexican movies, I felt a sense of homecoming as well as alienation. People who were to amount to something didn't go to Mexican movies, or *bailes*, or tune their radios to *bolero*, *rancherita*, and *corrido* music.

The whole time I was growing up, there was *norteño* music sometimes called North Mexican border music, or Tex-Mex music, or Chicano music, or *cantina* (bar) music. I grew up listening to *conjuntos*, three- or four-piece bands made up of folk musicians playing guitar, *bajo sexto*, drums, and button accordion, which Chicanos had borrowed from the German immigrants who had come to Central Texas and Mexico to farm and build breweries. In the Rio Grande Valley, Steve Jordan and Little Joe Hernández were popular, and Flaco Jiménez was the accordion king. The rhythms of Tex-Mex music are those of the polka, also adapted from the Germans, who in turn had borrowed the polka from the Czechs and Bohemians.

I remember the hot, sultry evenings when *corridos* — songs of love and death on the Texas-Mexican borderlands — reverberated out of cheap amplifiers from the local *cantinas* and wafted in through my bedroom window.

Corridos first became widely used along the South Texas/Mexican border during the early conflict between Chicanos and Anglos. The *corridos* are usually about Mexican heroes who do valiant deeds against the Anglo oppressors. Pancho Villa's song, *"La cucaracha,"* is the most famous one. *Corridos* of John F. Kennedy and his death are still very popular in the Valley. Older Chicanos remember Lydia Mendoza, one of the great border *corrido* singers who was called *la Gloria de Tejas*. Her *"El tango negro,"* sung during the Great Depression, made her a singer of the people. The everpresent *corridos* narrated one hundred years of border history, bringing news of events as well as entertaining. These folk musicians and folk songs are our chief cultural mythmakers, and they made our hard lives seem bearable.

I grew up feeling ambivalent about our music. Country-western and rock-and-roll had more status. In the 50s and 60s, for the slightly educated and *agringado* Chicanos, there existed a sense of shame at being caught listening to our music. Yet I couldn't stop my feet from thumping to the music, could not stop humming the words, nor hide from myself the exhilaration I felt when I heard it.

There are more subtle ways that we internalize identification, espe- 35 cially in the forms of images and emotions. For me food and certain

8

smells are tied to my identity, to my homeland. Woodsmoke curling up to an immense blue sky; woodsmoke perfuming my grandmother's clothes, her skin. The stench of cow manure and the yellow patches on the ground; the crack of a .22 rifle and the reek of cordite. Homemade white cheese sizzling in a pan, melting inside a folded *tortilla*. My sister Hilda's hot, spicy *menudo, chile colorado* making it deep red, pieces of *panza* and hominy floating on top. My brother Carito barbequing *fajitas* in the backyard. Even now and 3,000 miles away, I can see my mother spicing the ground beef, pork, and venison with *chile*. My mouth salivates at the thought of the hot steaming *tamales* I would be eating if I were home.

Si le preguntas a mi mamá, "¿Qué eres?"

"Identity is the essential core of who we are as individuals, the conscious experience of the self inside."
—GERSHEN KAUFMAN[9]

Nosotros los Chicanos straddle the borderlands. On one side of us, we are constantly exposed to the Spanish of the Mexicans, on the other side we hear the Anglos' incessant clamoring so that we forget our language. Among ourselves we don't say *nosotros los americanos, o nosotros los españoles, o nosotros los hispanos.* We say *nosotros los mexicanos* (by *mexicanos* we do not mean citizens of Mexico; we do not mean a national identity, but a racial one). We distinguish between *mexicanos del otro lado* and *mexicanos de este lado.* Deep in our hearts we believe that being Mexican has nothing to do with which country one lives in. Being Mexican is a state of soul—not one of mind, not one of citizenship. Neither eagle nor serpent, but both. And like the ocean, neither animal respects borders.

Dime con quien andas y te diré quien eres.
(Tell me who your friends are and I'll tell you who you are.)
—MEXICAN SAYING

Si le preguntas a mi mamá, "¿Qué eres?" te dirá, *"Soy mexicana."* My brothers and sister say the same. I sometimes will answer *"soy mexicana"* and at others will say *"soy Chicana" o "soy tejana."* But I identified as *"Raza"* before I ever identified as *"mexicana"* or "Chicana."

As a culture, we call ourselves Spanish when referring to ourselves as a linguistic group and when copping out. It is then that we forget our predominant Indian genes. We are 70–80 percent Indian.[10] We call ourselves Hispanic[11] or Spanish-American or Latin American or Latin when

9

linking ourselves to other Spanish-speaking peoples of the Western hemisphere and when copping out. We call ourselves Mexican-American[12] to signify we are neither Mexican nor American, but more the noun "American" than the adjective "Mexican" (and when copping out).

Chicanos and other people of color suffer economically for not acculturating. This voluntary (yet forced) alienation makes for psychological conflict, a kind of dual identity—we don't identify with the Anglo-American cultural values and we don't totally identify with the Mexican cultural values. We are a synergy of two cultures with various degrees of Mexicanness or Angloness. I have so internalized the borderland conflict that sometimes I feel like one cancels out the other and we are zero, nothing, no one. *A veces no soy nada ni nadie. Pero hasta cuando no lo soy, lo soy.*

When not copping out, when we know we are more than nothing, we call ourselves Mexican, referring to race and ancestry; *mestizo* when affirming both our Indian and Spanish (but we hardly ever own our Black ancestry); Chicano when referring to a politically aware people born and/or raised in the U.S.; *Raza* when referring to Chicanos; *tejanos* when we are Chicanos from Texas. 40

Chicanos did not know we were a people until 1965 when Ceasar Chavez and the farmworkers united and *I Am Joaquín* was published and *la Raza Unida* party was formed in Texas. With that recognition, we became a distinct people. Something momentous happened to the Chicano soul—we became aware of our reality and acquired a name and a language (Chicano Spanish) that reflected that reality. Now that we had a name, some of the fragmented pieces began to fall together—who we were, what we were, how we had evolved. We began to get glimpses of what we might eventually become.

Yet the struggle of identities continues, the struggle of borders is our reality still. One day the inner struggle will cease and a true integration take place. In the meantime, *tenémos que hacer la lucha. ¿Quién está protegiendo los ranchos de mi gente? ¿Quién está tratando de cerrar la fisura entre la india y el blanco en nuestra sangre? El Chicano, si, el Chicano que anda como un ladrón en su propia casa.*

Los Chicanos, how patient we seem, how very patient. There is the quiet of the Indian about us.[13] We know how to survive. When other races have given up their tongue, we've kept ours. We know what it is to live under the hammer blow of the dominant *norteamericano* culture. But more than we count the blows, we count the days the weeks the years the centuries the eons until the white laws and commerce and customs will rot in the deserts they've created, lie bleached. *Humildes* yet proud, *quietos* yet wild, *nosotros los mexicanos-Chicanos* will walk by the crumbling ashes as we go about our business. Stubborn, persevering, impenetrable as stone, yet possessing a malleability that renders us unbreakable, we, the *mestizas* and *mestizos*, will remain.

Notes

1. Ray Gwyn Smith, *Moorland Is Cold Country*, unpublished book.

2. Irena Klepfisz, "*Di rayze aheym*/The Journey Home," in *The Tribe of Dina: A Jewish Women's Anthology*, Melanie Kaye/Kantrowitz and Irena Klepfisz, eds. (Montpelier, VT: Sinister Wisdom Books, 1986), 49.

3. R. C. Ortega, *Dialectología Del Barrio*, trans. Hortencia S. Alwan (Los Angeles, CA: R. C. Ortega Publisher & Bookseller, 1977), 132.

4. Eduardo Hernandéz-Chávez, Andrew D. Cohen, and Anthony F. Beltramo, *El Lenguaje de los Chicanos: Regional and Social Characteristics of Language Used by Mexican Americans* (Arlington, VA: Center for Applied Linguistics, 1975), 39.

5. Hernandéz-Chávez, xvii.

6. Irena Klepfisz, "Secular Jewish Identity: Yidishkayt in America," in *The Tribe of Dina*, Kaye/Kantrowitz and Klepfisz, eds., 43.

7. Melanie Kaye/Kantrowitz, "Sign," in *We Speak in Code: Poems and Other Writings* (Pittsburgh, PA: Motheroot Publications, Inc., 1980), 85.

8. Rodolfo Gonzales, *I Am Joaquín/Yo Soy Joaquín* (New York, NY: Bantam Books, 1972). It was first published in 1967.

9. Gershen Kaufman, *Shame: The Power of Caring* (Cambridge, MA: Schenkman Books, Inc., 1980), 68.

10. John R. Chávez, *The Lost Land: The Chicano Images of the Southwest* (Albuquerque, NM: University of New Mexico Press, 1984), 88–90.

11. "Hispanic" is derived from *Hispanis* (*España*, a name given to the Iberian Peninsula in ancient times when it was a part of the Roman Empire) and is a term designated by the U.S. government to make it easier to handle us on paper.

12. The Treaty of Guadalupe Hidalgo created the Mexican-American in 1848.

13. Anglos, in order to alleviate their guilt for dispossessing the Chicano, stressed the Spanish part of us and perpetrated the myth of the Spanish Southwest. We have accepted the fiction that we are Hispanic, that is Spanish, in order to accommodate ourselves to the dominant culture and its abhorrence of Indians. Chávez, 88–91.

[1987]

11

LEE ANN FISHER BARON

The Influence of "Junk Science" and the Role of Science Education

Lee Ann Fisher Baron graduated with a B.A. from Wittenberg University in 1977 and an M.S. and Ph.D. from the University of Michigan in 1979 and 1984, respectively. She is currently the Savona Professor of Natural Sciences and Professor of Chemistry at Hillsdale College, where she has been teaching since 1989. A pioneer in science education, Baron has developed science programs intended to attract middle-school girls to futures in scientific fields, study guides for high school summer science camps, and science curricula for elementary schools. She has been honored with numerous awards for teaching, including an Emily Daugherty Award for Teaching Excellence, a Lubrizol Award, a Paul F. Bagley Fellowship, and a Dow Chemical Foundation Fellowship, along with membership in the Phi Lambda Upsilon and Sigma Zeta Honorary societies and the American Chemical Society. Baron earned acclaimed recognition in the 2000 edition of *Who's Who among America's Teachers*.

Baron's "The Influence of 'Junk Science' and the Role of Science Education," first published in *Imprimis*, the monthly journal of Hillsdale College, mourns the failure of the American educational system to maintain high standards in science instruction. Baron criticizes the food industry and homeopathists for knowingly misleading "unwary consumers" who buy into the claims of "junk science." More emphatically, however, she stresses the necessity for all citizens to possess a working knowledge of the scientific method in order to make wise choices regarding their physical health.

Science is exciting partly because single discoveries can change the course of history. Think of the effects on human health and longevity of the discovery of antibiotics, the multi-faceted impact on our lives of the discovery of polymers, or the far-reaching importance of the Human

Genome Project. Unfortunately, however, most of the "revolutionary discoveries" made throughout history have turned out to be wrong.

Error is a regular part of science. That is why reports of new findings or discoveries, no matter where or how widely they are reported, should be regarded with healthy skepticism. The proper scientific approach to such claims involves a set of procedures called the scientific method. This method requires the design of tests or experiments that can be repeated with the same results by anyone. These tests must also contain controls to ensure that the results are statistically significant.

Let me illustrate the importance of controls by describing briefly an experiment in which my daughter participated as a subject some years ago at the University of Michigan Medical School. Its purpose was to determine whether the vaccine for tuberculosis could lengthen the interval during which newly-diagnosed type 1 diabetics do not experience severe high or low blood sugar. The subjects were divided into a group of those who received the vaccine and a control group of those who received a placebo. The subjects did not know who got the vaccine and, just as importantly, neither did the researchers—a type of control referred to as a "double-blind." By using two groups, the researchers were able to measure the "placebo effect"—a phenomenon in which patients improve because they falsely believe that they are receiving medicine. And by keeping themselves ignorant of the breakdown of the groups, the researchers were prevented from reading their hypotheses into the results.

"JUNK SCIENCE"

Most erroneous conclusions by scientists are discovered during the process of publishing their research. Other scientists review submitted articles, often repeating any relevant tests or experiments and always evaluating the conclusions that have been drawn from them. So-called "junk science" bypasses this system of peer review. Presented directly to the public by people variously described as "experts" or "activists," often with little or no supporting evidence, this "junk science" undermines the ability of elected representatives, jurists, and others—including everyday consumers—to make rational decisions.

An example of "junk science" I like to use with my students is the myth of "fat-free foods" invented by the food industry with the help of federal regulators. By regulatory definition, these foods may contain monoglycerides and diglycerides, but not triglycerides. From the point of view of solid science this definition makes no practical sense, given that the body metabolizes mono-, di- and triglycerides in essentially the same

5

way. Meanwhile unwary consumers take the "fat-free" label as a license to eat these foods to excess, and Americans are more obese now than ever before.

A more amusing example is "Vitamin O," a wonder supplement advertised to "maximize your nutrients, purify your blood stream, and eliminate toxins and poisons—in other words, [to supply] all the processes necessary to prevent disease and promote health." It was described on its label as "stabilized oxygen molecules in a solution of distilled water and sodium chloride." In other words, the 60,000 consumers purchasing "Vitamin O"—to the tune of $20 a month—were taking salt water! Although this product was legally exempted from certain FDA requirements by virtue of its status as a "natural" diet supplement, the FTC was able to file a complaint against it in 1999, based on false claims by its promoters that it was being used by NASA astronauts. Otherwise "Vitamin O" would still be one of the world's best-selling placebos.

The potential lasting power of "junk science" is demonstrated by the story of German physician Samuel Hahnemann, who took quinine back in 1776 to investigate its use against malaria. After taking the quinine he experienced chills and fever, which are the symptoms of malaria. For this he concluded, wrongly, that "likes cure likes," i.e., that diseases should be treated with medicines that produce similar symptoms to the diseases. In the course of testing this theory with other herbal remedies, Hahnemann discovered that many "natural" herbs are toxic and made his patients worse. To reduce the toxic effects, he diluted the remedies until they seemed to be working. On that basis he formulated a "law of infinitesimals" stating that higher dilutions of herbal cures increase their medicinal benefits. To be fair, Hahnemann conducted these experiments more than 70 years before scientists understood that a dilution weaker than one part in 6.02×10^{23} may not contain even a single molecule of the dissolved substance. Thus he did not realize that upon administering to his patients 30x preparations—dilutions of one part herb to 10^{30} parts water—the placebo effect was all that was really left to measure.

Incredibly, homeopathic medicine today still relies on Hahnemann's theories. Not only does it often come in 30x preparations, it comes in 200c dilutions—solutions of one part herb to 100 parts of water 200 times, resulting in one molecule of the herb per 10^{400} molecules of water! Modern homeopathists obviously can't deny that such preparations are beyond the dilution limit, but they insist that the dilutions still work because their water or alcohol/water mixtures somehow "remember" the herbs. Despite this preposterous claim, the market for these remedies is enormous.

Just as many homeopathic preparations are diluted to the point that they are nothing but water, many "natural" herbs on the market contain drugs and chemicals which interact with the human body like prescription drugs. For example, Echinacea stimulates the immune system, which could prove harmful to people with type 1 diabetes, rheumatoid arthritis, or other autoimmune diseases. It is therefore unwise—to put it gently—to take herbal remedies or supplements of any kind without consulting a doctor and/or the *Physician's Desk Reference for Herbal Medicines*. But many Americans do so, equating "natural" with "harmless" and "good."

CAUSE AND SOLUTION

I have addressed here the corrupting influence of "junk science" in the   10
area of consumer foods, vitamins and diet supplements. The same dynamic increasingly affects other aspects of our individual and collective lives as well. But I believe the root cause is the same: Americans are losing the common-sense skepticism toward scientific claims that animates the scientific method itself. And one of the reasons for this is a slow but steady degradation of our educational system. In short, as Charles J. Sykes explains in *Dumbing Down Our Kids*, theories such as "outcome-based education," "cooperative learning," and "maximization of self-esteem" are fast replacing reading, writing, and arithmetic as the goals of education.

Anecdotal evidence of this trend is vast and compelling. For instance, when average SAT math scores fell from 500 to 424, the College Board responded by allowing the use of calculators. When that didn't work, they "recentered" the test by adding approximately 20 points to the math scores (while also adding 80 points on the verbal side, for a total of 100), regardless of achievement. At the state level, many high school competency exams are written at an eighth-grade level. And coloring for credit in elementary-level math classes is now fairly common. Is it any wonder that so many of the kids we now graduate from high school enter the workforce unable to add in their heads or make correct change, or arrive at college incapable of solving the simplest equations?

The situation is no better in the sciences. Students at a Seattle middle school spend two weeks studying the eating habits of birds by trying to pick up Cheerios with tongue depressors, toothpicks, spoons, and clothespins between their teeth. "Educationalists" call this creative and engaging. But it doesn't create useful or important knowledge. And surely it is not true that such activity is more engaging than learning about Newton's Laws or DNA.

A popular high school chemistry book moves from "Supplying Our Water Needs," which includes a discussion of acid rain, to "Chemistry

15

and the Atmosphere," which addresses the ozone layer. This approach would not be all bad if the chemistry behind these issues was rigorously taught and if important topics unrelated to social controversies were also included. Unfortunately they are not. When I called the American Chemical Society—which, sadly, produced this textbook—one of those responsible justified its approach by pointing out that most high school graduates don't pursue science in college. Furthermore, he said, students introduced to chemistry in this way enjoy it more and find it easier to handle, resulting in higher self-esteem. I asked if it had occurred to him that perhaps students don't pursue college science because they don't obtain the requisite skills or knowledge in high school. Regardless, when the American Chemical Society endorses a high school science text that doesn't even list the scientific method in its index, we shouldn't be surprised that so many Americans gorge themselves on "fat-free foods," throw their money at "Vitamin O," or risk their health by taking "natural" herbs without investigating their effects.

The solution to the problem I have outlined is easy to see, and is by no means impossible to accomplish. Individually, we must be careful to take our bearings from the scientific method when confronted with scientific claims, employing healthy skepticism and asking questions before believing what we hear or read. Together, we must work diligently to revive real standards in primary and secondary science education.

PETER ELBOW [b. 1935]

Freewriting

Peter Elbow received his Ph.D. from Brandeis University in 1969. He has taught at several universities, including M.I.T., the University of Massachusetts at Amherst, and SUNY at Stony Brook, where he directed the writing program. Having experienced the inability to write as a graduate student, he has since written widely on the writing process. Often attempting to demystify the process, Elbow offers practical advice on achieving one's writing goals, tackling such issues as writer's block, freewriting, and, for instructors, teaching and evaluating writing. His most well-known books include *Writing With Power: Techniques for Mastering the Writing Process* (1981), *Embracing Contraries: Essays on Learning and Teaching* (1986), *What Is English?* (1990), and, most recently, *Being a Writer* (2002).

The essay "Freewriting" is taken from Elbow's revolutionary work *Writing Without Teachers* (1973) and discusses the rules of freewriting, which amount to not stopping and not editing as you go. Editing is good to do once a piece of writing has been produced, but editing while producing kills the writer's unique voice.

The most effective way I know to improve your writing is to do freewriting exercises regularly. At least three times a week. They are sometimes called "automatic writing," "babbling," or "jabbering" exercises. The idea is simply to write for ten minutes (later on, perhaps fifteen or twenty). Don't stop for anything. Go quickly without rushing. Never stop to look back, to cross something out, to wonder how to spell something, to wonder what word or thought to use, or to think about what you are doing. If you can't think of a word or a spelling, just use a squiggle or else write, "I can't think of it." Just put down something. The easiest thing is just to put down whatever is in your mind. If you get stuck it's fine to write "I can't think what to say, I can't think what to say" as many times as you want; or to repeat the last word you wrote over and over again; or anything else. The only requirement is that you *never* stop.

What happens to a freewriting exercise is important. It must be a piece of writing which, even if someone reads it, doesn't send any ripples back to you. It is like writing something and putting it in a bottle in the sea. The teacherless class helps your writing by providing maximum feedback. Freewritings help you by providing no feedback at all. When I assign one, I invite the writer to let me read it. But I also tell him to keep it if he prefers. I read it quickly and make no comments at all and I do not speak with him about it. The main thing is that a freewriting must never be evaluated in any way; in fact there must be no discussion or comment at all.

Here is an example of a fairly coherent exercise (sometimes they are very incoherent, which is fine):

I think I'll write what's on my mind, but the only thing on my mind right now is what to write for ten minutes. I've never done this before and I'm not prepared in any way—the sky is cloudy today, how's that? now I'm afraid I won't be able to think of what to write when I get to the end of the sentence—well, here I am at the end of the sentence—here I am again, again, again, at least I'm still writing—Now I ask is there some reason to be happy that I'm still writing—ah yes! Here comes the question again — What am I getting out of this? What point is there in it? It's almost obscene to always ask it but I seem to question everything that way and I was gonna say something else pertaining to that but I got so busy writing down the first part that I forgot what I was leading into. This is kind of fun oh don't stop writing—cars and trucks speeding by somewhere out the window, pens clittering across peoples' papers. The sky is still cloudy—is it symbolic that I should be mentioning it? Huh? I dunno. Maybe I should try colors, blue, red, dirty words—wait a minute—no can't do that, orange, yellow, arm tired, green pink violet magenta lavender red brown black green—now that I can't think of any more colors—just about done—relief? maybe.

Freewriting may seem crazy but actually it makes simple sense. Think of the difference between speaking and writing. Writing has the advantage of permitting more editing. But that's its downfall too. Almost everybody interposes a massive and complicated series of editings between the time words start to be born into consciousness and when they finally come off the end of the pencil or typewriter onto the page. This is partly because schooling makes us obsessed with the "mistakes" we make in writing. Many people are constantly thinking about spelling and grammar as they try to write. I am always thinking about the awkwardness, wordiness, and general mushiness of my natural verbal product as I try to write down words.

18

But it's not just "mistakes" or "bad writing" we edit as we write. We 5
also edit unacceptable thoughts and feelings, as we do in speaking. In
writing there is more time to do it so the editing is heavier: when speaking, there's someone right there waiting for a reply and he'll get bored or
think we're crazy if we don't come out with *something*. Most of the time
in speaking, we settle for the catch-as-catch-can way in which the words
tumble out. In writing, however, there's a chance to try to get them right.
But the opportunity to get them right is a terrible burden: you can work
for two hours trying to get a paragraph "right" and discover it's not right
at all. And then give up.

Editing, *in itself*, is not the problem. Editing is usually necessary if we
want to end up with something satisfactory. The problem is that editing
goes on *at the same time* as producing. The editor is, as it were, constantly looking over the shoulder of the producer and constantly fiddling
with what he's doing while he's in the middle of trying to do it. No wonder the producer gets nervous, jumpy, inhibited, and finally can't be
coherent. It's an unnecessary burden to try to think of words and also
worry at the same time whether they're the right words.

The main thing about freewriting is that it is *nonediting*. It is an exercise in bringing together the process of producing words and putting
them down on the page. Practiced regularly, it undoes the ingrained
habit of editing at the same time you are trying to produce. It will make
writing less blocked because words will come more easily. You will use
up more paper, but chew up fewer pencils.

Next time you write, notice how often you stop yourself from writing
down something you were going to write down. Or else cross it out after
it's written. "Naturally," you say, "it wasn't any good." But think for a
moment about the occasions when you spoke well. Seldom was it
because you first got the beginning just right. Usually it was a matter of a
halting or even garbled beginning, but you kept going and your speech
finally became coherent and even powerful. There is a lesson here for
writing: trying to get the beginning just right is a formula for failure—
and probably a secret tactic to make yourself give up writing. Make
some words, whatever they are, and then grab hold of that line and reel
in as hard as you can. Afterwards you can throw away lousy beginnings
and make new ones. This is the quickest way to get into good writing.

The habit of compulsive, premature editing doesn't just make writing
hard. It also makes writing dead. Your voice is damped out by all the
interruptions, changes, and hesitations between the consciousness and
the page. In your natural way of producing words there is a sound, a tex-
ture, a rhythm—a voice—which is the main source of power in your
writing. I don't know how it works, but this voice is the force that will
make a reader listen to you, the energy that drives the meanings through

19

his thick skull. Maybe you don't *like* your voice; maybe people have made fun of it. But it's the only voice you've got. It's your only source of power. You better get back into it, no matter what you think of it. If you keep writing in it, it may change into something you like better. But if you abandon it, you'll likely never have a voice and never be heard.

Freewritings are vacuums. Gradually you will begin to carry over into 10 your regular writing some of the voice, force, and connectedness that creep into those vacuums.

FREDERICK DOUGLASS [1818–1895]

Learning to Read and Write

Frederick Douglass was born a slave in 1818 in Maryland. He learned to read and write, escaped to New York, and became a leader in the abolitionist movement. He engaged in speaking tours and edited North Star, a newspaper named for the one guide escaping southern slaves could rely on to find their way to freedom. Douglass is best known for his autobiography, *Narrative of the Life of Frederick Douglass* (1845), from which "Learning to Read and Write" is excerpted. In this selection, Douglass tells the story of his coming to literacy. As you read, keep your eye on the ways in which Douglass describes the world opening up for him as he learns his letters and the range of emotions this process evokes in him.

I lived in Master Hugh's family about seven years. During this time, I succeeded in learning to read and write. In accomplishing this, I was compelled to resort to various stratagems. I had no regular teacher. My mistress, who had kindly commenced to instruct me, had, in compliance with the advice and direction of her husband, not only ceased to instruct, but had set her face against my being instructed by any one else. It is due, however, to my mistress to say of her, that she did not adopt this course of treatment immediately. She at first lacked the depravity indispensable to shutting me up in mental darkness. It was at least necessary for her to have some training in the exercise of irresponsible power, to make her equal to the task of treating me as though I were a brute.

My mistress was, as I have said, a kind and tender-hearted woman; and in the simplicity of her soul she commenced, when I first went to live with her, to treat me as she supposed one human being ought to treat another. In entering upon the duties of a slaveholder, she did not seem to perceive that I sustained to her the relation of a mere chattel, and that for her to treat me as a human being was not only wrong, but dangerously so. Slavery proved as injurious to her as it did to me. When I went there, she was a pious, warm, and tender-hearted woman. There was no sorrow or suffering for which she had not a tear. She had bread for the hungry, clothes for the naked, and comfort for every mourner that came within her reach. Slavery soon proved its ability to divest her of these heavenly qualities. Under its influence, the tender heart became stone, and the lamb-like disposition gave way to one of tiger-like fierce-ness. The first step in her downward course was in her ceasing to in-struct me. She now commenced to practise her husband's precepts. She finally became even more violent in her opposition than her husband himself. She was not satisfied with simply doing as well as he had com-manded; she seemed anxious to do better. Nothing seemed to make her more angry than to see me with a newspaper. She seemed to think that here lay the danger. I have had her rush at me with a face made all up of fury, and snatch from me a newspaper, in a manner that fully re-vealed her apprehension. She was an apt woman; and a little experience soon demonstrated, to her satisfaction, that education and slavery were incompatible with each other.

From this time I was most narrowly watched. If I was in a separate room any considerable length of time, I was sure to be suspected of hav-ing a book, and was at once called to give an account of myself. All this, however, was too late. The first step had been taken. Mistress, in teach-ing me the alphabet, had given me the *inch*, and no precaution could prevent me from taking the *ell*.

The plan which I adopted, and the one by which I was most success-ful, was that of making friends of all the little white boys whom I met in the street. As many of these as I could, I converted into teachers. With their kindly aid, obtained at different times and in different places, I fi-nally succeeded in learning to read. When I was sent of errands, I always took my book with me, and by going one part of my errand quickly, I found time to get a lesson before my return. I used also to carry bread with me, enough of which was always in the house, and to which I was always welcome; for I was much better off in this regard than many of the poor white children in our neighborhood. This bread I used to be-stow upon the hungry little urchins, who, in return, would give me that more valuable bread of knowledge. I am strongly tempted to give the names of two or three of those little boys, as a testimonial of the grati-tude and affection I bear them; but prudence forbids:—not that it would injure me, but it might embarrass them; for it is almost an unpardonable offence to teach slaves to read in this Christian country. It is enough to say of the dear little fellows, that they lived on Philpot Street, very near Durgin and Bailey's ship-yard. I used to talk this matter of slavery over with them. I would sometimes say to them, I wished I could be as free as they would be when they got to be men. "You will be free as soon as you are twenty-one, *but I am a slave for life*! Have not I as good a right to be free as you have?" These words used to trouble them; they would express for me the liveliest sympathy, and console me with the hope that some-thing would occur by which I might be free.

I was now about twelve years old, and the thought of being *a slave for* 5

22

life began to bear heavily upon my heart. Just about this time, I got hold of a book entitled "The Columbian Orator." Every opportunity I got, I used to read this book. Among much of other interesting matter, I found in it a dialogue between a master and his slave. The slave was represented as having run away from his master three times. The dialogue represented the conversation which took place between them, when the slave was retaken the third time. In this dialogue, the whole argument in behalf of slavery was brought forward by the master, all of which was disposed of by the slave. The slave was made to say some very smart as well as impressive things in reply to his master — things which had the desired though unexpected effect; for the conversation resulted in the voluntary emancipation of the slave on the part of the master.

In the same book, I met with one of Sheridan's mighty speeches on and in behalf of Catholic emancipation. These were choice documents to me. I read them over and over again with unabated interest. They gave tongue to interesting thoughts of my own soul, which had frequently lashed through my mind, and died away for want of utterance. The moral which I gained from the dialogue was the power of truth over the conscience of even a slaveholder. What I got from Sheridan was a bold denunciation of slavery, and a powerful vindication of human rights. The reading of these documents enabled me to utter my thoughts, and to meet the arguments brought forward to sustain slavery; but while they relieved me of one difficulty, they brought on another even more painful than the one of which I was relieved. The more I read, the more I was led to abhor and detest my enslavers. I could regard them in no other light than a band of successful robbers, who had left their homes, and gone to Africa, and stolen us from our homes, and in a strange land reduced us to slavery. I loathed them as being the meanest as well as the most wicked of men. As I read and contemplated the subject, behold! that very discontentment which Master Hugh had predicted would follow my learning to read had already come, to torment and sting my soul to unutterable anguish. As I writhed under it, I would at times feel that learning to read had been a curse rather than a blessing. It had given me a view of my wretched condition, without the remedy. It opened my eyes to the horrible pit, but to no ladder upon which to get out. In moments of agony, I envied my fellow-slaves for their stupidity. I have often wished myself a beast. I preferred the condition of the meanest reptile to my own. Any thing, no matter what, to get rid of thinking! It was this everlasting thinking of my condition that tormented me. There was no getting rid of it. It was pressed upon me by every object within sight or hearing, animate or inanimate. The silver trump of freedom had roused my soul to eternal wakefulness. Freedom now appeared, to disappear no more forever. It was heard in every sound, and seen in every thing. It was

23

ever present to torment me with a sense of my wretched condition. I saw nothing without seeing it, I heard nothing without hearing it, and felt nothing without feeling it. It looked from every star, it smiled in every calm, breathed in every wind, and moved in every storm.

I often found myself regretting my own existence, and wishing myself dead; and but for the hope of being free, I have no doubt but that I should have killed myself, or done something for which I should have been killed. While in this state of mind, I was eager to hear any one speak of slavery. I was a ready listener. Every little while, I could hear something about the abolitionists. It was some time before I found what the word meant. It was always used in such connections as to make it an interesting word to me. If a slave ran away and succeeded in getting clear, or if a slave killed his master, set fire to a barn, or did any thing very wrong in the mind of a slaveholder, it was spoken of as the fruit of *abolition.* Hearing the word in this connection very often, I set about learning what it meant. The dictionary afforded me little or no help. I found it was "the act of abolishing"; but then I did not know what was to be abolished. Here I was perplexed. I did not dare to ask any one about its meaning, for I was satisfied that it was something they wanted me to know very little about. After a patient waiting, I got one of our city papers, containing an account of the number of petitions from the north, praying for the abolition of slavery in the District of Columbia, and of the slave trade between the States. From this time I understood the words *abolition* and *abolitionist,* and always drew near when that word was spoken, expecting to hear something of importance to myself and fellow-slaves. The light broke in upon me by degrees. I went one day down on the wharf of Mr. Waters; and seeing two Irishmen unloading a scow of stone, I went, unasked, and helped them. When we had finished, one of them came to me and asked me if I were a slave. I told him I was. He asked, "Are ye a slave for life?" I told him that I was. The good Irishman seemed to be deeply affected by the statement. He said to the other that it was a pity so fine a little fellow as myself should be a slave for life. He said it was a shame to hold me. They both advised me to run away to the north; that I should find friends there, and that I should be free. I pretended not to be interested in what they said, and treated them as if I did not understand them; for I feared they might be treacherous. White men have been known to encourage slaves to escape, and then, to get the reward, catch them and return them to their masters. I was afraid that these seemingly good men might use me so; but I nevertheless remembered their advice, and from that time I resolved to run away. I looked forward to a time at which it would be safe for me to escape. I was too young to think of doing so immediately; besides, I wished to learn how to write, as I might have occasion to write my own pass. I consoled myself with the hope that I should one day find a good chance. Meanwhile, I would learn to write.

The idea as to how I might learn to write was suggested to me by being in Durgin and Bailey's ship-yard, and frequently seeing the ship carpenters, after hewing, and getting a piece of timber ready for use, write on the timber the name of that part of the ship for which it was intended. When a piece of timber was intended for the larboard side, it would be marked thus—"L." When a piece was for the starboard side, it would be marked thus—"S." A piece for the larboard side forward, would be marked thus—"L. F." When a piece was for starboard side forward, it would be marked thus—"S. F." For larboard aft, it would be marked thus—"L. A." For starboard aft, it would be marked thus—"S. A." I soon learned the names of these letters, and for what they were intended when placed upon a piece of timber in the ship-yard. I immediately commenced copying them, and in a short time was able to make the four letters named. After that, when I met with any boy who I knew could write, I would tell him I could write as well as he. The next word would be, "I don't believe you. Let me see you try it." I would then make the letters which I had been so fortunate as to learn, and ask him to beat that. In this way I got a good many lessons in writing, which it is quite possible I should never have gotten in any other way. During this time, my copy-book was the board fence, brick wall, and pavement; my pen and ink was a lump of chalk. With these, I learned mainly how to write. I then commenced and continued copying the Italics in Webster's Spelling Book, until I could make them all without looking on the book. By this time, my little Master Thomas had gone to school, and learned how to write, and had written over a number of copy-books. These had been brought home, and shown to some of our near neighbors, and then laid aside. My mistress used to go to class meeting at the Wilk Street meetinghouse every Monday afternoon, and leave me to take care of the house. When left thus, I used to spend the time in writing in the spaces left in Master Thomas's copy-book, copying what he had written. I continued to do this until I could write a hand very similar to that of Master Thomas. Thus, after a long, tedious effort for years, I finally succeeded in learning how to write.

[1845]

PAULO FREIRE [1921–1997]

The "Banking"
Concept of Education

Paulo Freire was raised in Recife, Brazil, and graduated from the
University of Recife. In the late 1940s and 1950s, Freire worked among
poor, mostly illiterate laborers, where he developed methods for teaching reading and writing to adults, and began developing his pedagogical theory, which was heavily influenced by both Marxism and
Christianity. In 1962, the literacy program he developed was used to
teach three hundred manual laborers to read and write in forty-five
days. After a coup in 1964, Freire was briefly imprisoned in Brazil.
After his imprisonment, he travelled first to Bolivia and then to Chile.
Freire's first book was published in 1967, *Education as the Practice of
Freedom*. In 1969, Freire took a visiting professorship at Harvard University, where he taught until 1979 when he received political amnesty
and returned to Brazil. In São Paulo, Freire joined the Workers' Party,
supervised the city's adult literacy project, and was appointed secretary of education. His most famous book, *Pedagogy of the Oppressed*,
was published first in Portuguese in 1968 and two years later in Spanish and English. However, due to political reasons, it was not published
in Brazil until 1974. Freire advocated equalizing the relationships
between teachers and students, by teaching, learning from, and respect-
ing one another. Freire received many honorary degrees, awards, and
prizes for his work, including the UNESCO Prize for Peace Education
in 1986.

The following selection is taken from *The Pedagogy of the Oppressed*.
In it, Freire compares the current education model to banking, with its
deposits and withdrawals, and discusses how this model fails students.

A careful analysis of the teacher-student relationship at any level, inside
or outside the school, reveals its fundamentally *narrative* character. This
relationship involves a narrating Subject (the teacher) and patient, listening objects (the students). The contents, whether values or empirical

dimensions of reality, tend in the process of being narrated to become lifeless and petrified. Education is suffering from narration sickness.

The teacher talks about reality as if it were motionless, static, compartmentalized, and predictable. Or else he expounds on a topic completely alien to the existential experience of the students. His task is to "fill" the students with the contents of his narration—contents which are detached from reality, disconnected from the totality that engendered them and could give them significance. Words are emptied of their concreteness and become a hollow, alienated, and alienating verbosity.

The outstanding characteristic of this narrative education, then, is the sonority of words, not their transforming power. "Four times four is sixteen; the capital of Pará is Belém." The student records, memorizes, and repeats these phrases without perceiving what four times four really means, or realizing the true significance of "capital" in the affirmation "the capital of Pará is Belém," that is, what Belém means for Pará and what Pará means for Brazil.

Narration (with the teacher as narrator) leads the students to memorize mechanically the narrated content. Worse yet, it turns them into "containers," into "receptacles" to be "filled" by the teacher. The more completely she fills the receptacles, the better a teacher she is. The more meekly the receptacles permit themselves to be filled, the better students they are.

Education thus becomes an act of depositing, in which the students 5 are the depositories and the teacher is the depositor. Instead of communicating, the teacher issues communiqués and makes deposits which the students patiently receive, memorize, and repeat. This is the "banking" concept of education, in which the scope of action allowed to the students extends only as far as receiving, filing, and storing the deposits. They do, it is true, have the opportunity to become collectors or cataloguers of the things they store. But in the last analysis, it is the people themselves who are filed away through the lack of creativity, transformation, and knowledge in this (at best) misguided system. For apart from inquiry, apart from the praxis, individuals cannot be truly human. Knowledge emerges only through invention and re-invention, through the restless, impatient, continuing, hopeful inquiry human beings pursue in the world, with the world, and with each other.

In the banking concept of education, knowledge is a gift bestowed by those who consider themselves knowledgeable upon those whom they consider to know nothing. Projecting an absolute ignorance onto others, a characteristic of the ideology of oppression, negates education and knowledge as processes of inquiry. The teacher presents himself to his students as their necessary opposite; by considering their ignorance absolute, he justifies his own existence. The students, alienated like the slave in the Hegelian dialectic, accept their ignorance as justifying the teacher's existence—but, unlike the slave, they never discover that they educate the teacher.

The *raison d'être* of libertarian education, on the other hand, lies in its drive towards reconciliation. Education must begin with the solution of the teacher-student contradiction, by reconciling the poles of the contradiction so that both are simultaneously teachers *and* students.

This solution is not (nor can it be) found in the banking concept. On the contrary, banking education maintains and even stimulates the contradiction through the following attitudes and practices, which mirror oppressive society as a whole:

a.   the teacher teaches and the students are taught;

b.   the teacher knows everything and the students know nothing;

c.   the teacher thinks and the students are thought about;

d.   the teacher talks and the students listen—meekly;

e.   the teacher disciplines and the students are disciplined;

f.   the teacher chooses and enforces his choice, and the students comply;

g.   the teacher acts and the students have the illusion of acting through the action of the teacher;

h.   the teacher chooses the program content, and the students (who were not consulted) adapt to it;

i.   the teacher confuses the authority of knowledge with his or her own professional authority, which she and he sets in opposition to the freedom of the students;

j.   the teacher is the Subject of the learning process, while the pupils are mere objects.

It is not surprising that the banking concept of education regards men as adaptable, manageable beings. The more students work at storing the deposits entrusted to them, the less they develop the critical consciousness which would result from their intervention in the world as transformers of that world. The more completely they accept the passive role imposed on them, the more they tend simply to adapt to the world as it is and to the fragmented view of reality deposited in them.

The capability of banking education to minimize or annul the students' creative power and to stimulate their credulity serves the interests of the oppressors, who care neither to have the world revealed nor to see it transformed. The oppressors use their "humanitarianism" to preserve a profitable situation. Thus they react almost instinctively against any experiment in education which stimulates the critical faculties and is

10

not content with a partial view of reality but always seeks out the ties which link one point to another and one problem to another.

Indeed, the interests of the oppressors lie in "changing the consciousness of the oppressed, not the situation which oppresses them";[1] for the more the oppressed can be led to adapt to that situation, the more easily they can be dominated. To achieve this end, the oppressors use the banking concept of education in conjunction with a paternalistic social action apparatus, within which the oppressed receive the euphemistic title of "welfare recipients." They are treated as individual cases, as marginal persons who deviate from the general configuration of a "good, organized, and just" society. The oppressed are regarded as the pathology of the healthy society, which must therefore adjust these "incompetent and lazy" folk to its own patterns by changing their mentality. These marginals need to be "integrated," "incorporated" into the healthy society that they have "forsaken."

The truth is, however, that the oppressed are not "marginals," are not people living "outside" society. They have always been "inside"—inside the structure which made them "beings for others." The solution is not to "integrate" them into the structure of oppression, but to transform that structure so that they can become "beings for themselves." Such transformation, of course, would undermine the oppressors' purposes; hence their utilization of the banking concept of education to avoid the threat of student *conscientização*.

The banking approach to adult education, for example, will never propose to students that they critically consider reality. It will deal instead with such vital questions as whether Roger gave green grass to the goat, and insist upon the importance of learning that, on the contrary, *Roger gave green grass to the rabbit*. The "humanism" of the banking approach masks the effort to turn women and men into automatons—the very negation of their ontological vocation to be more fully human.

Those who use the banking approach, knowingly or unknowingly (for there are innumerable well-intentioned bank-clerk teachers who do not realize that they are serving only to dehumanize), fail to perceive that the deposits themselves contain contradictions about reality. But, sooner or later, these contradictions may lead formerly passive students to turn against their domestication and the attempt to domesticate reality. They may discover through existential experience that their present way of life is irreconcilable with their vocation to become fully human. They may perceive through their relations with reality that reality is really a *process*, undergoing constant transformation. If men and women are searchers and their ontological vocation is humanization, sooner or later they may perceive the contradiction in which banking education seeks to maintain them, and then engage themselves in the struggle for their liberation.

But the humanist, revolutionary educator cannot wait for this possibility 15 to materialize. From the outset, her efforts must coincide with those of the students to engage in critical thinking and the quest for mutual humanization. His efforts must be imbued with a profound trust in people and their creative power. To achieve this, they must be partners of the students in their relations with them.

The banking concept does not admit to such partnership—and necessarily so. To resolve the teacher-student contradiction, to exchange the role of depositor, prescriber, domesticator, for the role of student among students would be to undermine the power of oppression and serve the cause of liberation.

Implicit in the banking concept is the assumption of a dichotomy between human beings and the world: a person is merely *in* the world, not *with* the world or with others; the individual is spectator, not re-creator. In this view, the person is not a conscious being *(corpo consciente);* he or she is rather the possessor of *a* consciousness: an empty "mind" passively open to the reception of deposits of reality from the world outside. For example, my desk, my books, my coffee cup, all the objects before me—as bits of the world which surrounds me—would be "inside" me, exactly as I am inside my study right now. This view makes no distinction between being accessible to consciousness and entering consciousness. The distinction, however, is essential: the objects which surround me are simply accessible to my consciousness, not located within it. I am aware of them, but they are not inside me.

It follows logically from the banking notion of consciousness that the educator's role is to regulate the way the world "enters into" the students. The teacher's task is to organize a process which already occurs spontaneously, to "fill" the students by making deposits of information which he or she considers to constitute true knowledge.[2] And since people "receive" the world as passive entities, education should make them more passive still, and adapt them to the world. The educated individual is the adapted person, because she or he is better "fit" for the world. Translated into practice, this concept is well suited to the purposes of the oppressors, whose tranquility rests on how well people fit the world the oppressors have created, and how little they question it.

The more completely the majority adapt to the purposes which the dominant minority prescribe for them (thereby depriving them of the right to their own purposes), the more easily the minority can continue to prescribe. The theory and practice of banking education serve this end quite efficiently. Verbalistic lessons, reading requirements,[3] the methods for evaluating "knowledge," the distance between the teacher and the taught, the criteria for promotion: everything in this ready-to-wear approach serves to obviate thinking.

30

The bank-clerk educator does not realize that there is no true security in 20 his hypertrophied role, that one must seek to live *with* others in solidarity. One cannot impose oneself, nor even merely co-exist with one's students. Solidarity requires true communication, and the concept by which such an educator is guided fears and proscribes communication.

Yet only through communication can human life hold meaning. The teacher's thinking is authenticated only by the authenticity of the students' thinking. The teacher cannot think for her students, nor can she impose her thoughts on them. Authentic thinking, thinking that is concerned about *reality*, does not take place in ivory tower isolation, but only in communication. If it is true that thought has meaning only when generated by action upon the world, the subordination of students to teachers becomes impossible.

Because banking education begins with a false understanding of men and women as objects, it cannot promote the development of what Fromm calls "biophily," but instead produces its opposite: "necrophily."

> While life is characterized by growth in a structured, functional manner, the necrophilous person loves all that does not grow, all that is mechanical. The necrophilous person is driven by the desire to transform the organic into the inorganic, to approach life mechanically, as if all living persons were things. . . . Memory, rather than experience; having, rather than being, is what counts. The necrophilous person can relate to an object—a flower or a person—only if he possesses it; hence a threat to his possession is a threat to himself; if he loses possession he loses contact with the world. . . . He loves control, and in the act of controlling he kills life.[4]

Oppression—overwhelming control—is necrophilic; it is nourished by love of death, not life. The banking concept of education, which serves the interests of oppression, is also necrophilic. Based on a mechanistic, static, naturalistic, spatialized view of consciousness, it transforms students into receiving objects. It attempts to control thinking and action, leads women and men to adjust to the world, and inhibits their creative power.

When their efforts to act responsibly are frustrated, when they find themselves unable to use their faculties, people suffer. "This suffering due to impotence is rooted in the very fact that the human equilibrium has been disturbed."[5] But the inability to act which causes people's anguish also causes them to reject their impotence, by attempting

> . . . to restore [their] capacity to act. But can [they], and how? One way is to submit to and identify with a person or group having power. By this symbolic participation in another person's life, [men have] the illusion of

31

acting, when in reality [they] only submit to and become part of those who act.[6]

Populist manifestations perhaps best exemplify this type of behavior 25 by the oppressed, who, by identifying with charismatic leaders, come to feel that they themselves are active and effective. The rebellion they express as they emerge in the historical process is motivated by that desire to act effectively. The dominant elites consider the remedy to be more domination and repression, carried out in the name of freedom, order, and social peace (that is, the peace of the elites). Thus they can condemn—logically, from their point of view—"the violence of a strike by workers and [can] call upon the state in the same breath to use violence in putting down the strike."[7]

Education as the exercise of domination stimulates the credulity of students, with the ideological intent (often not perceived by educators) of indoctrinating them to adapt to the world of oppression. This accusation is not made in the naïve hope that the dominant elites will thereby simply abandon the practice. Its objective is to call the attention of true humanists to the fact that they cannot use banking educational methods in the pursuit of liberation, for they would only negate that very pursuit. Nor may a revolutionary society inherit these methods from an oppressor society. The revolutionary society which practices banking education is either misguided or mistrusting of people. In either event, it is threatened by the specter of reaction.

Unfortunately, those who espouse the cause of liberation are themselves surrounded and influenced by the climate which generates the banking concept, and often do not perceive its true significance or its dehumanizing power. Paradoxically, then, they utilize this same instrument of alienation in what they consider an effort to liberate. Indeed, some "revolutionaries" brand as "innocents," "dreamers," or even "reactionaries" those who would challenge this educational practice. But one does not liberate people by alienating them. Authentic liberation—the process of humanization—is not another deposit to be made in men. Liberation is a praxis: the action and reflection of men and women upon their world in order to transform it. Those truly committed to the cause of liberation can accept neither the mechanistic concept of consciousness as an empty vessel to be filled, nor the use of banking methods of domination (propaganda, slogans—deposits) in the name of liberation.

Those truly committed to liberation must reject the banking concept in its entirety, adopting instead a concept of women and men as conscious beings, and consciousness as consciousness intent upon the world. They must abandon the educational goal of deposit-making and replace it with the posing of the problems of human beings in their relations with the world. "Problem-posing" education, responding to the essence of consciousness — *intentionality* — rejects communiqués and embodies communications. It epitomizes the special characteristic of consciousness: being *conscious of*, not only as intent on objects but as turned in upon itself in a Jasperian "split" — consciousness as conscious-ness *of* consciousness.

Liberating education consists in acts of cognition, not transferrals of information. It is a learning situation in which the cognizable object (far from being the end of the cognitive act) intermediates the cognitive actors — teacher on the one hand and students on the other. Accordingly, the practice of problem-posing education entails at the outset that the teacher-student contradiction be resolved. Dialogical relations — indis-pensable to the capacity of cognitive actors to cooperate in perceiving the same cognizable object — are otherwise impossible.

Indeed, problem-posing education, which breaks with the vertical pat-   30
terns characteristic of banking education, can fulfill its function as the practice of freedom only if it can overcome the above contradiction. Through dialogue, the teacher-of-the-students and the students-of-the-teacher cease to exist and a new term emerges: teacher-student with students-teachers. The teacher is no longer merely the-one-who-teaches, but one who is himself taught in dialogue with the students, who in turn while being taught also teach. They become jointly responsible for a process in which all grow. In this process, arguments based on "author-ity" are no longer valid; in order to function, authority must be *on the side of* freedom, not *against* it. Here, no one teaches another, nor is anyone self-taught. People teach each other, mediated by the world, by the cog-nizable objects which in banking education are "owned" by the teacher.

The banking concept (with its tendency to dichotomize everything) dis-tinguishes two stages in the action of the educator. During the first, he cognizes a cognizable object while he prepares his lessons in his study or his laboratory; during the second, he expounds to his students about that object. The students are not called upon to know, but to memorize the contents narrated by the teacher. Nor do the students practice any act of cognition, since the object towards which that act should be directed is the property of the teacher rather than a medium evoking the critical reflection of both teacher and students. Hence in the name of the "preser-vation of culture and knowledge" we have a system which achieves nei-ther true knowledge nor true culture.

The problem-posing method does not dichotomize the activity of the teacher-student: she is not "cognitive" at one point and "narrative" at another. She is always "cognitive," whether preparing a project or engag-ing in dialogue with the students. He does not regard cognizable objects as his private property, but as the object of reflection by himself and the

33

students. In this way, the problem-posing educator constantly re-forms his reflections in the reflection of the students. The students—no longer docile listeners—are now critical co-investigators in dialogue with the teacher. The teacher presents the material to the students for their consideration, and re-considers her earlier considerations as the students express their own. The role of the problem-posing educator is to create, together with the students, the conditions under which knowledge at the level of the *doxa* is superseded by true knowledge, at the level of the *logos*.

Whereas banking education anesthetizes and inhibits creative power, problem-posing education involves a constant unveiling of reality. The former attempts to maintain the *submersion* of consciousness; the latter strives for the *emergence* of consciousness and *critical intervention* in reality.

Students, as they are increasingly posed with problems relating to themselves in the world and with the world, will feel increasingly challenged and obliged to respond to that challenge. Because they apprehend the challenge as interrelated to other problems within a total context, not as a theoretical question, the resulting comprehension tends to be increasingly critical and thus constantly less alienated. Their response to the challenge evokes new challenges, followed by new understandings; and gradually the students come to regard themselves as committed.

Education as the practice of freedom—as opposed to education as the 35 practice of domination—denies that man is abstract, isolated, independent, and unattached to the world; it also denies that the world exists as a reality apart from people. Authentic reflection considers neither abstract man nor the world without people, but people in their relations with the world. In these relations consciousness and world are simultaneous: consciousness neither precedes the world nor follows it.

La conscience et le monde sont donnés d'un même coup: extérieur par essence à la conscience, le monde est, par essence relatif à elle.[8]

In one of our culture circles in Chile, the group was discussing (based on a codification) the anthropological concept of culture. In the midst of the discussion, a peasant who by banking standards was completely ignorant said: "Now I see that without man there is no world." When the educator responded: "Let's say, for the sake of argument, that all the men on earth were to die, but that the earth itself remained, together with trees, birds, animals, rivers, seas, the stars . . . wouldn't all this be a world?" "Oh no," the peasant replied emphatically. "There would be no one to say: 'This is a world.'"

34

The peasant wished to express the idea that there would be lacking the consciousness of the world which necessarily implies the world of consciousness. *I* cannot exist without a *non-I*. In turn, the *not-I* depends on that existence. The world which brings consciousness into existence becomes the world *of* that consciousness. Hence, the previously cited affirmation of Sartre: *"La conscience et le monde sont donnés d'un même coup."*

As women and men, simultaneously reflecting on themselves and on the world, increase the scope of their perception, they begin to direct their observations towards previously inconspicuous phenomena:

> In perception properly so-called, as an explicit awareness *[Gewahren]*, I am turned towards the object, to the paper, for instance. I apprehend it as being this here and now. The apprehension is a singling out, every object having a background in experience. Around and about the paper lie books, pencils, inkwell, and so forth, and these in a certain sense are also "perceived," perceptually there, in the "field of intuition"; but whilst I was turned towards the paper there was no turning in their direction, nor any apprehending of them, not even in a secondary sense. They appeared and yet were not singled out, were not posited on their own account. Every perception of a thing has such a zone of background intuitions or background awareness, if "intuiting" already includes the state of being turned towards, and this also is a "conscious experience," or more briefly a "consciousness of" all indeed that in point of fact lies in the co-perceived objective background.[9]

That which had existed objectively but had not been perceived in its deeper implications (if indeed it was perceived at all) begins to "stand out," assuming the character of a problem and therefore of challenge. Thus, men and women begin to single out elements from their "background awarenesses" and to reflect upon them. These elements are now objects of their consideration, and, as such, objects of their action and cognition.

In problem-posing education, people develop their power to perceive critically *the way they exist* in the world *with which* and *in which* they find themselves; they come to see the world not as a static reality, but as a reality in process, in transformation. Although the dialectical relations of women and men with the world exist independently of how these relations are perceived (or whether or not they are perceived at all), it is also true that the form of action they adopt is to a large extent a function of how they perceive themselves in the world. Hence, the teacher-student and the students-teachers reflect simultaneously on themselves and the world without dichotomizing this reflection from action, and thus establish an authentic form of thought and action.

35

Once again, the two educational concepts and practices under analysis come into conflict. Banking education (for obvious reasons) attempts, by mythicizing reality, to conceal certain facts which explain the way human beings exist in the world; problem-posing education sets itself the task of demythologizing. Banking education resists dialogue; problem-posing education regards dialogue as indispensable to the act of cognition which unveils reality. Banking education treats students as objects of assistance; problem-posing education makes them critical thinkers. Banking education inhibits creativity and domesticates (although it cannot completely destroy) the *intentionality* of consciousness by isolating consciousness from the world, thereby denying people their ontological and historical vocation of becoming more fully human. Problem-posing education bases itself on creativity and stimulates true reflection and action upon reality, thereby responding to the vocation of persons as beings who are authentic only when engaged in inquiry and creative transformation. In sum: banking theory and practice, as immobilizing and fixating forces, fail to acknowledge men and women as historical beings; problem-posing theory and practice take the people's historicity as their starting point.

Problem-posing education affirms men and women as beings in the 40 process of *becoming*—as unfinished, uncompleted beings in and with a likewise unfinished reality. Indeed, in contrast to other animals who are unfinished, but not historical, people know themselves to be unfinished; they are aware of their incompletion. In this incompletion and this awareness lie the very roots of education as an exclusively human manifestation. The unfinished character of human beings and the transformational character of reality necessitate that education be an ongoing activity.

Education is thus constantly remade in the praxis. In order to *be*, it must *become*. Its "duration" (in the Bergsonian meaning of the word) is found in the interplay of the opposites *permanence* and *change*. The banking method emphasizes permanence and becomes reactionary; problem-posing education—which accepts neither a "well-behaved" present nor a predetermined future—roots itself in the dynamic present and becomes revolutionary.

Problem-posing education is revolutionary futurity. Hence, it is prophetic (and, as such, hopeful). Hence, it corresponds to the historical nature of humankind. Hence, it affirms women and men as beings who transcend themselves, who move forward and look ahead, for whom immobility represents a fatal threat, for whom looking at the past must only be a means of understanding more clearly what and who they are so that they can more wisely build the future. Hence, it identifies with the movement which engages people as beings aware of their incompletion—an historical movement which has its point of departure, its Subjects and its objective.

The point of departure of the movement lies in the people themselves. But since people do not exist apart from the world, apart from reality, the movement must begin with the human-world relationship. Accordingly, the point of departure must always be with men and women in the "here and now," which constitutes the situation within which they are submerged, from which they emerge, and in which they intervene. Only by starting from this situation—which determines their perception of it—can they begin to move. To do this authentically they must perceive their state not as fated and unalterable, but merely as limiting—and therefore challenging.

Whereas the banking method directly or indirectly reinforces men's fatalistic perception of their situation, the problem-posing method presents this very situation to them as a problem. As the situation becomes the object of their cognition, the naïve or magical perception which produced their fatalism gives way to perception which is able to perceive itself even as it perceives reality, and can thus be critically objective about that reality.

A deepened consciousness of their situation leads people to apprehend 45 that situation as an historical reality susceptible of transformation. Resignation gives way to the drive for transformation and inquiry, over which men feel themselves to be in control. If people, as historical beings necessarily engaged with other people in a movement of inquiry, did not control that movement, it would be (and is) a violation of their humanity. Any situation in which some individuals prevent others from engaging in the process of inquiry is one of violence. The means used are not important; to alienate human beings from their own decision-making is to change them into objects.

This movement of inquiry must be directed towards humanization—the people's historical vocation. The pursuit of full humanity, however, cannot be carried out in isolation or individualism, but only in fellowship and solidarity; therefore it cannot unfold in the antagonistic relations between oppressors and oppressed. No one can be authentically human while he prevents others from being so. Attempting *to be more* human, individualistically, leads to *having more*, egotistically, a form of dehumanization. Not that it is not fundamental *to have* in order *to be* human. Precisely because it *is* necessary, some men's *having* must not be allowed to constitute an obstacle to others' *having*, must not consolidate the power of the former to crush the latter.

Problem-posing education, as a humanist and liberating praxis, posits as fundamental that the people subjected to domination must fight for their emancipation. To that end, it enables teachers and students to become Subjects of the educational process by overcoming authoritarianism and an alienating intellectualism; it also enables people to overcome their false perception of reality. The world—no longer something to be described with deceptive words—becomes the object of that transforming action by men and women which results in their humanization.

Problem-posing education does not and cannot serve the interests of the oppressor. No oppressive order could permit the oppressed to begin to question: Why? While only a revolutionary society can carry out this education in systematic terms, the revolutionary leaders need not take full power before they can employ the method. In the revolutionary process, the leaders cannot utilize the banking method as an interim measure, justified on grounds of expediency, with the intention of *later* behaving in a genuinely revolutionary fashion. They must be revolutionary—that is to say, dialogical—from the outset.

Notes

1. Simone de Beauvoir, *La pensée de droite, aujourd'hui* (Paris); ST, *El pensamiento político de la derecha* (Buenos Aires, 1963), p. 34.

2. This concept corresponds to what Sartre calls the "digestive" or "nutritive" concept of education, in which knowledge is "fed" by the teacher to the students to "fill them out." See Jean-Paul Sartre, "Une idée fundamentale de la phénoménologie de Husserl: L'intentionalité," *Situations* I (Paris, 1947).

3. For example, some professors specify in their reading lists that a book should be read from pages 10 to 15—and do this to "help" their students!

4. Eric Fromm, *The Heart of Man* (New York, 1966), p. 41.

5. Ibid., p. 31.

6. Ibid.

7. Reinhold Niebuhr, *Moral Man and Immoral Society* (New York, 1960), p. 130.

8. Sartre, op. cit., p. 32. [The passage is obscure but could be read as "Consciousness and the world are given at one and the same time: the exterior world as it enters consciousness is relative to our ways of seeing and understanding that world." —Editors' note]

9. Edmund Husserl, *Ideas—General Introduction to Pure Phenomenology* (London, 1969), pp. 105–06.

MALCOLM GLADWELL   [b. 1963]

Something Borrowed

Malcolm Gladwell was born in the United Kingdom, earned a degree in
history in Canada, and now lives and works as a writer in New York.
He has served as a science reporter for the *Washington Post* and as a
staff writer for the *New Yorker*. Gladwell's profile of inventor and mar-
keter Ron Popeil garnered a National Magazine Award in 2001; in
2005, Gladwell was named one of *Time* magazine's 100 Most Influential People. As a writer, he links topics relating to psychology, sociol-
ogy, politics, human communication, and consumer behavior. His
books include *The Tipping Point: How Little Things Can Make a Big Difference* (2000), *Blink: The Power of Thinking without Thinking* (2005),
and *Outliers: The Story of Success* (2008).

   In "Something Borrowed," Gladwell describes the plagiarism case of
the Broadway play *Frozen*, which contained verbatim excerpts from a
profile written by Gladwell. For this reason, the case was personal and
inspired him to pose the question of whether or not plagiarism charges
should ruin one's life. In the essay, this question and Gladwell's answer
is exposed.

One day this spring, a psychiatrist named Dorothy Lewis got a call from
her friend Betty, who works in New York City. Betty had just seen a
Broadway play called "Frozen," written by the British playwright Bryony
Lavery. "She said, 'Somehow it reminded me of you. You really ought to
see it,'" Lewis recalled. Lewis asked Betty what the play was about, and
Betty said that one of the characters was a psychiatrist who studied
serial killers. "And I told her, 'I need to see that as much as I need to go to
the moon.'"
   Lewis has studied serial killers for the past twenty-five years. With her
collaborator, the neurologist Jonathan Pincus, she has published a great
many research papers, showing that serial killers tend to suffer from
predictable patterns of psychological, physical, and neurological dysfunction: that they were almost all the victims of harrowing physical and
sexual abuse as children, and that almost all of them have suffered some
kind of brain injury or mental illness. In 1998, she published a memoir

Malcolm Gladwell, "Something Borrowed" from *The New Yorker*, November 22, 2004.
Reprinted by permission of the author.

of her life and work entitled "Guilty by Reason of Insanity." She was the last person to visit Ted Bundy before he went to the electric chair. Few people in the world have spent as much time thinking about serial killers as Dorothy Lewis, so when her friend Betty told her that she needed to see "Frozen" it struck her as a busman's holiday.

But the calls kept coming. "Frozen" was winning raves on Broadway, and it had been nominated for a Tony. Whenever someone who knew Dorothy Lewis saw it, they would tell her that she really ought to see it, too. In June, she got a call from a woman at the theatre where "Frozen" was playing. "She said she'd heard that I work in this field, and that I see murderers, and she was wondering if I would do a talk-back after the show," Lewis said. "I had done that once before, and it was a delight, so I said sure. And I said, would you please send me the script, because I wanted to read the play."

The script came, and Lewis sat down to read it. Early in the play, something caught her eye, a phrase: "it was one of those days." One of the murderers Lewis had written about in her book had used that same expression. But she thought it was just a coincidence. "Then, there's a scene of a woman on an airplane, typing away to her friend. Her name is Agnetha Gottmundsdottir. I read that she's writing to her colleague, a neurologist called David Nabkus. And with that I realized that more was going on, and I realized as well why all these people had been telling me to see the play."

Lewis began underlining line after line. She had worked at New York   5
University School of Medicine. The psychiatrist in "Frozen" worked at New York School of Medicine. Lewis and Pincus did a study of brain injuries among fifteen death-row inmates. Gottmundsdottir and Nabkus did a study of brain injuries among fifteen death-row inmates. Once, while Lewis was examining the serial killer Joseph Franklin, he sniffed her, in a grotesque, sexual way. Gottmundsdottir is sniffed by the play's serial killer, Ralph. Once, while Lewis was examining Ted Bundy, she kissed him on the cheek. Gottmundsdottir, in some productions of "Frozen," kisses Ralph. "The whole thing was right there," Lewis went on. "I was sitting at home reading the play, and I realized that it was I. I felt robbed and violated in some peculiar way. It was as if someone had stolen—I don't believe in the soul, but, if there was such a thing, it was as if someone had stolen my essence."

Lewis never did the talk-back. She hired a lawyer. And she came down from New Haven to see "Frozen." "In my book," she said, "I talk about where I rush out of the house with my black carry-on, and I have two black pocket-books, and the play opens with her"—Agnetha—"with one big black bag and a carry-on, rushing out to do a lecture." Lewis had written about biting her sister on the stomach as a child. Onstage, Agnetha fantasized out loud about attacking a stewardess on an airplane and "biting out her throat." After the play was over, the cast came onstage and took questions from the audience. "Somebody in the audience said, 'Where did Bryony Lavery get the idea for the psychiatrist?'" Lewis recounted. "And one of the cast members, the male lead, said, 'Oh, she said that she read it in an English medical magazine.'" Lewis is a tiny woman, with enormous, childlike eyes, and they were wide open now with the memory. "I wouldn't have cared if she did a play about a shrink who's interested in the frontal lobe and the limbic system. That's out there to do. I see things week after week on television, on 'Law & Order' or 'C.S.I.,' and I see that they are using material that Jonathan and I brought to light. And it's wonderful. That would have been acceptable. But she did more than that. She took things about my own life, and that is the part that made me feel violated."

At the request of her lawyer, Lewis sat down and made up a chart detailing what she felt were the questionable parts of Lavery's play. The chart was fifteen pages long. The first part was devoted to thematic similarities between "Frozen" and Lewis's book "Guilty by Reason of Insanity." The other, more damning section listed twelve instances of almost verbatim similarities—totalling perhaps six hundred and seventy-five words—between passages from "Frozen" and passages from a 1997 magazine profile of Lewis. The profile was called "Damaged." It appeared in the February 24, 1997, issue of *The New Yorker*. It was written by me.

Words belong to the person who wrote them. There are few simpler ethical notions than this one, particularly as society directs more and more energy and resources toward the creation of intellectual property. In the past thirty years, copyright laws have been strengthened. Courts have become more willing to grant intellectual-property protections. Fighting piracy has become an obsession with Hollywood and the recording industry, and, in the worlds of academia and publishing, plagiarism has gone from being bad literary manners to something much closer to a crime. When, two years ago, Doris Kearns Goodwin was found to have lifted passages from several other historians, she was asked to resign from the board of the Pulitzer Prize committee. And why not? If she had robbed a bank, she would have been fired the next day.

I'd worked on "Damaged" through the fall of 1996. I would visit Dorothy Lewis in her office at Bellevue Hospital, and watch the videotapes of her interviews with serial killers. At one point, I met up with her in Missouri. Lewis was testifying at the trial of Joseph Franklin, who claims responsibility for shooting, among others, the civil-rights leader Vernon Jordan and the pornographer Larry Flynt. In the trial, a videotape was shown of an interview that Franklin once gave to a television station. He was asked whether he felt any remorse. I wrote:

"I can't say that I do," he said. He paused again, then added, "The only thing I'm sorry about is that it's not legal."
"What's not legal?"
Franklin answered as if he'd been asked the time of day: "Killing Jews."

That exchange, almost to the word, was reproduced in "Frozen."   10
Lewis, the article continued, didn't feel that Franklin was fully responsible for his actions. She viewed him as a victim of neurological dysfunction and childhood physical abuse. "The difference between a crime of evil and a crime of illness," I wrote, "is the difference between a sin and a symptom." That line was in "Frozen," too—not once but twice. I faxed Bryony Lavery a letter:

I am happy to be the source of inspiration for other writers, and had you asked for my permission to quote—even liberally—from my piece, I would have been delighted to oblige. But to lift material, without my approval, is theft.

Almost as soon as I'd sent the letter, though, I began to have second thoughts. The truth was that, although I said I'd been robbed, I didn't feel that way. Nor did I feel particularly angry. One of the first things I had said to a friend after hearing about the echoes of my article in "Frozen" was that this was the only way I was ever going to get to Broadway—and I was only half joking. On some level, I considered Lavery's borrowing to be a compliment. A savvier writer would have changed all those references to Lewis, and rewritten the quotes from me, so that their origin was no longer recognizable. But how would I have been better off if Lavery had disguised the source of her inspiration?

Dorothy Lewis, for her part, was understandably upset. She was considering a lawsuit. And, to increase her odds of success, she asked me to assign her the copyright to my article. I agreed, but then I changed my mind. Lewis had told me that she "wanted her life back." Yet in order to get her life back, it appeared, she first had to acquire it from me. That seemed a little strange.

Then I got a copy of the script for "Frozen." I found it breathtaking, I realize that this isn't supposed to be a relevant consideration. And yet it was: instead of feeling that my words had been taken from me, I felt that they had become part of some grander cause. In late September the story broke. The *Times*, the *Observer* in England, and the Associated Press all ran stories about Lavery's alleged plagiarism, and the articles were picked up by newspapers around the world. Bryony Lavery had seen one of my articles, responded to what she read, and used it as she constructed a work of art. And now her reputation was in tatters. Something about that didn't seem right.

In 1992, the Beastie Boys released a song called "Pass the Mic," which 15 begins with a six-second sample taken from the 1976 composition "Choir," by the jazz flutist James Newton. The sample was an exercise in what is called multiphonics, where the flutist "overblows" into the instrument while simultaneously singing in a falsetto. In the case of "Choir," Newton played a C on the flute, then sang C, D-flat, C—and the distortion of the overblown C, combined with his vocalizing, created a surprisingly complex and haunting sound. In "Pass the Mic," the Beastie Boys repeated the Newton sample more than forty times. The effect was riveting.

In the world of music, copyrighted works fall into two categories—the recorded performance and the composition underlying that performance. If you write a rap song, and want to sample the chorus from Billy Joel's "Piano Man," you first have to get permission from the record label to use the "Piano Man" recording, and then get permission from Billy Joel (or whoever owns his music) to use the underlying composition. In the case of "Pass the Mic," the Beastie Boys got the first kind of permission—the rights to use the recording of "Choir"—but not the second. Newton sued, and he lost—and the reason he lost serves as a useful introduction to how to think about intellectual property.

At issue in the case wasn't the distinctiveness of Newton's performance. The Beastie Boys, everyone agreed, had properly licensed Newton's performance when they paid the copyright recording fee. And there was no question about whether they had copied the underlying music to the sample. At issue was simply whether the Beastie Boys were required to ask for that secondary permission: was the composition underneath those six seconds so distinctive and original that Newton could be said to own it? The court said that it wasn't.

The chief expert witness for the Beastie Boys in the "Choir" case was Lawrence Ferrara, who is a professor of music at New York University, and when I asked him to explain the court's ruling he walked over to the piano in the corner of his office and played those three notes: C, D-flat, C. "That's it!" he shouted. "There ain't nothing else! That's what was used. You know what this is? It's no more than a mordent, a turn. It's been done thousands upon thousands of times. No one can say they own that."

Ferrara then played the most famous four-note sequence in classical music, the opening of Beethoven's Fifth: G, G, G, E-flat. This was unmistakably Beethoven. But was it original? "That's a harder case," Ferrara

43

said. "Actually, though, other composers wrote that. Beethoven himself wrote that in a piano sonata, and you can find figures like that in composers who predate Beethoven. It's one thing if you're talking about *da-da-da dummm, da-da-da dummm* — those notes, with those durations. But just the four pitches, G, G, G, E-flat? Nobody owns those."

Ferrara once served as an expert witness for Andrew Lloyd Webber, 20 who was being sued by Ray Repp, a composer of Catholic folk music. Repp said that the opening few bars of Lloyd Webber's 1984 "Phantom Song," from "The Phantom of the Opera," bore an overwhelming resemblance to his composition "Till You," written six years earlier, in 1978. As Ferrara told the story, he sat down at the piano again and played the beginning of both songs, one after the other; sure enough, they sounded strikingly similar. "Here's Lloyd Webber," he said, calling out each note as he played it. "Here's Repp. Same sequence. The only difference is that Andrew writes a perfect fourth and Repp writes a sixth."

But Ferrara wasn't quite finished. "I said, let me have everything Andrew Lloyd Webber wrote prior to 1978 — 'Jesus Christ Superstar,' 'Joseph,' 'Evita.' " He combed through every score, and in "Joseph and the Amazing Technicolor Dreamcoat" he found what he was looking for. "It's the song 'Benjamin Calypso.' " Ferrara started playing it. It was immediately familiar. "It's the first phrase of 'Phantom Song.' It's even using the same notes. But wait — it gets better. Here's 'Close Every Door,' from a 1969 concert performance of 'Joseph.' " Ferrara is a dapper, animated man, with a thin, well-manicured mustache, and thinking about the Lloyd Webber case was almost enough to make him jump up and down. He began to play again. It was the second phrase of "Phantom." "The first half of 'Phantom' is in 'Benjamin Calypso.' The second half is in 'Close Every Door.' They are identical. On the button. In the case of the first theme, in fact, 'Benjamin Calypso' is closer to the first half of the theme at issue than the plaintiff's song. Lloyd Webber writes something in 1984, and he borrows from himself."

In the "Choir" case, the Beastie Boys' copying didn't amount to theft because it was too trivial. In the "Phantom" case, what Lloyd Webber was alleged to have copied didn't amount to theft because the material in question wasn't original to his accuser. Under copyright law, what matters is not that you copied someone else's work. What matters is *what* you copied, and *how much* you copied. Intellectual-property doctrine isn't a straightforward application of the ethical principle "Thou shalt not steal." At its core is the notion that there are certain situations where you *can* steal. The protections of copyright, for instance, are time-limited; once something passes into the public domain, anyone can copy it without restriction. Or suppose that you invented a cure for breast cancer in your basement lab. Any patent you received would protect your intellectual property for twenty years, but after that anyone could take your invention. You get an initial monopoly on your creation because we want to provide economic incentives for people to invent things like cancer drugs. But everyone gets to steal your breast-cancer cure—after a decent interval—because it is also in society's interest to let as many people as possible copy your invention; only then can others learn from it, and build on it, and come up with better and cheaper alternatives. This balance between the protecting and the limiting of intellectual property is, in fact, enshrined in the Constitution: "Congress shall have the power to promote the Progress of Science and useful Arts, by securing for limited"—note that specification, *limited*—"Times to Authors and Inventors the exclusive Right to their respective Writings and Discoveries."

So is it true that words belong to the person who wrote them, just as other kinds of property belong to their owners? Actually, no. As the Stanford law professor Lawrence Lessig argues in his new book "Free Culture":

> In ordinary language, to call a copyright a "property" right is a bit misleading, for the property of copyright is an odd kind of property. . . . I understand what I am taking when I take the picnic table you put in your backyard. I am taking a thing, the picnic table, and after I take it, you don't have it. But what am I taking when I take the good idea you had to put a picnic table in the backyard—by, for example, going to Sears, buying a table, and putting it in my backyard? What is the thing that I am taking then?
>
> The point is not just about the thingness of picnic tables versus ideas, though that is an important difference. The point instead is that in the ordinary case—indeed, in practically every case except for a narrow range of exceptions—ideas released to the world are free. I don't take anything from you when I copy the way you dress—though I might seem weird if I do it every day. . . . Instead, as Thomas Jefferson said (and this is especially true when I copy the way someone dresses), "He who receives an idea from me, receives instruction himself without lessening mine; as he who lights his taper at mine, receives light without darkening me."

Lessig argues that, when it comes to drawing this line between private interests and public interests in intellectual property, the courts and Congress have, in recent years, swung much too far in the direction of private interests. He writes, for instance, about the fight by some developing countries to get access to inexpensive versions of Western drugs through what is called "parallel importation"—buying drugs from another developing country that has been licensed to produce patented medicines.

The move would save countless lives. But it has been opposed by the United States not on the ground that it would cut into the profits of Western pharmaceutical companies (they don't sell that many patented drugs in developing countries anyway) but on the ground that it violates the sanctity of intellectual property. "We as a culture have lost this sense of balance," Lessig writes. "A certain property fundamentalism, having no connection to our tradition, now reigns in this culture."

Even what Lessig decries as intellectual-property extremism, however, 25 acknowledges that intellectual property has its limits. The United States didn't say that developing countries could never get access to cheap versions of American drugs. It said only that they would have to wait until the patents on those drugs expired. The arguments that Lessig has with the hard-core proponents of intellectual property are almost all arguments about *where* and *when* the line should be drawn between the right to copy and the right to protection from copying, not *whether* a line should be drawn.

But plagiarism is different, and that's what's so strange about it. The ethical rules that govern when it's acceptable for one writer to copy another are even more extreme than the most extreme position of the intellectual-property crowd: when it comes to literature, we have somehow decided that copying is *never* acceptable. Not long ago, the Harvard law professor Laurence Tribe was accused of lifting material from the historian Henry Abraham for his 1985 book, *God Save This Honorable Court*. What did the charge amount to? In an exposé that appeared in the conservative publication *The Weekly Standard*, Joseph Bottum produced a number of examples of close paraphrasing, but his smoking gun was this one borrowed sentence: "Taft publicly pronounced Pitney to be a 'weak member' of the Court to whom he could not assign cases." That's it. Nineteen words.

Not long after I learned about "Frozen," I went to see a friend of mine who works in the music industry. We sat in his living room on the Upper East Side, facing each other in easy chairs, as he worked his way through a mountain of CDs. He played "Angel," by the reggae singer Shaggy, and then "The Joker," by the Steve Miller Band, and told me to listen very carefully to the similarity in bass lines. He played Led Zeppelin's "Whole Lotta Love" and then Muddy Waters's "You Need Love," to show the extent to which Led Zeppelin had mined the blues for inspiration. He played "Twice My Age," by Shabba Ranks and Krystal, and then the saccharine seventies pop standard "Seasons in the Sun," until I could hear the echoes of the second song in the first. He played "Last Christmas," by Wham!, followed by Barry Manilow's "Can't Smile Without You" to explain why Manilow might have been startled when he first heard that song, and then "Joanna," by Kool and the Gang, because, in a different way, "Last Christmas" was an homage to Kool and the Gang as well. "That sound you hear in Nirvana," my friend said at one point, "that soft and then loud, kind of exploding thing, a lot of that was inspired by the Pixies. Yet Kurt Cobain"—Nirvana's lead singer and songwriter—"was such a genius that he managed to make it his own. And 'Smells Like Teen Spirit'?"—here he was referring to perhaps the best-known Nirvana song. "That's Boston's 'More Than a Feeling.' " He began to hum the riff of the Boston hit, and said, "The first time I heard 'Teen Spirit,' I said, 'That guitar lick is from "More Than a Feeling.' " But it was different—it was urgent and brilliant and new."

He played another CD. It was Rod Stewart's "Do Ya Think I'm Sexy," a huge hit from the nineteen-seventies. The chorus has a distinctive, catchy hook—the kind of tune that millions of Americans probably hummed in the shower the year it came out. Then he put on "Taj Mahal," by the Brazilian artist Jorge Ben Jor, which was recorded several years before the Rod Stewart song. In his twenties, my friend was a d.j. at various downtown clubs, and at some point he'd become interested in world music. "I caught it back then," he said. A small, sly smile spread across his face. The opening bars of "Taj Mahal" were very South American, a world away from what we had just listened to. And then I heard it. It was so obvious and unambiguous that I laughed out loud; virtually note for note, it was the hook from "Do Ya Think I'm Sexy." It was possible that Rod Stewart had independently come up with that riff, because resemblance is not proof of influence. It was also possible that he'd been in Brazil, listened to some local music, and liked what he heard.

My friend had hundreds of these examples. We could have sat in his living room playing at musical genealogy for hours. Did the examples upset him? Of course not, because he knew enough about music to know that these patterns of influence—cribbing, tweaking, transforming— were at the very heart of the creative process. True, copying could go too far. There were tunes when one artist was simply replicating the work of another, and to let that pass inhibited true creativity. But it was equally dangerous to be overly vigilant in policing creative expression, because if Led Zeppelin hadn't been free to mine the blues for inspiration we wouldn't have got "Whole Lotta Love," and if Kurt Cobain couldn't listen to "More Than a Feeling" and pick out and transform the part he really liked we wouldn't have "Smells Like Teen Spirit"—and, in the evolution of rock, "Smells Like Teen Spirit" was a real step forward from "More Than a Feeling." A successful music executive has to understand the distinction between borrowing that is transformative and borrowing that is merely derivative, and that distinction, I realized, was what was missing from the discussion of Bryony Lavery's borrowings. Yes, she had copied my work. But no one was asking why she had copied it, or what she had copied, or whether her copying served some larger purpose.

Bryony Lavery came to see me in early October. It was a beautiful Satur- 30 day afternoon, and we met at my apartment. She is in her fifties, with short tousled blond hair and pale-blue eyes, and was wearing jeans and a loose green shirt and clogs. There was something rugged and raw about her. In the *Times* the previous day, the theatre critic Ben Brantley had not been kind to her new play, "Last Easter." This was supposed to be her moment of triumph. "Frozen" had been nominated for a Tony. "Last Easter" had opened Off Broadway. And now? She sat down heavily at my kitchen table. "I've had the absolute gamut of emotions," she said, playing nervously with her hands as she spoke, as if she needed a cigarette. "I think when one's working, one works between absolute confidence and absolute doubt, and I got a huge dollop of each. I was terribly confident that I could write well after 'Frozen,' and then this opened a chasm of doubt." She looked up at me. "I'm terribly sorry," she said.

Lavery began to explain: "What happens when I write is that I find that I'm somehow zoning on a number of things. I find that I've cut things out of newspapers because the story or something in them is interesting to me, and seems to me to have a place onstage. Then it starts coagulating. It's like the soup starts thickening. And then a story, which is also a structure, starts emerging. I'd been reading thrillers like 'The Silence of the Lambs,' about fiendishly clever serial killers. I'd also seen a documentary of the victims of the Yorkshire killers, Myra Hindley and Ian Brady, who were called the Moors Murderers. They spirited away several children. It seemed to me that killing somehow wasn't fiendishly clever. It was the opposite of clever. It was as banal and stupid and destructive as it could be. There are these interviews with the survivors, and what struck me was that they appeared to be frozen in time. And one of them said, 'If that man was out now, I'm a forgiving man but I couldn't forgive him. I'd kill him.' That's in 'Frozen.' I was thinking about that. Then my mother went into hospital for a very simple operation, and the surgeon punctured her womb, and therefore her intestine, and she got peritonitis and died."

When Lavery started talking about her mother, she stopped, and had to collect herself. "She was seventy-four, and what occurred to me is that I utterly forgave him. I thought it was an honest mistake. I'm very sorry it happened to my mother, but it's an honest mistake." Lavery's feelings confused her, though, because she could think of people in her own life whom she had held grudges against for years, for the most trivial of reasons. "In a lot of ways, 'Frozen' was an attempt to understand the nature of forgiveness," she said.

Lavery settled, in the end, on a play with three characters. The first is a serial killer named Ralph, who kidnaps and murders a young girl. The second is the murdered girl's mother, Nancy. The third is a psychiatrist from New York, Agnetha, who goes to England to examine Ralph. In the course of the play, the three lives slowly intersect — and the characters gradually change and become "unfrozen" as they come to terms with the idea of forgiveness. For the character of Ralph, Lavery says that she drew on a book about a serial killer titled "The Murder of Childhood," by Ray Wyre and Tim Tate. For the character of Nancy, she drew on an article written in the *Guardian* by a woman named Marian Partington, whose sister had been murdered by the serial killers Frederick and Rosemary West. And, for the character of Agnetha, Lavery drew on a reprint of my article that she had read in a British publication. "I wanted a scientist who would understand," Lavery said — a scientist who could explain how it was possible to forgive a man who had killed your daughter, who could explain that a serial killing was not a crime of evil but a crime of illness. "I wanted it to be *accurate*," she added.

So why didn't she credit me and Lewis? How could she have been so meticulous about accuracy but not about attribution? Lavery didn't have an answer. "I thought it was O.K. to use it," she said with an embarrassed shrug. "It never occurred to me to ask you. I thought it was *news*." She was aware of how hopelessly inadequate that sounded, and when she went on to say that my article had been in a big folder of source material that she had used in the writing of the play, and that the folder had got lost during the play's initial run, in Birmingham, she was aware of how inadequate that sounded, too.

But then Lavery began to talk about Marian Partington, her other important inspiration, and her story became more complicated. While she was writing "Frozen," Lavery said, she wrote to Partington to inform her of how much she was relying on Partington's experiences. And when "Frozen" opened in London she and Partington met and talked. In reading through articles on Lavery in the British press, I found this, from the *Guardian* two years ago, long before the accusations of plagiarism surfaced:

> Lavery is aware of the debt she owes to Partington's writing and is eager to acknowledge it.
> "I always mention it, because I am aware of the enormous debt that I owe to the generosity of Marian Partington's piece. . . . You have to be hugely careful when writing something like this, because it touches on people's shattered lives and you wouldn't want them to come across it unawares."

Lavery wasn't indifferent to other people's intellectual property, then; she was just indifferent to my intellectual property. That's because, in

49

her eyes, what she took from me was different. It was, as she put it, "news." She copied my description of Dorothy Lewis's collaborator, Jonathan Pincus, conducting a neurological examination. She copied the description of the disruptive neurological effects of prolonged periods of high stress. She copied my transcription of the television interview with Franklin. She reproduced a quote that I had taken from a study of abused children, and she copied a quotation from Lewis on the nature of evil. She didn't copy my musings, or conclusions, or structure. She lifted sentences like "It is the function of the cortex—and, in particular, those parts of the cortex beneath the forehead, known as the frontal lobes—to modify the impulses that surge up from within the brain, to provide judgment, to organize behavior and decision-making, to learn and adhere to rules of everyday life." It is difficult to have pride of authorship in a sentence like that. My guess is that it's a reworked version of something I read in a textbook. Lavery knew that failing to credit Partington would have been wrong. Borrowing the personal story of a woman whose sister was murdered by a serial killer matters because that story has real emotional value to its owner. As Lavery put it, it touches on someone's shattered life. Are boilerplate descriptions of physiological functions in the same league?

It also matters *how* Lavery chose to use my words. Borrowing crosses the line when it is used for a derivative work. It's one thing if you're writing a history of the Kennedys, like Doris Kearns Goodwin, and borrow, without attribution, from another history of the Kennedys. But Lavery wasn't writing another profile of Dorothy Lewis. She was writing a play about something entirely new—about what would happen if a mother met the man who killed her daughter. And she used my descriptions of Lewis's work and the outline of Lewis's life as a building block in making that confrontation plausible. Isn't that the way creativity is supposed to work? Old words in the service of a new idea aren't the problem. What inhibits creativity is new words in the service of an old idea.

And this is the second problem with plagiarism. It is not merely extremist. It has also become disconnected from the broader question of what does and does not inhibit creativity. We accept the right of one writer to engage in a full-scale knockoff of another—think how many serial-killer novels have been cloned from "The Silence of the Lambs." Yet, when Kathy Acker incorporated parts of a Harold Robbins sex scene verbatim in a satiric novel, she was denounced as a plagiarist (and threatened with a lawsuit). When I worked at a newspaper, we were routinely dispatched to "match" a story from the *Times*: to do a new version of someone else's idea. But had we "matched" any of the *Times'* words—even the most banal of phrases—it could have been a firing offense. The ethics of plagiarism have turned into the narcissism of

50

small differences: because journalism cannot own up to its heavily derivative nature, it must enforce originality on the level of the sentence.

Dorothy Lewis says that one of the things that hurt her most about   40
"Frozen" was that Agnetha turns out to have had an affair with her collaborator, David Nabkus. Lewis feared that people would think she had
had an affair with her collaborator, Jonathan Pincus. "That's slander,"
Lewis told me. "I'm recognizable in that. Enough people have called me
and said, 'Dorothy, its about you,' and if everything up to that point is
true, then the affair becomes true in the mind. So that is another reason
that I feel violated. If you are going to take the life of somebody, and
make them absolutely identifiable, you don't create an affair, and you
certainly don't have that as a climax of the play."

It is easy to understand how shocking it must have been for Lewis to
sit in the audience and see her "character" admit to that indiscretion.
But the truth is that Lavery has every right to create an affair for
Agnetha, because Agnetha is not Dorothy Lewis. She is a fictional character, drawn from Lewis's life but endowed with a completely imaginary
set of circumstances and actions. In real life, Lewis kissed Ted Bundy on
the cheek, and in some versions of "Frozen" Agnetha kisses Ralph. But
Lewis kissed Bundy only because he kissed her first, and there's a big difference between responding to a kiss from a killer and initiating one.
When we first see Agnetha, she's rushing out of the house and thinking
murderous thoughts on the airplane. Dorothy Lewis also charges out of
her house and thinks murderous thoughts. But the dramatic function of
that scene is to make us think, in that moment, that Agnetha is crazy.
And the one inescapable fact about Lewis is that she is not crazy: she has
helped get people to rethink their notions of criminality because of her
unshakable command of herself and her work. Lewis is upset not just
about how Lavery copied her life story, in other words, but about how
Lavery *changed* her life story. She's not merely upset about plagiarism.
She's upset about art—about the use of old words in the service of a new
idea—and her feelings are perfectly understandable, because the alter-
ations of art can be every bit as unsettling and hurtful as the thievery of
plagiarism. It's just that art is not a breach of ethics.

When I read the original reviews of "Frozen," I noticed that time and
again critics would use, without attribution, some version of the sentence "The difference between a crime of evil and a crime of illness is the
difference between a sin and a symptom." That's my phrase, of course. I
wrote it. Lavery borrowed it from me, and now the critics were borrowing it from her. The plagiarist was being plagiarized. In this case, there is
no "art" defense: nothing new was being done with that line. And this
was not "news." Yet do I really own "sins and symptoms"? There is a
quote by Gandhi, it turns out, using the same two words, and I'm sure

that if I were to plow through the body of English literature I would find the path littered with crimes of evil and crimes of illness. The central fact about the "Phantom" case is that Ray Repp, if he was borrowing from Andrew Lloyd Webber, certainly didn't realize it, and Andrew Lloyd Webber didn't realize that he was borrowing from himself. Creative property, Lessig reminds us, has many lives—the newspaper arrives at our door, it becomes part of the archive of human knowledge, then it wraps fish. And, by the time ideas pass into their third and fourth lives, we lose track of where they came from, and we lose control of where they are going. The final dishonesty of the plagiarism fundamentalists is to encourage us to pretend that these chains of influence and evolution do not exist, and that a writer's words have a virgin birth and an eternal life. I suppose that I could get upset about what happened to my words. I could also simply acknowledge that I had a good, long ride with that line—and let it go.

"It's been absolutely bloody, really, because it attacks my own notion of my character," Lavery said, sitting at my kitchen table. A bouquet of flowers she had brought were on the counter behind her. "It feels absolutely terrible. I've had to go through the pain for being careless. I'd like to repair what happened, and I don't know how to do that. I just didn't think I was doing the wrong thing . . . and then the article comes out in the *New York Times* and every continent in the world." There was a long silence. She was heartbroken. But, more than that, she was confused, because she didn't understand how six hundred and seventy-five rather ordinary words could bring the walls tumbling down. "It's been horrible and bloody." She began to cry. "I'm still composting what happened. It will be for a purpose . . . whatever that purpose is."

[2004]

DONALD HALL   [b. 1928]

Four Ways of Reading

Born in New Haven, Connecticut, esteemed poet **Donald Hall** found his
calling in his teens, both attending the Bread Loaf Writers' Conference
and publishing his first work at the age of sixteen. He earned his B.A.
from Harvard University in 1951 and went on to earn a B. Litt. from
Oxford University in 1953. After spending a year as a Creative Writing
Fellow at Stanford and then three years in the Society of Fellows at
Harvard, he took a position teaching English at the University of Michigan at Ann Arbor from 1957 to 1975, during which time he met and
married his late wife, poet Jane Kenyon. Following his retirement from
teaching, Hall and Kenyon moved to his grandparents' New Hampshire
farm in order that he might pursue writing full-time. Much like his
mentor Robert Frost, Hall employs themes of simple living, nature, and
mortality in his writing. Prolific, he has published poetry, prose, essays,
drama, and children's books, including *Kicking the Leaves* (1978); *The
Happy Man* (1986); and *Without* (1998), which commemorates his
wife's life and fight with leukemia. Hall has been honored with two
Guggenheim Fellowships, a Robert Frost Medal, the National Book
Critics Circle Award for Poetry, and a Caldecott Medal, and he has been
nominated three times for the National Book Award. Hall served as the
poet laureate of New Hampshire from 1984 to 1989 and in June 2006
he was named the fourteenth United States Poet Laureate.

In "Four Ways of Reading," originally published in the *New York
Times* (1969), Hall ponders the significance attributed to the act of
reading and distinguishes between four ways of reading: the brisk scan
to acquire information; the reflective read in pursuit of higher concepts; the escapist reading to protect against reality; and the savory
and thoughtful reading to delight in the actual words and imagination
of literature.

Everywhere one meets the idea that reading is an activity desirable in
itself. It is understandable that publishers and librarians—and even
writers—should promote this assumption, but it is strange that the idea
should have general currency. People surround the idea of reading with

Donald Hall, "Four Ways of Reading" from the *New York Times*, January 26, 1969.
Copyright © 1969 by the New York Times. Reprinted by permission.

piety, and do not take into account the purpose of reading or the value of what is being read. Teachers and parents praise the child who reads, and praise themselves, whether the text be *The Reader's Digest* or *Moby Dick*. The advent of TV has increased the false values ascribed to reading, since TV provides a vulgar alternative. But this piety is silly; and most reading is no more cultural nor intellectual nor imaginative than shooting pool or watching *What's My Line*.

It is worth asking how the act of reading became something to value in itself, as opposed for instance to the act of conversation or the act of taking a walk. Mass literacy is a recent phenomenon, and I suggest that the aura which decorates reading is a relic of the importance of reading to our great-great-grandparents. Literacy used to be a mark of social distinction, separating a small portion of humanity from the rest. The farm laborer who was ambitious for his children did not daydream that they would become schoolteachers or doctors; he daydreamed that they would learn to read, and that a world would therefore open up to them in which they did not have to labor in the fields fourteen hours a day for six days a week in order to buy salt and cotton. On the next rank of society, ample time for reading meant that the reader was free from the necessity to spend most of his waking hours making a living of any kind.... Reading is an inactivity, and therefore a badge of social class. Of course, these reasons for the piety attached to reading are never acknowledged. They show themselves in the shape of our attitudes toward books; reading gives off an air of gentility.

It seems to me possible to name four kinds of reading, each with a characteristic manner and purpose. The first is reading for information —reading to learn about a trade, or politics, or how to accomplish something. We read a newspaper this way, or most textbooks, or directions on how to assemble a bicycle. With most of this sort of material, the reader can learn to scan the page quickly, coming up with what he needs and ignoring what is irrelevant to him, like the rhythm of the sentence, or the play of metaphor. Courses in speed reading can help us read for this purpose, training the eye to jump quickly across the page. If we read *The New York Times* with the attention we should give a novel or a poem, we will have time for nothing else, and our mind will be cluttered with clichés and dead metaphor. Quick eye-reading is a necessity to anyone who wants to keep up with what's happening, or learn much of what has happened in the past. The amount of reflection, which interrupts and slows down the reading, depends on the material.

But it is not the same activity as reading literature. There ought to be another word. If we read a work of literature properly, we read slowly, and we hear all the words. If our lips do not actually move, it's only laziness. The muscles in our throats move, and come together when we see the word "squeeze." We hear the sounds so accurately that if a syllable is missing in a line of poetry we hear the lack, though we may not know what we are lacking. In prose we accept the rhythms, and hear the adjacent sounds. We also register a track of feeling through the metaphors and associations of words. Careless writing prevents this sort of attention, and becomes offensive. But the great writers reward this attention. Only by the full exercise of our powers to receive language can we absorb their intelligence and their imagination. This kind of reading goes through the ear — though the eye takes in the print, and decodes it into sound — to the throat and the understanding, and it can never be quick. It is slow and sensual, a deep pleasure that begins with touch and ends with the sort of comprehension that we associate with dream.

Too many intellectuals read in order to reduce images to abstractions. 5 With a philosopher one reads slowly, as if it were literature, but much time must be spent with the eyes turned away from the pages, reflecting on the text. To read literature this way is to turn it into something it is not — to concepts clothed in character, or philosophy sugar-coated. I think that most literary intellectuals read this way, including the brighter Professors of English, with the result that they miss literature completely, and concern themselves with a minor discipline called the history of ideas. I remember a course in Chaucer at my University in which the final exam largely required the identification of a hundred or more fragments of Chaucer, none as long as a line. If you liked poetry, and read Chaucer through a couple of times slowly, you found yourself knowing them all. If you were a literary intellectual, well-informed about the great chain of being, chances are you had a difficult time. To read literature is to be intimately involved with the words on the page, and never to think of them as the embodiments of ideas which can be expressed in other terms. On the other hand, intellectual writing — closer to mathematics on a continuum that has at its opposite pole lyric poetry — requires intellectual reading, which is slow because it is reflective and because the reader must pause to evaluate concepts.

But most of the reading which is praised for itself is neither literary nor intellectual. It is narcotic. Novels, stories, and biographies — historical sagas, monthly regurgitations of book clubs, four- and five-thousand word daydreams of the magazines — these are the opium of the suburbs. The drug is not harmful except to the addict himself, and is no more injurious to him than Johnny Carson or a bridge club, but it is nothing to be proud of. This reading is the automated daydream, the mild trip of the housewife and the tired businessman, interested not in experience and feeling but in turning off the possibilities of experience and feeling. Great literature, if we read it well, opens us up to the world, and makes us more sensitive to it, as if we acquired eyes that could see through things and ears that could hear smaller sounds. But by narcotic reading, one can reduce great literature to the level of *The Valley of the Dolls*. One can read *Anna Karenina* passively and inattentively, and float down the river of lethargy as if one were reading a confession magazine: "I Spurned My Husband for a Count."

I think that everyone reads for narcosis occasionally, and perhaps most consistently in late adolescence, when great readers are born. I remember reading to shut the world out, away at a school where I did not want to be; I invented a word to name my disease: "bibliolepsy," on the analogy of narcolepsy. But after a while the books became a window on the world, and not a screen against it. This change doesn't always happen. I think that late adolescent narcotic reading accounts for some of the badness of English departments. As a college student, the boy loves reading and majors in English because he would be reading anyway. Deciding on a career, he takes up English teaching for the same reason. Then in graduate school he is trained to be a scholar, which is painful and irrelevant, and finds he must write papers and publish them to be a Professor—and at about this time he no longer requires reading for narcosis, and he is left with nothing but a Ph.D. and the prospect of fifty years of teaching literature; and he does not even like literature.

Narcotic reading survives the impact of television, because this type of reading has even less reality than melodrama; that is, the reader is in control: once the characters reach into the reader's feelings, he is able to stop reading, or glance away, or superimpose his own daydream. The trouble with television is that it writes its own script. Literature is often valued precisely because of its distance from the tangible. Some readers prefer looking into the text of a play to seeing it performed. Reading a play, it is possible to stage it oneself by an imaginative act; but it is also possible to remove it from real people. Here is Virginia Woolf, who was lavish in her praise of the act of reading, talking about reading a play rather than seeing it: "Certainly there is a good deal to be said for reading *Twelfth Night* in the book if the book can be read in a garden, with no sound but the thud of an apple falling to the earth, or of the wind ruffling the branches of the trees." She sets her own stage; the play is called *Virginia Woolf Reads Twelfth Night in a Garden*. Piety moves into narcissism, and the high metaphors of Shakespeare's lines dwindle into the flowers of an English garden; actors in ruffles wither, while the wind ruffles branches.

PERRI KLASS   [b. 1958]

Learning the Language

Perri Klass received her M.D. from Harvard Medical School in 1986. A practicing pediatrician in Massachusetts, she is the president and medical director of the national program Reach Out and Read, which stresses the importance of reading aloud and of general literacy in the context of pediatric primary care. Klass's short stories have won five O. Henry awards and have been collected in two volumes. Her interests are varied, and she regularly writes about travel, food, and knitting for such publications as the *New York Times Magazine, Discover, Mademoiselle, Esquire, Vogue, Knitters,* and *Gourmet.* She has written several novels, including *Other Women's Children* (1990) and *The Mystery of Breathing* (2004). She cowrote *Every Mother Is a Daughter* (2006) with her mother and *Quirky Kids: Understanding and Helping Your Child Who Doesn't Fit In* (2003), with Eileen Costello, M.D. Klass is known for writing with great humor and compassion. She has said, "Writers and doctors, I would argue, have many overlapping traits—a fascination with the many stories out there in the world, an eagerness to probe for detail and complexity, a willingness to reformulate and retell."

The following essay, about learning the jargon of doctors and medical school, is taken from *A Not Entirely Benign Procedure: Four Years as a Medical Student* (1987).

"Mrs. Tolstoy is your basic LOL in NAD, admitted for a soft rule-out MI," the intern announces. I scribble that on my patient list. In other words, Mrs. Tolstoy is a Little Old Lady in No Apparent Distress who is in the hospital to make sure she hasn't had a heart attack (rule out a Myocardial Infarction). And we think it's unlikely that she has had a heart attack (a *soft* rule-out).

If I learned nothing else during my first three months of working in the hospital as a medical student, I learned endless jargon and abbreviations. I started out in a state of primeval innocence, in which I didn't even know that "s̄ CP, SOB, N/V" meant "without chest pain, shortness of breath, or nausea and vomiting." By the end I took the abbreviations so much for granted that I would complain to my mother the English professor, "And can you believe I had to put down *three* NG tubes last night?"

"You'll have to tell me what an NG tube is if you want me to sympathize properly," my mother said. NG, nasogastric—isn't it obvious?

I picked up not only the specific expressions but also the patterns of speech and the grammatical conventions; for example, you never say that a patient's blood pressure fell or that his cardiac enzymes rose. Instead, the patient is always the subject of the verb: "He dropped his pressure." "He bumped his enzymes." This sort of construction probably reflects the profound irritation of the intern when the nurses come in the middle of the night to say that Mr. Dickinson has disturbingly low blood pressure. "Oh, he's gonna hurt me bad tonight," the intern might say, inevitably angry at Mr. Dickinson for dropping his pressure and creating a problem.

When chemotherapy fails to cure Mrs. Bacon's cancer, what we say is,   5 "Mrs. Bacon failed chemotherapy."

"Well, we've already had one hit today, and we're up next, but at least we've got mostly stable players on our team." This means that our team (group of doctors and medical students) has already gotten one new admission today, and it is our turn again, so we'll get whoever is admitted next in emergency, but at least most of the patients we already have are fairly stable, that is, unlikely to drop their pressures or in any other way get suddenly sicker and hurt us bad. Baseball metaphor is pervasive. A no-hitter is a night without any new admissions. A player is always a patient—a nitrate player is a patient on nitrates, a unit player is a patient in the intensive care unit, and so on, until you reach the terminal player.

It is interesting to consider what it means to be winning, or doing well, in this perennial baseball game. When the intern hangs up the phone and announces, "I got a hit," that is not cause for congratulations. The team is not scoring points; rather, it is getting hit, being bombarded with new patients. The object of the game from the point of view of the doctors, considering the players for whom they are already responsible, is to get as few new hits as possible.

This special language contributes to a sense of closeness and professional spirit among people who are under a great deal of stress. As a medical student, I found it exciting to discover that I'd finally cracked the code, that I could understand what doctors said and wrote, and could use the same formulations myself. Some people seem to become enamored of the jargon for its own sake, perhaps because they are so deeply thrilled with the idea of medicine, with the idea of themselves as doctors.

I knew a medical student who was referred to by the interns on the team as Mr. Eponym because he was so infatuated with eponymous terminology, the more obscure the better. He never said "capillary pulsations" if he could say "Quincke's pulses." He would lovingly tell over the multinamed syndromes—Wolff-Parkinson-White, Lown-Ganong-Levine, Schönlein-Henoch—until the temptation to suggest Schleswig-Holstein or Stevenson-Kefauver or Baskin-Robbins became irresistible to his less reverent colleagues.

And there is the jargon that you don't ever want to hear yourself using. You know that your training is changing you, but there are certain changes you think would be going a little too far. 10

The resident was describing a man with devastating terminal pancreatic cancer. "Basically he's CTD," the resident concluded. I reminded myself that I had resolved not to be shy about asking when I didn't understand things. "CTD?" I asked timidly.

The resident smirked at me. "Circling The Drain."

The images are vivid and terrible. "What happened to Mrs. Melville?"

"Oh, she boxed last night." To box is to die, of course.

Then there are the more pompous locutions that can make the beginning medical student nervous about the effects of medical training. A 15 friend of mine was told by his resident, "A pregnant woman with sickle-cell represents a failure of genetic counseling."

Mr. Eponym, who tried hard to talk like the doctors, once explained to me, "An infant is basically a brainstem preparation." The term "brainstem preparation," as used in neurological research, refers to an animal whose higher brain functions have been destroyed so that only the most primitive reflexes remain, like the sucking reflex, the startle reflex, and the rooting reflex.

And yet at other times the harshness dissipates into a strangely elusive euphemism. "As you know, this is a not entirely benign procedure," some doctor will say, and that will be understood to imply agony, risk of complications, and maybe even a significant mortality rate.

The more extreme forms aside, one most important function of medical jargon is to help doctors maintain some distance from their patients. By reformulating a patient's pain and problems into a language that the patient doesn't even speak, I suppose we are in some sense taking those pains and problems under our jurisdiction and also reducing their emotional impact. This linguistic separation between doctors and patients allows conversations to go on at the bedside that are unintelligible to the patient. "Naturally, we're worried about adeno-CA," the intern can say to the medical student, and lung cancer need never be mentioned.

I learned a new language this past summer. At times it thrills me to hear myself using it. It enables me to understand my colleagues, to communicate effectively in the hospital. Yet I am uncomfortably aware that I will never again notice the peculiarities and even atrocities of medical language as keenly as I did this summer. There may be specific expressions I manage to avoid, but even as I remark them, promising myself I will never use them, I find that this language is becoming my professional speech. It no longer sounds strange in my ears—or coming from my mouth. And I am afraid that as with any new language, to use it properly you must absorb not only the vocabulary but also the structure, the logic, the attitudes. At first you may notice the new and alien assumptions every time you put together a sentence, but with time and increased fluency you stop being aware of them at all. And as you lose that awareness, for better or for worse, you move closer and closer to being a doctor instead of just talking like one.

C. H. KNOBLAUCH [b. 1945]

Literacy and the Politics of Education

Born in 1945, C. H. Knoblauch is an associate professor of English and associate dean of undergraduate studies at the State University of New York–Albany. Specializing in rhetoric, his essays have appeared in *CCC, College English, Rhetoric Society Quarterly,* and *Eighteenth Century Studies,* among others. Knoblauch has cowritten two books with his wife Lil Brannon, associate professor of English and director of the Writing Center at SUNY Albany: *Rhetorical Traditions and the Teaching of Writing* (1984), which bemoans the fact that contemporary education relies more heavily on the outdated classical rhetorical style of Aristotle than on modern rhetoric, and *Critical Teaching and the Idea of Literacy* (1993), which explores the pedagogical repercussions on the classroom of American educational policy.

"Literacy and the Politics of Education," first presented at the 1988 Right to Literacy Conference, examines the concept of literacy and how and why it is considered essential for the nonliterate. Realizing that being literate can ensure prosperity in the modern world, Knoblauch looks at the motivations of those who would confer literacy and assigns levels of literacy—functional, cultural, and critical—to its practitioners. He concludes that the myriad definitions of literacy provide little clarity, and literacy itself conveys little empowerment, unless understood from the political perspective of the already literate and their veiled paternalism.

Literacy is one of those mischievous concepts, like virtuousness and craftsmanship, that appear to denote capacities but that actually convey value judgments. It is rightly viewed, Linda Brodkey has noted, "as a social trope" and its sundry definitions "as cultural Rorschachs" (47). The labels *literate* and *illiterate* almost always imply more than a degree or deficiency of skill. They are, grossly or subtly, sociocultural judgments laden with approbation, disapproval, or pity about the character and place, the worthiness and prospects, of persons and groups. A revealing exercise would be to catalog the definitions of literacy that lie explicit or implicit in the pages of this collection, definitions that motivate judgments, political no less than scholarly, about which people belong in literate and illiterate categories; the numbers in each group; why and in what ways literacy is important; what should be done for or about those who are not literate or are less literate than others; and who has the power to say so. It would be quickly apparent that there is no uniformity of view, since the values that surround reading and writing abilities differ from argument to argument. Instead, there are competing views, responsive to the agendas of those who characterize the ideal. Invariably, definitions of literacy are also rationalizations of its importance. Furthermore, they are invariably offered by the literate, constituting, therefore, implicit rationalizations of the importance of literate people, who are powerful (the reasoning goes) because they are literate and, as such, deserving of power.

The concept of literacy is embedded, then, in the ideological dispositions of those who use the concept, those who profit from it, and those who have the standing and motivation to enforce it as a social requirement. It is obviously not a cultural value in all times and places; when Sequoya brought his syllabic writing system to the Cherokee,° their first inclination was to put him to death for dabbling in an evil magic. The majority of the world's languages have lacked alphabets, though they have nonetheless articulated rich oral traditions in societies that have also produced many other varieties of cultural achievement. To be sure, there is ready agreement, at least among the literate, about the necessity of literacy in the so-called modern world; this agreement is reinforced by explanations that typically imply a more developed mode of existence among literate people. I. J. Gelb has written, for instance: "As language distinguishes man from animal, so writing distinguishes civilized man from barbarian," going on to point out that "an illiterate person cannot expect to participate successfully in human progress, and what is true of individuals is also true of any group of individuals, social strata, or ethnic units" (221–222). This argument offers a common and pernicious half-truth, representing the importance of literacy, which is unquestionable, in absolutist and ethnocentric terms.

However, if literacy today is perceived as a compelling value, the reason lies not in such self-interested justifications but in its continuing association with forms of social reality that depend on its primacy. During the Middle Ages, clerks were trained to read and write so that they could keep accounts for landowners, merchants, and government

Sequoya (c. 1773–1843): Sequoya created a syllabic writing system, approved by tribal elders in 1821, that enabled the Cherokee language to be reproduced in printed form.

officials. Bureaucratic documentation was not conceived so that people could acquire literacy. Christian missionaries in nineteenth-century Africa spread literacy so that people could read the Bible; they did not teach the Bible so that the illiterate could become readers and writers. There is no question that literacy is necessary to survival and success in the contemporary world—a world where the literate claim authority to set the terms of survival and success, a world that reading and writing abilities have significantly shaped in the first place. But it is important to regard that necessity in the context of political conditions that account for it, or else we sacrifice the humanizing understanding that life can be otherwise than the way we happen to know it and that people who are measured positively by the yardstick of literacy enjoy their privileges because of their power to choose and apply that instrument on their own behalf, not because of their point of development or other innate worthiness. Possessing that understanding, educators in particular but other citizens as well may advance their agendas for literacy with somewhat less likelihood of being blinded by the light of their own benevolence to the imperial designs that may lurk in the midst of their compassion.

In the United States today, several arguments about the nature and importance of literacy vie for power in political and educational life. Sketching the more popular arguments may remind us of the extent to which definitions of the concept incorporate the social agendas of the definers, serving the needs of the nonliterate only through the mediation of someone's vision of the way the world should be. Literacy never stands alone in these perspectives as a neutral denoting of skills; it is always literacy for something—for professional competence in a technological world, for civic responsibility and the preservation of heritage, for personal growth and self-fulfilment, for social and political change. The struggle of any one definition to dominate the others entails no merely casual or arbitrary choice of values, nor does it allow for a conflating of alternatives in some grand compromise or list of cumulative benefits. At stake are fundamentally different perceptions of social reality; the nature of language and discourse; the importance of culture, history, and tradition; the functions of schools, as well as other commitments, few of which are regarded as negotiable. At the same time, since no definition achieves transcendent authority, their dialectical interaction offers a context of choices within which continually changing educational and other social policies find their justification. The process of choosing is visible every day, for better and worse, in legislative assemblies, television talk shows, newspaper editorials, and classrooms throughout the country.

The most familiar literacy argument comes from the functionalist 5 perspective, with its appealingly pragmatic emphasis on readying people for the necessities of daily life—writing checks, reading sets of instructions—as well as for the professional tasks of a complex technological society. Language abilities in this view are often represented by the metaphors of information theory: Language is a code that enables the sending of messages and the processing of information. The concern of a functionalist perspective is the efficient transmission of useful messages in a value-neutral medium. Basic-skill and technical-writing programs in schools, many on-the-job training programs in business and industry, and the training programs of the United States military—all typically find their rationalization in the argument for functional literacy, in each case presuming that the ultimate value of language lies in its utilitarian capacity to pass information back and forth for economic or other material gain.

The functionalist argument has the advantage of tying literacy to concrete needs, appearing to promise socioeconomic benefit to anyone who can achieve the appropriate minimal competency. But it has a more hidden advantage as well, at least from the standpoint of those whose literacy is more than minimal: It safeguards the socioeconomic status quo. Whatever the rhetoric of its advocates concerning the "self-determined objectives" (Hunter and Harman 7) of people seeking to acquire skills, functionalism serves the world as it is, inviting outsiders to enter that world on the terms of its insiders by fitting themselves to roles that they are superficially free to choose but that have been prepared as a range of acceptable alternatives. Soldiers will know how to repair an MX missile by reading the field manual but will not question the use of such weapons because of their reading of antimilitarist philosophers; clerks will be able to fill out and file their order forms but will not therefore be qualified for positions in higher management. Functionalist arguments presume that a given social order is right simply because it exists, and their advocates are content to recommend the training of persons to take narrowly beneficial places in that society. The rhetoric of technological progressivism is often leavened with a mixture of fear and patriotism (as in *A Nation at Risk*)° in order to defend a social program that maintains managerial classes—whose members are always more than just functionally literate—in their customary places while outfitting workers with the minimal reading and writing skills needed for usefulness to the modern information economy.

Cultural literacy offers another common argument about the importance of reading and writing, one frequently mounted by traditionalist educators but sustained in populist versions as well, especially among people who

A Nation at Risk: This 1983 report by the National Commission on Excellence in Education couched many of its criticisms and recommendations in terms of the present and future position of the United States as a world leader.

feel insecure about their own standing and their future prospects when confronted by the volatile mix of ethnic heritages and socioeconomic interests that make up contemporary American life. The argument for cultural literacy moves beyond a mechanist conception of basic skills and toward an affirmation of supposedly stable and timeless cultural values inscribed in the verbal memory—in particular, the canonical literature of Western European society. Its reasoning is that true literacy entails more than technical proficiency, a minimal ability to make one's way in the world; that literacy also includes an awareness of cultural heritage, a capacity for higher-order thinking, even some aesthetic discernment—faculties not automatically available to the encoders and decoders of the functionalist perspective. Language is no mere tool in this view but is, rather, a repository of cultural values and to that extent a source of social cohesion. To guard the vitality of the language, the advocates of cultural literacy say, citizens must learn to speak and write decorously, as well as functionally, and must also read great books, where the culture is enshrined. In some popular versions of cultural literacy, English is regarded as the only truly American language and is, therefore, the appropriate medium of commerce and government. The economic self-interest that pervades the functionalist perspective frequently gives way here to jingoistic protectionism; cultural literacy advocates presume that the salvation of some set of favored cultural norms or language practices lies necessarily in the marginalizing or even extinction of others.

The argument for cultural literacy often presents itself within a myth of the fall from grace: Language and, by extension, culture once enjoyed an Edenlike existence but are currently degenerating because of internal decay and sundry forces of barbarism. People no longer read, write, or think with the strength of insight of which they were once capable. They no longer remember and, therefore, no longer venerate. The age of high culture has passed; minds and characters have been weakened by television or rock music or the 1960s. The reasons vary, but the message is clear: Unless heritage is protected, the former purity of language reconstituted, the past life of art and philosophy retrieved, we risk imminent cultural decay. However extravagant such predictions appear to unbelievers, there is no mistaking the melancholy energy of contemporary proponents of cultural literacy or, if we are to judge from the recent best-seller lists, the number of solemn citizens—anxious perhaps about recent influxes of Mexicans, Vietnamese, and other aliens—who take their warnings to heart.

Arguments for cultural and functional literacy plainly dominate the American imagination at the moment and for obvious reasons. They articulate the needs, hopes, anxieties, and frustrations of the conservative temper. They reveal in different ways the means of using an ideal of literacy to preserve and advance the world as it is, a world in which the interests of traditionally privileged groups dominate the interests of the traditionally less privileged. Schools reflect such conservatism to the extent that they view themselves as agencies for preserving established institutions and values, not to mention the hierarchical requirements of the American economy. But still other arguments, if not quite so popular, reflect the priorities and the agendas of liberal and even radical ideologies struggling to project their altered visions of social reality, seeking their own power over others under the banner of literacy. The liberal argument, for instance, emphasizes literacy for personal growth, finding voice in the process-writing movement in American high schools or in the various practices of personalized learning. The liberal argument has been successful, up to a point, in schools because it borrows from long-hallowed American myths of expressive freedom and boundless individual opportunity, romantic values to which schools are obliged to pay at least lip service even when otherwise promoting more authoritarian curricula.

The assumption of a literacy-for-personal-growth argument is that 10 language expresses the power of the individual imagination, so that nurturing a person's reading and writing abilities enables the development of that power, thereby promoting the progress of society through the progress of the individual learner. The political agenda behind this liberalism tends to be educational and other social change; its concern for personal learning draws attention to school practices that supposedly thwart the needs of individual students or that disenfranchise some groups of students in the interest of maintaining the values of the status quo. The kinds of change that the personal-growth argument recommends are, on the whole, socially tolerable because they are moderate in character: Let students read enjoyable novels, instead of basal reader selections; let young women and young Hispanics find images of themselves in schoolwork, not just images of white males. Using the rhetoric of moral sincerity, the personal-growth argument speaks compassionately on behalf of the disadvantaged. Meanwhile, it avoids, for the most part, the suggestion of any fundamental restructuring of institutions, believing that the essential generosity and fair-mindedness of American citizens will accommodate some liberalization of outmoded curricula and an improved quality of life for the less privileged as long as fundamental political and economic interests are not jeopardized. Frequently, Americans do hear such appeals, though always in the context of an implicit agreement that nothing important is going to change. Accordingly, advocates of expressive writing, personalized reading programs, whole-language curricula, and open classrooms have been permitted to carry out their educational programs, with politicians and school officials quick to realize the ultimate gain in administrative control that comes from allowing such modest symbols of self-determination to release built-up pressures of dissatisfaction.

A fourth argument, substantially to the left of the personal-growth advocates, is one for what Henry Giroux, among others, calls critical literacy (226). Critical literacy is a radical perspective whose adherents, notably Paulo Freire,° have been influential primarily in the Third World, especially Latin America. Strongly influenced by marxist philosophical premises, critical literacy is not a welcome perspective in this country, and it finds voice currently in only a few academic enclaves, where it exists more as a facsimile of oppositional culture than as a practice, and in an even smaller number of community-based literacy projects, which are typically concerned with adult learners. Its agenda is to identify reading and writing abilities with a critical consciousness of the social conditions in which people find themselves, recognizing the extent to which language practices objectify and rationalize these conditions and the extent to which people with authority to name the world dominate others whose voices they have been able to suppress. Literacy, therefore, constitutes a means to power, a way to seek political enfranchisement—not with the naive expectation that merely being literate is sufficient to change the distribution of prerogatives but with the belief that the ability to speak alone enables entrance to the arena in which power is contested. At stake, from this point of view, is, in principle, the eventual reconstituting of the class structure of American life, specifically a change of those capitalist economic practices that assist the dominance of particular groups.

For that reason, if for no other, such a view of literacy will remain suspect as a theoretical enterprise and will be considered dangerous, perhaps to the point of illegality, in proportion to its American adherents' attempts to implement it practically in schools and elsewhere. The scholarly Right has signaled this institutional hostility in aggressive attacks on Jonathan Kozol's *Illiterate America*, the most popular American rendering of critical-literacy arguments, for its supposedly inaccurate statistics about illiteracy and in calculatedly patronizing Kozol's enthusiasm for radical change. Meanwhile, although critical literacy is trendy in some academic circles, those who commend it also draw their wages from the capitalist economy it is designed to challenge. Whether its advocates will take Kozol's risks in bringing so volatile a practice into community schools is open to doubt. Whether something important would change if they did take the risks is also doubtful. Whether, if successful, they would still approve a world in which their own privileges were withheld may be

Paulo Freire (b. 1921): Author of *The Politics of Education: Culture, Power, and Liberation* (1985) and *Pedagogy of the Oppressed* (1970).

more doubtful still. In any case, one can hardly imagine NCTE or the MLA,° let alone the Department of Education, formally sanctioning such a fundamental assault on their own institutional perquisites.

Definitions of literacy could be multiplied far beyond these popular arguments. But enumerating others would only belabor my point, which is that no definition tells, with ontological or objective reliability, what literacy is; definitions only tell what some person or group—motivated by political commitments—wants or needs literacy to be. What makes any such perspective powerful is the ability of its adherents to make it invisible or, at least, transparent—a window on the world, revealing simple and stable truths—so that the only problem still needing to be addressed is one of implementation: how best to make the world—other people—conform to that prevailing vision. At the same time, what makes any ideology visible as such and, therefore, properly limited in its power to compel unconscious assent is critical scrutiny, the only safe-guard people have if they are to be free of the designs of others. To the extent that literacy advocates of one stripe or another remain uncon-scious of or too comfortable with those designs, their offerings of skills constitute a form of colonizing, a benign but no less mischievous pater-nalism that rationalizes the control of others by representing it as a means of liberation. To the extent that the nonliterate allow themselves to be objects of someone else's "kindness," they will find no power in literacy, however it is defined, but only altered terms of dispossession. When, for instance, the memberships of U.S. English and English First,° totaling around half a million citizens, argue for compulsory English, they may well intend the enfranchisement of those whose lack of English-language abilities has depressed their economic opportunities. But they also intend the extinction of cultural values inscribed in languages other than their own and held to be worthwhile by people different from them-selves. In this or any other position on literacy, its advocates, no less than its intended beneficiaries, need to hear—for all our sakes—a critique of whatever assumptions and beliefs are fueling their passionate benevolence.

The **NCTE** (National Council of Teachers of English) and the **MLA** (Modern Language Association): The two largest professional associations of English teach-ers in the country.   **U.S. English and English First:** Active in the 1980s, the politi-cal organizations English First, a project of the Committee to Protect the Family, and U.S. English petitioned for a constitutional amendment to make English the official language of the United States.

GUNTHER KRESS

From Literacy in the New Media Age

Originally from Australia, **Gunther Kress** is a professor of semiotics
and education at the University of London. Kress's research interests
focus on the impact of technology and new modes of communication
on language and literacy, and his work has been profoundly influential
in the development of multimodal curricula in education. His books
include *Before Writing: Rethinking the Paths to Literacy* (1997), *Reading
Images: The Grammar of Visual Design* (2006), and *Literacy in the New
Media Age* (2003).

 In the following excerpts from the first chapter of *Literacy in the
New Media Age*, Kress argues that new media transforms both our
understanding of the world and our production of knowledge. Literacy, therefore, is redefined and reformed by new media, according to
Kress. While explaining the shifting hierarchy that exists between the
logic of words and images, he critiques the "democratic potentials and
effects" of digital technology, arguing that technology is a site of conflict over power.

It is no longer possible to think about literacy in isolation from a vast
array of social, technological and economic factors. Two distinct yet
related factors deserve to be particularly highlighted. These are, on the
one hand, the broad move from the now centuries-long dominance of
writing to the new dominance of the image and, on the other hand, the
move from the dominance of the medium of the book to the dominance
of the medium of the screen. These two together are producing a revolution in the uses and effects of literacy and of associated means for representing and communicating at every level and in every domain. Together
they raise two questions: what is the likely future of literacy, and what
are the likely larger-level social and cultural effects of that change?

 One might say the following with some confidence. Language-as-speech
will remain the major mode of communication; language-as-writing will

increasingly be displaced by image in many domains of public communication, though writing will remain the preferred mode of the political and cultural elites. The combined effects on writing of the dominance of the mode of image and of the medium of the screen will produce deep changes in the forms and functions of writing. This in turn will have profound effects on human, cognitive/affective, cultural and bodily engagement with the world, and on the forms and shapes of knowledge. *The world told* is a different world to *the world shown*. The effects of the move to the screen as the major medium of communication will produce far-reaching shifts in relations of power, and not just in the sphere of communication. Where significant changes to distribution of power threaten, there will be fierce resistance by those who presently hold power, so that predictions about the democratic potentials and effects of the new information and communication technologies have to be seen in the light of inevitable struggles over power yet to come. It is already clear that the effects of the two changes taken together will have the widest imaginable political, economic, social, cultural, conceptual/cognitive and epistemological consequences. . . .

It may be as well to try and answer here and now three objections that will be made. One is that more books are published now than ever before; the second is, that there is more writing than ever before, including writing on the screen. The third, the most serious, takes the form of a question: what do we lose if many of the forms of writing that we know disappear?

To the first objection I say: the books that are published now are in very many cases books which are already influenced by the new logic of the screen, and in many cases they are not "books" as that word would have been understood thirty or forty years ago. I am thinking here particularly of textbooks, which then were expositions of coherent "bodies of knowledge" presented in the mode of writing. The move from chapter to chapter was a stately and orderly progression through the unfolding matter of the book. The contemporary textbook—since the late 1970s for lower years of secondary school and by now for all the years of secondary school—is often a collection of "worksheets," organised around the issues of the curriculum, and put between more or less solid covers. This is still called a book. But there are no chapters, there is none of that sense of a reader engaging with and absorbing a coherent exposition of a body of knowledge, authoritatively presented. Instead there is a sense that the issue now is to involve students in action around topics, of learning by doing. Above all, the matter is presented through image more than through writing—and writing and image are given different representational and communicational functions.

These are still called "book," though I think we need to be wary of ⁵ being fooled by the seeming stability of the word. These are not books that can be "read," for instance, in anything like that older sense of the word "read." These are books for working with, for acting on. So yes, there are more "books" published now than ever before, but in many cases the "books" of now are not the "books" of then. And I am not just thinking of factual, information books but of books of all kinds.

And yes, there is more writing than ever before. Let me make two points. The first is, who is writing more? Who is filling the pages of websites with writing? Is it the young? Or is it those who grew up in the era when writing was clearly the dominant mode? The second point goes to the question of the future of writing. Image has coexisted with writing, as of course has speech. In the era of the dominance of writing, when the logic of writing organised the page, image appeared on the page subject to the logic of writing. In simple terms, it fitted in how, where and when the logic of the written text and of the page suggested. In the era of the dominance of the screen, writing appears on the screen subject to the logic of the image. Writing fits in how, where and when the logic of the image-space suggests. The effects on writing, as is already "visible" in any number of ways, tiny at times, larger at others, will be inescapable.

That leaves the third objection. It cannot be dealt with quickly. It requires a large project, much debate, and an uncommon generosity of view. On one level the issue is one of gains and losses; on another level it will require from us a different kind of reflection on what writing is, what forms of imagination it fosters. It asks questions of a profounder kind, about human potentials, wishes, desires—questions which go beyond immediate issues of utility for social or economic needs.

[2003]

ANNE LAMOTT [b. 1954]

Shitty First Drafts

Born in San Francisco in 1954, **Anne Lamott** is the best-selling author of six novels and several works of nonfiction, including *Operating Instructions*, a brutally honest account of motherhood in her son's first year of life, *Bird by Bird: Some Instructions on Writing and Life*, a riotous handbook for aspiring writers, and *Traveling Mercies*, a collection of autobiographical essays on living with faith. The recipient of a Guggenheim fellowship, a one-time food critic for *California* magazine and book reviewer for *Mademoiselle*, Lamott has taught at the University of California, Davis and at numerous writers' conferences. "Word by Word," her biweekly personal reflections contributed to the online *Salon Magazine* from 1996 to 1999, were voted *The Best of the Web* by *Time* magazine. A self-identified recovering alcoholic and born-again Christian, Lamott's writing is frank, candid, and utterly sincere. Her sharp words and strong sense of humor make for a poignantly entertaining read.

"Shitty First Drafts," an excerpt from her book *Bird by Bird: Some Instructions on Writing and Life*, encourages writers to trust in their writing processes. Lamott shares her own writing methods and drolly suggests ways of blocking out even the most annoying distractions.

For me and most of the other writers I know, writing is not rapturous. In fact, the only way I can get anything written at all is to write really, really crummy first drafts.

The first draft is the child's draft, where you let it all pour out and then let it romp all over the place, knowing that no one is going to see it and that you can shape it later. You just let this childlike part of you channel whatever voices and visions come through and onto the page. If one of the characters wants to say "Well, so what, Mr. Poopy Pants?" you let her. No one is going to see it. If the kid wants to get into really sentimental, weepy, emotional territory, you let him. Just get it all down on paper, because there may be something great in those six crazy pages that you would never have gotten to by more rational, grown-up means. There may be something in the very last line of the very last paragraph on page six that you just love, that is so beautiful or wild that you now know what you're supposed to be writing about, more or less, or in what direction you might go—but there was no way to get to this without first getting through the first five and a half pages.

I used to write food reviews for *California* magazine before it folded. (My writing food reviews had nothing to do with the magazine folding, although every single review did cause a couple of canceled subscriptions. Some readers took umbrage at my comparing mounds of vegetable puree with various ex-presidents' brains.) These reviews always took two days to write. First I'd go to a restaurant several times with a few opinionated, articulate friends in tow. I'd sit there writing down everything anyone said that was at all interesting or funny. Then on the following Monday I'd sit down at my desk with my notes, and try to write the review. Even after I'd been doing this for years, panic would set in. I'd try to write a lead, but instead I'd write a couple of dreadful sentences, XX them out, try again, XX everything out, and then feel despair and worry settle on my chest like an x-ray apron. It's over, I'd think, calmly. I'm not going to be able to get the magic to work this time. I'm ruined. I'm through. I'm toast. Maybe, I'd think, I can get my old job back as a clerk-typist. But probably not. I'd get up and study my teeth in the mirror for a while. Then I'd stop, remember to breathe, make a few phone calls, hit the kitchen and chow down. Eventually I'd go back and sit down at my desk, and sigh for the next ten minutes. Finally I would pick up my one-inch picture frame, stare into it as if for the answer, and every time the answer would come: all I had to do was to write a really crummy first draft of, say, the opening paragraph. And no one was going to see it.

So I'd start writing without reining myself in. It was almost just typing, just making my fingers move. And the writing would be *terrible*. I'd write a lead paragraph that was a whole page, even though the entire review could only be three pages long, and then I'd start writing up descriptions of the food, one dish at a time, bird by bird, and the critics would be sitting on my shoulders, commenting like cartoon characters. They'd be pretending to snore, or rolling their eyes at my overwrought descriptions, no matter how hard I tried to tone those descriptions down, no matter how conscious I was of what a friend said to me gently in my early days of restaurant reviewing. "Annie," she said, "it is just a piece of *chicken*. It is just a bit of *cake*."

But because by then I had been writing for so long, I would eventually 5 let myself trust the process—sort of, more or less. I'd write a first draft that was maybe twice as long as it should be, with a self-indulgent and boring beginning, stupefying descriptions of the meal, lots of quotes from my black-humored friends that made them sound more like the

73

Manson girls° than food lovers, and no ending to speak of. The whole thing would be so long and incoherent and hideous that for the rest of the day I'd obsess about getting creamed by a car before I could write a decent second draft. I'd worry that people would read what I'd written and believe that the accident had really been a suicide, that I had panicked because my talent was waning and my mind was shot.

The next day, though, I'd sit down, go through it all with a colored pen, take out everything I possibly could, find a new lead somewhere on the second page, figure out a kicky place to end it, and then write a second draft. It always turned out fine, sometimes even funny and weird and helpful. I'd go over it one more time and mail it in.

Then, a month later, when it was time for another review, the whole process would start again, complete with the fears that people would find my first draft before I could rewrite it.

Almost all good writing begins with terrible first efforts. You need to start somewhere. Start by getting something—anything—down on paper. A friend of mine says that the first draft is the down draft—you just get it down. The second draft is the up draft—you fix it up. You try to say what you have to say more accurately. And the third draft is the dental draft, where you check every tooth, to see if it's loose or cramped or decayed, or even, God help us, healthy.

What I've learned to do when I sit down to work on a crummy first draft is to quiet the voices in my head. First there's the vinegar-lipped Reader Lady, who says primly, "Well, *that's* not very interesting, is it?" And there's the emaciated German male who writes these Orwellian memos detailing your thought crimes. And there are your parents, agonizing over your lack of loyalty and discretion; and there's William Burroughs, dozing off or shooting up because he finds you as bold and articulate as a houseplant; and so on. And there are also the dogs: let's not forget the dogs, the dogs in their pen who will surely hurtle and snarl their way out if you ever *stop* writing, because writing is, for some of us, the latch that keeps the door of the pen closed, keeps those crazy, ravenous dogs contained. [. . .]

Close your eyes and get quiet for a minute, until the chatter starts up. 10 Then isolate one of the voices and imagine the person speaking as a mouse. Pick it up by the tail and drop it into a mason jar. Then isolate another voice, pick it up by the tail, drop it in the jar. And so on. Drop in any high-maintenance parental units, drop in any contractors, lawyers, colleagues, children, anyone who is whining in your head. Then put the lid on, and watch all these mouse people clawing at the glass, jabbering away, trying to make you feel crummy because you won't do what they

Manson girls: Young, troubled, members of a cult led by Charles Manson (b. 1934). In 1969 Manson and some of his followers were convicted of murder in California.

want—won't give them more money, won't be more successful, won't see them more often. Then imagine that there is a volume-control button on the bottle. Turn it all the way up for a minute, and listen to the stream of angry, neglected, guilt-mongering voices. Then turn it all the way down and watch the frantic mice lunge at the glass, trying to get to you. Leave it down, and get back to your crummy first draft.

A writer friend of mine suggests opening the jar and shooting them all in the head. But I think he's a little angry, and I'm sure nothing like this would ever occur to you.

JENNIFER LEE

I Think, Therefore IM

Jennifer Lee is a freelance writer whose nonfiction writing has appeared in the *New York Times* and other publications. In her essay "I Think, Therefore IM," she explores the current phenomenon of instant messaging among young people. In addressing this issue, Lee documents student use of "the conversational style of the Internet" to condense language into a shorthand that eliminates capitalization, punctuation, and formal syntax. The result is a blurring of students' social and academic worlds in a lingua franca that subverts traditional classroom English. Lee's article shows two sides: a belief that this new language undermines formal written English as well as a more accommodating response that views this tendency a "part of a larger arc of language evolution." Lee's article appeared in the September 19, 2002, issue of the *New York Times*.

Each September Jacqueline Harding prepares a classroom presentation on the common writing mistakes she sees in her students' work.

Ms. Harding, an eighth-grade English teacher at Viking Middle School in Guernee, Ill., scribbles the words that have plagued generations of schoolchildren across her whiteboard:

There. Their. They're.

Your. You're.

To. Too. Two.

Its. It's.

This September, she has added a new list: u, r, ur, b4, wuz, cuz, 2.

When she asked her students how many of them used shortcuts like these in their writing, Ms. Harding said, she was not surprised when most of them raised their hands. This, after all, is their online lingua franca: English adapted for the spitfire conversational style of Internet instant messaging.

Ms. Harding, who had seen such shortcuts creep into student papers over the last two years, said she gave her students a warning: "If I see this in your assignments, I will take points off."

"Kids should know the difference," said Ms. Harding, who decided to 5
address this issue head-on this year. "They should know where to draw
the line between formal writing."

As more and more teenagers socialize online, middle school and high
school teachers like Ms. Harding are increasingly seeing a breezy form of
Internet English jump from e-mail into schoolwork. To their dismay,
teachers say that papers are being written with shortened words,
improper capitalization and punctuation, and characters like &, $ and @.

Teachers have deducted points, drawn red circles and tsk-tsked at
their classes. Yet the errant forms continue. "It stops being funny after
you repeat yourself a couple of times," Ms. Harding said.

But teenagers, whose social life can rely as much these days on text
communication as the spoken word, say that they use instant-messaging
shorthand without thinking about it. They write to one another as much
as they write in school, or more.

"You are so used to abbreviating things, you just start doing it unconsciously on schoolwork and reports and other things," said Eve Brecker, 15,
a student at Montclair High School in New Jersey.

Ms. Brecker once handed in a midterm exam riddled with instant- 10
messaging shorthand. "I had an hour to write an essay on *Romeo and
Juliet*," she said. "I just wanted to finish before my time was up. I was
writing fast and carelessly. I spelled 'you' 'u.'" She got a C.

Even terms that cannot be expressed verbally are making their way
into papers. Melanie Weaver was stunned by some of the term papers
she received from a 10th-grade class she recently taught as part of an
internship. "They would be trying to make a point in a paper, they would
put a smiley face in the end," said Ms. Weaver, who teaches at Alvernia
College in Reading, PA. "If they were presenting an argument and they
needed to present an opposite view, they would put a frown."

As Trisha Fogarty, a sixth-grade teacher at Houlton Southside School
in Houlton, Maine, puts it, today's students are "Generation Text."

Almost 60 percent of the online population under age 17 uses instant
messaging, according to Nielsen/NetRatings. In addition to cellphone
text messaging, Weblogs and e-mail, it has become a popular means of
flirting, setting up dates, asking for help with homework and keeping in
contact with distant friends. The abbreviations are a natural outgrowth
of this rapid-fire style of communication.

"They have a social life that centers around typed communication,"
said Judith S. Donath, a professor at the Massachusetts Institute of
Technology's Media Lab who has studied electronic communication.
"They have a writing style that has been nurtured in a teenage social
milieu."

77

Some teachers see the creeping abbreviations as part of a continuing 15 assault of technology on formal written English. Others take it more lightly, saying that it is just part of the larger arc of language evolution.

"To them it's not wrong," said Ms. Harding, who is 28. "It's acceptable because it's in their culture. It's hard enough to teach them the art of formal writing. Now we've got to overcome this new instant-messaging language."

Ms. Harding noted that in some cases the shorthand isn't even shorter. "I understand 'cuz,' but what's with the 'wuz'? It's the same amount of letters as 'was,' so what's the point?" she said.

Deborah Bova, who teaches eighth-grade English at Raymond Park Middle School in Indianapolis, thought her eyesight was failing several years ago when she saw the sentence "B4 we perform, ppl have 2 practice" on a student assignment.

"I thought, 'My God, what is this?' " Ms. Bova said. "Have they lost their minds?"

The student was summoned to the board to translate the sentence into 20 standard English: "Before we perform, people have to practice." She realized that the students thought she was out of touch. "It was like 'Get with it, Bova,' " she said. Ms. Bova had a student type up a reference list of translations for common instant-messaging expressions. She posted a copy on the bulletin board by her desk and took another one home to use while grading.

Students are sometimes unrepentant.

"They were astonished when I began to point these things out to them," said Henry Assetto, a social studies teacher at Twin Valley High School in Elverson, Pa. "Because I am a history teacher, they did not think a history teacher would be checking up on their grammar or their spelling," said Mr. Assetto, who has been teaching for 34 years.

But Montana Hodgen, 16, another Montclair student, said she was so accustomed to instant-messaging abbreviations that she often read right past them. She proofread a paper last year only to get it returned with the messaging abbreviations circled in red.

"I was so used to reading what my friends wrote to me on Instant Messenger that I didn't even realize that there was something wrong," she said. She said her ability to separate formal and informal English declined the more she used instant messages. "Three years ago, if I had seen that, I would have been 'What is that?' "

The spelling checker doesn't always help either, students say. For one, 25 Microsoft Word's squiggly red spell-check lines don't appear beneath single letters and numbers such as u, r, c, 2 and 4. Nor do they catch words which have numbers in them such as "l8r" and "b4" by default.

Teenagers have essentially developed an unconscious "accent" in their typing, Professor Donath said. "They have gotten facile at typing and they are not paying attention."

Teenagers have long pushed the boundaries of spoken language, introducing words that then become passe with adult adoption. Now teenagers are taking charge and pushing the boundaries of written language. For them, expressions like "oic" (oh I see), "nm" (not much), "jk" (just kidding) and "lol" (laughing out loud), "brb" (be right back), "ttyl" (talk to you later) are as standard as conventional English.

"There is no official English language," said Jesse Sheidlower, the North American editor of the *Oxford English Dictionary*. "Language is spread not because anyone dictates any one thing to happen. The decisions are made by the language and the people who use the language."

Some teachers find the new writing style alarming. "First of all, it's very rude, and it's very careless," said Lois Moran, a middle school English teacher at St. Nicholas school in Jersey City.

"They should be careful to write properly and not to put these little 30 codes in that they are in such a habit of writing to each other," said Ms. Moran, who has lectured her eighth-grade class on such mistakes.

Others say that the instant-messaging style might simply be a fad, something that students will grow out of. Or they see it as an opportunity to teach students about the evolution of language.

"I turn it into a very positive teachable moment for kids in the class," said Erika V. Karres, an assistant professor at the University of North Carolina at Chapel Hill who trains student teachers. She shows students how English has evolved since Shakespeare's time. Imagine Langston Hughes's writing in quick texting instead of 'Langston writing,'" she said. "It makes teaching and learning so exciting."

Other teachers encourage students to use messaging shorthand to spark their thinking processes. "When my children are writing first drafts, I don't care how they spell anything, as long as they are writing," said Ms. Fogarty, the sixth-grade teacher from Houlton, Maine. "If this lingo gets their thoughts and ideas onto paper quicker, the more power to them." But during editing and revising, she expects her students to switch to standard English.

Ms. Bova shares the view that instant-messaging language can help free up their creativity. With the help of students, she does not even need the cheat sheet to read the shorthand anymore.

"I think it's a plus," she said. "And I would say that with a + sign." 35

MIN-ZHAN LU

From Silence to Words: Writing as Struggle

Having completed graduate work in both the Composition Program and the Cultural and Critical Studies Program at the University of Pittsburgh, **Min-Zhan Lu** is currently a professor of English at the University of Louisville, teaching courses in literature, rhetoric, and composition. Among Lu's research interests is the question of how to best serve the needs of basic, multilingual, and transnational writers in the composition classroom, and in 2005, she received the Richard Braddock Award for her writing on the teaching of English. Lu has published widely in academic journals such as *College English* and *College Composition and Communication*. In collaboration with Bruce Horner, she coedited *Cross-Language Relations in Composition* (2010) and coauthored *Representing the "Other": Basic Writers and the Teaching of Basic Writing* (1999) and *Writing Conventions* (2008). Lu's memoir *Shanghai Quartet: The Crossings of Four Women of China*, in which she relates the story of four generations of women in her family, was published in 2001.

In her literacy narrative "From Silence to Words: Writing as Struggle," crafted following her mother's death and originally published in *College English*, Lu considers her experiences as a child learning English and Marxist ideologies while growing up in China during the Cultural Revolution. She describes the dissonance between her home life and school life, as well as her struggles to reconcile the two. Through her experiences, Lu expresses her concern about conceptions of language as taught in composition classes.

Imagine that you enter a parlor. You come late. When you arrive, others have long preceded you, and they are engaged in a heated discussion. . . . You listen for a while, until you decide that you have caught the tenor of the argument; then you put in your oar. Someone answers; you answer him; another comes to your

Min-Zhan Lu, "From Silence to Words: Writing as Struggle." From *College English*, Volume 49, No. 4, April 1987, pp. 437–77. Copyright © by the National Council of Teachers of English. Reprinted by permission.

defense; another aligns himself against you, to either the embar-
rassment or gratification of your opponent, depending upon the
quality of your ally's assistance. However, the discussion is inter-
minable. The hour grows late, you must depart. And you do
depart, with the discussion still vigorously in progress.
   — KENNETH BURKE, *The Philosophy of Literary Form*

Men are not built in silence, but in word, in work, in action-
reflection. — PAULO FREIRE, *Pedagogy of the Oppressed*

My mother withdrew into silence two months before she died. A few
nights before she fell silent, she told me she regretted the way she had
raised me and my sisters. I knew she was referring to the way we had
been brought up in the midst of two conflicting worlds—the world of
home, dominated by the ideology of the Western humanistic tradition,
and the world of a society dominated by Mao Tse-tung's Marxism. My
mother had devoted her life to our education, an education she knew
had made us suffer political persecution during the Cultural Revolution.
I wanted to find a way to convince her that, in spite of the persecution, I
had benefited from the education she had worked so hard to give me.
But I was silent. My understanding of my education was so dominated
by memories of confusion and frustration that I was unable to reflect on
what I could have gained from it.

   This paper is my attempt to fill up that silence with words, words I
didn't have then, words that I have since come to by reflecting on my
earlier experience as a student in China and on my recent experience as
a composition teacher in the United States. For in spite of the frustration
and confusion I experienced growing up caught between two conflicting
worlds, the conflict ultimately helped me to grow as a reader and writer.
Constantly having to switch back and forth between the discourse of
home and that of school made me sensitive and self-conscious about the
struggle I experienced every time I tried to read, write, or think in either
discourse. Eventually, it led me to search for constructive uses for such
struggle.

   From early childhood, I had identified the differences between home
and the outside world by the different languages I used in each. My parents had wanted my sisters and me to get the best education they could
conceive of—Cambridge. They had hired a live-in tutor, a Scot, to make
us bilingual. I learned to speak English with my parents, my tutor, and
my sisters. I was allowed to speak Shanghai dialect only with the servants. When I was four (the year after the Communist Revolution of
1949), my parents sent me to a local private school where I learned to

speak, read, and write in a new language—Standard Chinese, the official written language of New China.

In those days I moved from home to school, from English to Standard
Chinese to Shanghai dialect, with no apparent friction. I spoke each language with those who spoke the language. All seemed quite "natural"—
servants spoke only Shanghai dialect because they were servants;
teachers spoke Standard Chinese because they were teachers; languages
had different words because they were different languages. I thought of
English as my family language, comparable to the many strange dialects
I didn't speak but had often heard some of my classmates speak with
their families. While I was happy to have a special family language, until
second grade I didn't feel that my family language was any different than
some of my classmates' family dialects.

My second grade homeroom teacher was a young graduate from a   5
missionary school. When she found out I spoke English, she began to
practice her English on me. One day she used English when asking me
to run an errand for her. As I turned to close the door behind me, I
noticed the puzzled faces of my classmates. I had the same sensation I
had often experienced when some stranger in a crowd would turn on
hearing me speak English. I was more intensely pleased on this occasion, however, because suddenly I felt that my family language had been
singled out from the family languages of my classmates. Since we were
not allowed to speak any dialect other than Standard Chinese in the
classroom, having my teacher speak English to me in class made English
an official language of the classroom. I began to take pride in my ability
to speak it.

This incident confirmed in my mind what my parents had always told
me about the importance of English to one's life. Time and again they
had told me of how my paternal grandfather, who was well versed in
classic Chinese, kept losing good-paying jobs because he couldn't speak
English. My grandmother reminisced constantly about how she had
slaved and saved to send my father to a first-rate missionary school. And
we were made to understand that it was my father's fluent English that
had opened the door to his success. Even though my family had always
stressed the importance of English for my future, I used to complain bit-
terly about the extra English lessons we had to take after school. It was
only after my homeroom teacher had "sanctified" English that I began to
connect English with my education. I became a much more eager student in my tutorials.

What I learned from my tutorials seemed to enhance and reinforce
what I was learning in my classroom. In those days each word had one
meaning. One day I would be making a sentence at school: "The national
flag of China is red." The next day I would recite at home, "My love is like

a red, red rose." There seemed to be an agreement between the Chinese "red" and the English "red," and both corresponded to the patch of color printed next to the word. "Love" was my love for my mother at home and my love for my "motherland" at school; both "loves" meant how I felt about my mother. Having two loads of homework forced me to develop a quick memory for words and a sensitivity to form and style. What I learned in one language carried over to the other. I made sentences such as, "I saw a red, red rose among the green leaves," with both the English lyric and the classic Chinese lyric—red flower among green leaves—running through my mind, and I was praised by both teacher and tutor for being a good student.

Although my elementary schooling took place during the fifties, I was almost oblivious to the great political and social changes happening around me. Years later, I read in my history and political philosophy textbooks that the fifties were a time when "China was making a transition from a semi-feudal, semi-capitalist, and semi-colonial country into a socialist country," a period in which "the Proletarians were breaking into the educational territory dominated by Bourgeois Intellectuals." While people all over the country were being officially classified into Proletarians, Petty-bourgeois, National-bourgeois, Poor-peasants, and Intellectuals, and were trying to adjust to their new social identities, my parents were allowed to continue the upper middle-class life they had established before the 1949 Revolution because of my father's affiliation with British firms. I had always felt that my family was different from the families of my classmates, but I didn't perceive society's view of my family until the summer vacation before I entered high school.

First, my aunt was caught by her colleagues talking to her husband over the phone in English. Because of it, she was criticized and almost labeled a Rightist. (This was the year of the Anti-Rightist movement, a movement in which the Intellectuals became the target of the "socialist class-struggle.") I had heard others telling my mother that she was foolish to teach us English when Russian had replaced English as the "official" foreign language. I had also learned at school that the American and British Imperialists were the arch-enemies of New China. Yet I had made no connection between the arch-enemies and the English our family spoke. What happened to my aunt forced the connection on me. I began to see my parents' choice of a family language as an anti-Revolutionary act and was alarmed that I had participated in such an act. From then on, I took care not to use English outside home and to conceal my knowledge of English from my new classmates.

Certain words began to play important roles in my new life at the junior high. On the first day of school, we were handed forms to fill out with our parents' class, job, and income. Being one of the few people 10

83

not employed by the government, my father had never been officially classified. Since he was a medical doctor, he told me to put him down as an Intellectual. My homeroom teacher called me into the office a couple of days afterwards and told me that my father couldn't be an Intellectual if his income far exceeded that of a Capitalist. He also told me that since my father worked for Foreign Imperialists, my father should be classified as an Imperialist Lackey. The teacher looked nonplussed when I told him that my father couldn't be an Imperialist Lackey because he was a medical doctor. But I could tell from the way he took notes on my form that my father's job had put me in an unfavorable position in his eyes.

The Standard Chinese term "class" was not a new word for me. Since first grade, I had been taught sentences such as, "The Working class are the masters of New China." I had always known that it was good to be a worker, but until then, I had never felt threatened for not being one. That fall, "class" began to take on a new meaning for me. I noticed a group of Working-class students and teachers at school. I was made to understand that because of my class background, I was excluded from that group.

Another word that became important was "consciousness." One of the slogans posted in the school building read, "Turn our students into future Proletarians with socialist consciousness and education!" For several weeks we studied this slogan in our political philosophy course, a subject I had never had in elementary school. I still remember the definition of "socialist consciousness" that we were repeatedly tested on through the years: "Socialist consciousness is a person's political soul. It is the consciousness of the Proletarians represented by Marxist Mao Tse-tung thought. It takes expression in one's action, language, and lifestyle. It is the task of every Chinese student to grow up into a Proletarian with a socialist consciousness so that he can serve the people and the motherland." To make the abstract concept accessible to us, our teacher pointed out that the immediate task for students from Working-class families was to strengthen their socialist consciousnesses. For those of us who were from other class backgrounds, the task was to turn ourselves into Workers with socialist consciousnesses. The teacher never explained exactly how we were supposed to "turn" into Workers. Instead, we were given samples of the ritualistic annual plans we had to write at the beginning of each term. In these plans, we performed "self-criticism" on our consciousnesses and made vows to turn ourselves into Workers with socialist consciousnesses. The teacher's division between those who did and those who didn't have a socialist consciousness led me to reify the notion of "consciousness" into a thing one possesses. I equated this intangible "thing" with a concrete way of dressing, speaking, and writing. For instance, I never doubted that my political philosophy teacher had a socialist consciousness because she was from a steel-worker's family (she announced this the first day of class) and was a Party member who wore grey cadre suits and talked like a philosophy textbook. I noticed other things about her. She had beautiful eyes and spoke Standard Chinese with such a pure accent that I thought she should be a film star. But I was embarrassed that I had noticed things that ought not to have been associated with her. I blamed my observation on my Bourgeois consciousness.

At the same time, the way reading and writing were taught through memorization and imitation also encouraged me to reduce concepts and ideas to simple definitions. In literature and political philosophy classes, we were taught a large number of quotations from Marx, Lenin, and Mao Tse-tung. Each concept that appeared in these quotations came with a definition. We were required to memorize the definitions of the words along with the quotations. Every time I memorized a definition, I felt I had learned a word: "The national red flag symbolizes the blood shed by Revolutionary ancestors for our socialist cause"; "New China rises like a red sun over the eastern horizon." As I memorized these sentences, I reduced their metaphors to dictionary meanings: "red" meant "Revolution" and "red sun" meant "New China" in the "language" of the Working class. I learned mechanically but eagerly. I soon became quite fluent in this new language.

As school began to define me as a political subject, my parents tried to buildup my resistance to the "communist poisoning" by exposing me to the "great books" — novels by Charles Dickens, Nathaniel Hawthorne, Emily Bronte, Jane Austen, and writers from around the turn of the century. My parents implied that these writers represented how I, their child, should read and write. My parents replaced the word "Bourgeois" with the word "cultured." They reminded me that I was in school only to learn math and science. I needed to pass the other courses to stay in school, but I was not to let the "Red doctrines" corrupt my mind. Gone were the days when I could innocently write, "I saw the red, red rose among the green leaves," collapsing, as I did, English and Chinese cultural traditions. "Red" came to mean Revolution at school, "the Commies" at home, and adultery in *The Scarlet Letter*. Since I took these symbols and metaphors as meanings natural to people of the same class, I abandoned my earlier definitions of English and Standard Chinese as the language of home and the language of school. I now defined English as the language of the Bourgeois and Standard Chinese as the language of the Working class. I thought of the language of the Working class as someone else's language and the language of the Bourgeois as my language. But I also believed that, although the language of the Bourgeois was my real language, I could and would adopt the language of the Working class when I was at school. I began to put on and take off my Working class language in the same way I put on and took off my school clothes to avoid being criticized for wearing Bourgeois clothes.

In my literature classes, I learned the Working-class formula for read- 15 ing. Each work in the textbook had a short "Author's Biography": "XXX, born in 19-- in the province of XX, is from a Worker's family. He joined the Revolution in 19--. He is a Revolutionary realist with a passionate love for the Party and Chinese Revolution. His work expresses the thoughts and emotions of the masses and sings praise to the prosperous socialist construction on all fronts of China." The teacher used the "Author's Biography" as a yardstick to measure the texts. We were taught to locate details in the texts that illustrated these summaries, such as words that expressed Workers' thoughts and emotions or events that illustrated the Workers' lives.

I learned a formula for Working-class writing in the composition classes. We were given sample essays and told to imitate them. The theme was always about how the collective taught the individual a lesson. I would write papers about labor-learning experiences or school-cleaning days, depending on the occasion of the collective activity closest to the assignment. To make each paper look different, I dressed it up with details about the date, the weather, the environment, or the appearance of the Master-worker who had taught me "the lesson." But as I became more and more fluent in the generic voice of the Working-class Student, I also became more and more self-conscious about the language we used at home.

For instance, in senior high we began to have English classes ("to study English for the Revolution," as the slogan on the cover of the textbook said), and I was given my first Chinese-English dictionary. There I discovered the English version of the term "class-struggle." (The Chinese characters for a school "class" and for a social "class" are different.) I had often used the English word "class" at home in sentences such as, "So and so has class," but I had not connected this sense of "class" with "class-struggle." Once the connection was made, I heard a second layer of meaning every time someone at home said a person had "class." The expression began to mean the person had the style and sophistication characteristic of the Bourgeoisie. The word lost its innocence. I was uneasy about hearing that second layer of meaning because I was sure my parents did not hear the word that way. I felt that therefore I should not be hearing it that way either. Hearing the second layer of meaning made me wonder if I was losing my English.

My suspicion deepened when I noticed myself unconsciously merging and switching between the "reading" of home and the "reading" of school. Once I had to write a report on *The Revolutionary Family*, a book about an illiterate woman's awakening and growth as a Revolutionary through the deaths of her husband and all her children for the cause of the Revolution. In one scene the woman deliberated over whether or not she should encourage her youngest son to join the Revolution. Her memory of her husband's death made her afraid to encourage her son. Yet she also remembered her earlier married life and the first time her husband tried to explain the meaning of the Revolution to her. These memories made her feel she should encourage her son to continue the cause his father had begun.

I was moved by this scene. "Moved" was a word my mother and sisters used a lot when we discussed books. Our favorite moments in novels were moments of what I would now call internal conflict, moments which we said "moved" us. I remember that we were "moved" by Jane Eyre when she was torn between her sense of ethics, which compelled her to leave the man she loved, and her impulse to stay with the only man who had ever loved her. We were also moved by Agnes in *David Copperfield* because of the way she restrained her love for David so that he could live happily with the woman he loved. My standard method of doing a book report was to model it on the review by the Publishing Bureau and to dress it up with detailed quotations from the book. The review of *The Revolutionary Family* emphasized the woman's Revolutionary spirit. I decided to use the scene that had moved me to illustrate this point. I wrote the report the night before it was due. When I had finished, I realized I couldn't possibly hand it in. Instead of illustrating her Revolutionary spirit, I had dwelled on her internal conflict, which could be seen as a moment of weak sentimentality that I should never have emphasized in a Revolutionary heroine. I wrote another report, taking care to illustrate the grandeur of her Revolutionary spirit by expanding on a quotation in which she decided that if the life of her son could change the lives of millions of sons, she should not begrudge his life for the cause of Revolution. I handed in my second version but kept the first in my desk.

I never showed it to anyone. I could never show it to people outside 20 my family, because it had deviated so much from the reading enacted by the jacket review. Neither could I show it to my mother or sisters, because I was ashamed to have been so moved by such a "Revolutionary" book. My parents would have been shocked to learn that I could like such a book in the same way they liked Dickens. Writing this book report increased my fear that I was losing the command over both the "language of home" and the "language of school" that I had worked so hard to gain. I tried to remind myself that, if I could still tell when my reading or writing sounded incorrect, then I had retained my command over both languages. Yet I could no longer be confident of my command over either language because I had discovered that when I was not careful — or even when I was — my reading and writing often surprised me with its impurity. To prevent such impurity, I became very suspicious of my thoughts when I read or wrote. I was always asking myself why I was using this word, how I was using it, always afraid that I wasn't reading or writing correctly. What confused and frustrated me most was that I could not figure out why I was no longer able to read or write correctly without such painful deliberation.

I continued to read only because reading allowed me to keep my thoughts and confusion private. I hoped that somehow, if I watched myself carefully, I would figure out from the way I read whether I had really mastered the "languages." But writing became a dreadful chore. When I tried to keep a diary, I was so afraid that the voice of school might slip in that I could only list my daily activities. When I wrote for school, I worried that my Bourgeois sensibilities would betray me.

The more suspicious I became about the way I read and wrote, the more guilty I felt for losing the spontaneity with which I had learned to "use" these "languages." Writing the book report made me feel that my reading and writing in the "language" of either home or school could not be free of the interference of the other. But I was unable to acknowledge, grasp, or grapple with what I was experiencing, for both my parents and my teachers had suggested that, if I were a good student, such interference would and should not take place. I assumed that once I had "acquired" a discourse, I could simply switch it on and off every time I read and wrote as I would some electronic tool. Furthermore, I expected my readings and writings to come out in their correct forms whenever I switched the proper discourse on. I still regarded the discourse of home as natural and the discourse of school alien, but I never had doubted before that I could acquire both and switch them on and off according to the occasion.

When my experience in writing conflicted with what I thought should happen when I used each discourse, I rejected my experience because it contradicted what my parents and teachers had taught me. I shied away from writing to avoid what I assumed I should not experience. But trying to avoid what should not happen did not keep it from recurring whenever I had to write. Eventually my confusion and frustration over these recurring experiences compelled me to search for an explanation: how and why had I failed to learn what my parents and teachers had worked so hard to teach me?

I now think of the internal scene for my reading and writing about *The Revolutionary Family* as a heated discussion between myself, the voices of home, and those of school. The review on the back of the book, the sample student papers I came across in my composition classes, my philosophy teacher—these I heard as voices of one group. My parents and my home readings were the voices of an opposing group. But the conversation between these opposing voices in the internal scene of my writing was not as polite and respectful as the parlor scene Kenneth Burke has portrayed (see epigraph). Rather, these voices struggled to dominate the discussion, constantly incorporating, dismissing, or suppressing the arguments of each other, like the battles between the hegemonic and counterhegemonic forces described in Raymond Williams' *Marxism and Literature* (108–14).

When I read *The Revolutionary Family* and wrote the first version of 25 my report, I began with a quotation from the review. The voices of both home and school answered, clamoring to be heard. I tried to listen to one group and turn a deaf ear to the other. Both persisted. I negotiated my way through these conflicting voices, now agreeing with one, now agreeing with the other. I formed a reading out of my interaction with both. Yet I was afraid to have done so because both home and school had implied that I should speak in unison with only one of these groups and stand away from the discussion rather than participate in it.

My teachers and parents had persistently called my attention to the intensity of the discussion taking place on the external social scene. The story of my grandfather's failure and my father's success had from my early childhood made me aware of the conflict between Western and traditional Chinese cultures. My political education at school added another dimension to the conflict: the war of Marxist-Maoism against them both. Yet when my parents and teachers called my attention to the conflict, they stressed the anxiety of having to live through China's transformation from a semi-feudal, semi-capitalist, and semi-colonial society to a socialist one. Acquiring the discourse of the dominant group was, to them, a means of seeking alliance with that group and thus of surviving the whirlpool of cultural currents around them. As a result, they modeled their pedagogical practices on this utilitarian view of language. Being the eager student, I adopted this view of language as a tool for survival. It came to dominate my understanding of the discussion on the social and historical scene and to restrict my ability to participate in that discussion.

To begin with, the metaphor of language as a tool for survival led me to be passive in my use of discourse, to be a bystander in the discussion. In Burke's "parlor," everyone is involved in the discussion. As it goes on through history, what we call "communal discourses"—arguments specific to particular political, social, economic, ethnic, sexual, and family groups—form, re-form and transform. To use a discourse in such a scene is to participate in the argument and to contribute to the formation of the discourse. But when I was growing up, I could not take on the burden of such an active role in the discussion. For both home and school presented the existent conventions of the discourse each taught me as absolute laws for my action. They turned verbal action into a tool, a set of conventions produced and shaped prior to and outside of my own verbal acts. Because I saw language as a tool, I separated the process of producing the tool from the process of using it. The tool was made by someone else and was then acquired and used by me. How the others made it before I acquired it determined and guaranteed what it produced when I used it. I imagined that the more experienced and powerful members of the community were the ones responsible for making the tool. They were the ones who participated in the discussion and fought with opponents. When I used what they made, their labor and accomplishments would ensure the quality of my reading and writing. By using it, I could survive the heated discussion. When my immediate experience in writing the book report suggested that knowing the conventions of school did not guarantee the form and content of my report, when it suggested that I had to write the report with the work and responsibility I had assigned to those who wrote book reviews in the Publishing Bureau, I thought I had lost the tool I had earlier acquired.

Another reason I could not take up an active role in the argument was that my parents and teachers contrived to provide a scene free of conflict for practicing my various languages. It was as if their experience had made them aware of the conflict between their discourse and other discourses and of the struggle involved in reproducing the conventions of any discourse on a scene where more than one discourse exists. They seemed convinced that such conflict and struggle would overwhelm someone still learning the discourse. Home and school each contrived a purified space where only one discourse was spoken and heard. In their choice of textbooks, in the way they spoke, and in the way they required me to speak, each jealously silenced any voice that threatened to break the unison of the scene. The homogeneity of home and of school implied that only one discourse could and should be relevant in each place. It led me to believe I should leave behind, turn a deaf ear to, or forget the discourse of the other when I crossed the boundary dividing them. I expected myself to set down one discourse whenever I took up another just as I would take off or put on a particular set of clothes for school or home.

Despite my parents' and teachers' attempts to keep home and school discrete, the internal conflict between the two discourses continued whenever I read or wrote. Although I tried to suppress the voice of one discourse in the name of the other, having to speak aloud in the voice I had just silenced each time I crossed the boundary kept both voices active in my mind. Every "I think . . ." from the voice of home or school brought forth a "However . . ." or a "But . . ." from the voice of the opponents. To identify with the voice of home or school, I had to negotiate through the conflicting voices of both by restating, taking back, qualifying my thoughts. I was unconsciously doing so when I did my book report. But I could not use the interaction comfortably and constructively. Both my parents and my teachers had implied that my job was to prevent that interaction from happening. My sense of having failed to accomplish what they had taught silenced me.

To use the interaction between the discourses of home and school constructively, I would have to have seen reading or writing as a process in which I worked my way towards a stance through a dialectical process of identification and division. To identify with an ally, I would have to have grasped the distance between where he or she stood and where I was positioning myself. In taking a stance against an opponent, I would have to have grasped where my stance identified with the stance of my allies. Teetering along the "wavering line of pressure and counterpressure" from both allies and opponents, I might have worked my way towards a stance of my own (Burke, *A Rhetoric of Motives* 23). Moreover, I would have to have understood that the voices in my mind, like the participants in the parlor scene, were in constant flux. As I came into contact with new and different groups of people or read different books, voices entered and left. Each time I read or wrote, the stance I negotiated out of these voices would always be at some distance from the stances I worked out in my previous and my later readings or writings.

I could not conceive such a form of action for myself because I saw reading and writing as an expression of an established stance. In delineating the conventions of a discourse, my parents and teachers had synthesized the stance they saw as typical for a representative member of the community. Burke calls this the stance of a "god" or the "prototype"; Williams calls it the "official" or "possible" stance of the community. Through the metaphor of the survival tool, my parents and teachers had led me to assume I could automatically reproduce the official stance of the discourse I used. Therefore, when I did my book report on *The Revolutionary Family*, I expected my knowledge of the official stance set by the book review to ensure the actual stance of my report. As it happened, I began by trying to take the official stance of the review. Other voices interrupted. I answered back. In the process, I worked out a stance approximate but not identical to the official stance I began with. Yet the experience of having to labor to realize my knowledge of the official stance or to prevent myself from wandering away from it frustrated and confused me. For even though I had been actually reading and writing in a Burkean scene, I was afraid to participate actively in the discussion. I assumed it was my role to survive by staying out of it.

Not long ago, my daughter told me that it bothered her to hear her friend "talk wrong." Having come to the United States from China with little English, my daughter has become sensitive to the way English, as spoken by her teachers, operates. As a result, she has amazed her teachers with her success in picking up the language and in adapting to life at school. Her concern to speak the English taught in the classroom "correctly" makes her uncomfortable when she hears people using "ain't" or double negatives, which her teacher considers "improper." I see in her the me that had eagerly learned and used the discourse of the Working class at school. Yet while I was torn between the two conflicting worlds of school and home, she moves with seeming ease from the conversations she hears over the dinner table to her teacher's words in the classroom. My husband and I are proud of the good work she does at school. We are glad she is spared the kinds of conflict between home and school I experienced at her age. Yet as we watch her becoming more and more fluent in the language of the classroom, we wonder if, by enabling her to "survive" school, her very fluency will silence her when the scene of her reading and writing expands beyond that of the composition classroom.

For when I listen to my daughter, to students, and to some composition teachers talking about the teaching and learning of writing, I am often alarmed by the degree to which the metaphor of a survival tool dominates their understanding of language as it once dominated my own. I am especially concerned with the way some composition classes focus on turning the classroom into a monological scene for the students' reading and writing. Most of our students live in a world similar to my daughter's, somewhere between the purified world of the classroom and the complex world of my adolescence. When composition classes encourage these students to ignore those voices that seem irrelevant to the purified world of the classroom, most students are often able to do so without much struggle. Some of them are so adept at doing it that the whole process has for them become automatic.

However, beyond the classroom and beyond the limited range of these students' immediate lives lies a much more complex and dynamic social and historical scene. To help these students become actors in such a scene, perhaps we need to call their attention to voices that may seem irrelevant to the discourse we teach rather than encourage them to shut them out. For example, we might intentionally complicate the classroom scene by bringing into it discourses that stand at varying distances from the one we teach. We might encourage students to explore ways of practicing the conventions of the discourse they are learning by negotiating through these conflicting voices. We could also encourage them to see themselves as responsible for forming or transforming as well as preserving the discourse they are learning.

As I think about what we might do to complicate the external and 35 internal scenes of our students' writing, I hear my parents and teachers saying: "Not now. Keep them from the wrangle of the marketplace until they have acquired the discourse and are skilled at using it." And I answer: "Don't teach them to 'survive' the whirlpool of crosscurrents by avoiding it. Use the classroom to moderate the currents. Moderate the currents, but teach them from the beginning to struggle." When I think of the ways in which the teaching of reading and writing as classroom activities can frustrate the development of students, I am almost grateful for the overwhelming complexity of the circumstances in which I grew up. For it was this complexity that kept me from losing sight of the effort and choice involved in reading or writing with and through a discourse.

[1987]

Works Cited

Burke, Kenneth. *The Philosophy of Literary Form: Studies in Symbolic Action.* 2nd ed. Baton Rouge: Louisiana State UP, 1967.
———. *A Rhetoric of Motives.* Berkeley: U of California P, 1969.
Freire, Paulo. *Pedagogy of the Oppressed.* Trans. M. B. Ramos. New York: Continuum, 1970.
Williams, Raymond. *Marxism and Literature.* New York: Oxford UP, 1977.

SCOTT McCLOUD   [b. 1960]

Understanding Comics

Born in Boston, Massachusetts, and raised in Lexington, Scott McCloud
is a cartoonist and comics theorist. After graduating from Syracuse
University with a fine arts degree in illustration, McCloud worked in
the production department of DC Comics before creating *Zot!*—a
lighthearted, thirty-six-issue alternative series published by Eclipse
Comics between 1984 and 1991—in response to the darker, violent
comics that dominated the scene during the 1980s. McCloud followed
Zot! with *Destroy!!* (1986), a single, oversized volume parodying the
archetypal, violent superhero; *The New Adventures of Abraham Lincoln*
(1998), his first attempt with computer-generated artwork; and *Superman: Adventures of the Man of Steel* (1998), a compilation of the first
six of twelve superman stories scripted for DC Comics. Cited as the
"Aristotle of comics," McCloud is best known as the author of *Understanding Comics: The Invisible Art* (1993), in which his self-caricature
guides the reader through a study of sequential art, by tracing the relationship between words and images. Following the belated success of
Understanding Comics, he published *Reinventing Comics* (2000) and
Making Comics (2006), in which his self-caricature reemerged.

In the following excerpts from *Understanding Comics*, McCloud suggests that the influence of new media on the written word is often misunderstood, and that comics are more than simple juxtapositions of
words and images. Drawing first on the idea of "show and tell,"
McCloud proposes "unlimited" benefits to the interdependent use of
words and images in comics, comparing the two to dance partners:
"[E]ach one takes turns leading."

THE ART FORM OF COMICS IS MANY CENTURIES OLD, BUT IT'S *PERCEIVED* AS A RECENT INVENTION AND SUFFERS THE CURSE OF *ALL* NEW MEDIA.

THE CURSE OF BEING JUDGED BY THE STANDARDS OF THE OLD.

EVER SINCE THE INVENTION OF THE WRITTEN WORD, NEW MEDIA HAVE BEEN *MISUNDERSTOOD.*

CAREFUL, JACOB! IF YOU KEEP DOING THIS, YOU'LL STOP USING YOUR *MEMORY!*

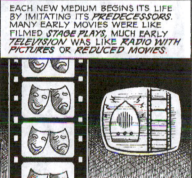

EACH NEW MEDIUM BEGINS ITS LIFE BY IMITATING ITS *PREDECESSORS.* MANY EARLY MOVIES WERE LIKE FILMED *STAGE PLAYS,* MUCH EARLY *TELEVISION* WAS LIKE *RADIO WITH PICTURES* OR *REDUCED MOVIES.*

FAR TOO MANY COMICS CREATORS HAVE NO HIGHER GOAL THAN TO MATCH THE ACHIEVEMENTS OF OTHER MEDIA, AND VIEW ANY CHANCE TO *WORK* IN OTHER MEDIA AS A *STEP UP.*

AND *AGAIN,* AS LONG AS WE VIEW COMICS AS A *GENRE* OF WRITING OR A *STYLE* OF GRAPHIC ART THIS ATTITUDE MAY *NEVER* DISAPPEAR.

WORDS AND PICTURES IN COMBINATION MAY NOT BE MY *DEFINITION* OF COMICS, BUT THE COMBINATION HAS HAD *TREMENDOUS INFLUENCE* ON ITS *GROWTH*.

com·ics (kom'iks)**n.** p... form, used with a singula... Juxtaposed pictoria... ...er images in deliberat... ...ence, intended to conve... ...n and/or to prod... response in t... 2. Superher... costumes, figh... villains, who work... ...he words in violent si... ...nse...

A HUGE RANGE OF HUMAN EXPERIENCES CAN BE *PORTRAYED* IN COMICS THROUGH EITHER WORDS OR PICTURES.

AS A RESULT--AND DESPITE ITS MANY *OTHER* POTENTIAL USES-- COMICS HAVE BECOME *FIRMLY IDENTIFIED* WITH THE ART OF *STORYTELLING*.

AND *INDEED*, WORDS AND PICTURES HAVE *GREAT* POWERS TO TELL STORIES WHEN CREATORS FULLY EXPLOIT THEM *BOTH*.

DADA

BIOGRAPHY   HORROR

ROMANCE   SURREALISM

BLANK VERSE

EPIC POETRY

SOCIAL ALLEGORY

ADAPTATIONS

STREAM OF CONSCIOUSNESS

SATIRE

HISTORICAL FICTION

FOLK TALES

EROTICA

MYSTERY

RELIGIOUS TOPICS

SEQUENTIAL ART

AND SO FAR, WE'VE ONLY SEEN THE *TIP OF THE ICEBERG!*

AS CHILDREN, WE "SHOW AND 'TELL" *INTERCHANGEABLY*, WORDS AND IMAGES COMBINING TO TRANSMIT A *CONNECTED SERIES OF IDEAS*.

IT'S GOT ONE OF *THESE THINGS*.

THE DIFFERENT WAYS IN WHICH WORDS AND PICTURES CAN *COMBINE* IN COMICS IS VIRTUALLY *UNLIMITED*.

BUT LET'S TRY TO BREAK IT DOWN INTO SOME DISTINCT *CATEGORIES*.

[1993]

DONALD MURRAY   [1924–2007]

The Maker's Eye: Revising Your Own Manuscripts

Donald Murray, an acclaimed novelist, poet, and journalist, was born in Boston, Massachusetts. He graduated from the University of New Hampshire, where he later worked as an English professor. Murray is considered an expert on the writing process, and he has written several composition textbooks and sourcebooks. These works include *A Writer Teaches Writing: A Complete Revision* (1985), *Learning by Teaching* (1982), and *Write to Learn* (Seventh Edition, 2004). Murray's editorials in *The Boston Globe* won him the Pulitzer Prize in 1954. He died from heart failure on December 30, 2007.

In his essay "The Maker's Eye: Revising Your Own Manuscripts," Murray emphasizes that writers can only rely on themselves to bring their work to success. While stressing the importance of revising and rewriting, Murray challenges writers to be their own critics, to review their work as if they were seeing it for the first time, and to rework their writing through multiple drafts. In the essay, he outlines the steps necessary to "edit oneself" in order to yield the most polished work possible.

When students complete a first draft, they consider the job of writing done—and their teachers too often agree. When professional writers complete a first draft, they usually feel that they are at the start of the writing process. When a draft is completed, the job of writing can begin.

That difference in attitude is the difference between amateur and professional, inexperience and experience, journeyman and craftsman. Peter F. Drucker, the prolific business writer, calls his first draft "the zero draft"—after that he can start counting. Most writers share the feeling that the first draft, and all of those which follow, are opportunities to discover what they have to say and how best they can say it.

To produce a progression of drafts, each of which says more and says it more clearly, the writer has to develop a special kind of reading skill.

Donald M. Murray, "The Maker's Eye: Revising Your Own Manuscripts" from *The Writer*, October 1973. Copyright © 1973 by Donald M. Murray. Reprinted by permission of the Rosenberg Group on behalf of the author's estate.

In school we are taught to decode what appears on the page as finished writing. Writers, however, face a different category of possibility and responsibility when they read their own drafts. To them the words on the page are never finished. Each can be changed and rearranged, can set off a chain reaction of confusion or clarified meaning. This is a different kind of reading which is possibly more difficult and certainly more exciting.

Writers must learn to be their own best enemy. They must accept the criticism of others and be suspicious of it; they must accept the praise of others and be even more suspicious of it. Writers cannot depend on others. They must detach themselves from their own pages so that they can apply both their caring and their craft to their own work.

Such detachment is not easy. Science-fiction writer Ray Bradbury supposedly puts each manuscript away for a year to the day and then rereads it as a stranger. Not many writers have the discipline or the time to do this. We must read when our judgment may be at its worst, when we are close to the euphoric moment of creation. $\quad$ 5

Then the writer, counsels novelist Nancy Hale, "should be critical of everything that seems to him most delightful in his style. He should excise what he most admires, because he wouldn't thus admire it if he weren't . . . in a sense protecting it from criticism." John Ciardi, the poet, adds, "The last act of the writing must be to become one's own reader. It is, I suppose, a schizophrenic process, to begin passionately and to end critically, to begin hot and to end cold; and, more important, to be passion-hot and critic-cold at the same time."

Most people think that the principal problem is that writers are too proud of what they have written. Actually, a greater problem for most professional writers is one shared by the majority of students. They are overly critical, think everything is dreadful, tear up page after page, never complete a draft, see the task as hopeless.

The writer must learn to read critically but constructively, to cut what is bad, to reveal what is good. Eleanor Estes, the children's book author, explains: "The writer must survey his work critically, coolly, as though he were a stranger to it. He must be willing to prune, expertly and hard-heartedly. At the end of each revision, a manuscript may look . . . worked over, torn apart, pinned together, added to, deleted from, words changed and words changed back. Yet the book must maintain its original freshness and spontaneity."

Most readers underestimate the amount of rewriting it usually takes to produce spontaneous reading. This is a great disadvantage to the student writer, who sees only a finished product and never watches the craftsman who takes the necessary step back, studies the work carefully, returns to the task, steps back, returns, steps back, again and again. Anthony Burgess, one of the most prolific writers in the English-speaking world, admits, "I might revise a page twenty times." Roald Dahl, the popular children's writer, states, "By the time I'm nearing the end of a story, the first part will have been reread and altered and corrected at least 150 times. . . . Good writing is essentially rewriting. I am positive of this."

Rewriting isn't virtuous. It isn't something that ought to be done. It is 10 simply something that most writers find they have to do to discover what they have to say and how to say it. It is a condition of the writer's life.

There are, however, a few writers who do little formal rewriting, primarily because they have the capacity and experience to create and review a large number of invisible drafts in their minds before they approach the page. And some writers slowly produce finished pages, performing all the tasks of revision simultaneously, page by page, rather than draft by draft. But it is still possible to see the sequence followed by most writers most of the time in rereading their own work.

Most writers scan their drafts first, reading as quickly as possible to catch the larger problems of subject and form, and then move in closer and closer as they read and write, reread and rewrite.

The first thing writers look for in their drafts is *information*. They know that a good piece of writing is built from specific, accurate, and interesting information. The writer must have an abundance of information from which to construct a readable piece of writing.

Next writers look for *meaning* in the information. The specifics must build to a pattern of significance. Each piece of specific information must carry the reader toward meaning.

Writers reading their own drafts are aware of *audience*. They put 15 themselves in the reader's situation and make sure that they deliver information which a reader wants to know or needs to know in a manner which is easily digested. Writers try to be sure that they anticipate and answer the questions a critical reader will ask when reading the piece of writing.

Writers make sure that the *form* is appropriate to the subject and the audience. Form, or genre, is the vehicle which carries meaning to the reader, but form cannot be selected until the writer has adequate information to discover its significance and an audience which needs or wants that meaning.

Once writers are sure the form is appropriate, they must then look at the *structure*, the order of what they have written. Good writing is built on a solid framework of logic, argument, narrative, or motivation which runs through the entire piece of writing and holds it together. This is the time when many writers find it most effective to outline as a way of visualizing the hidden spine by which the piece of writing is supported.

The element on which writers may spend a majority of their time is *development*. Each section of a piece of writing must be adequately

103

developed. It must give readers enough information so that they are satisfied. How much information is enough? That's as difficult as asking
how much garlic belongs in a salad. It must be done to taste, but most
beginning writers underdevelop, underestimating the reader's hunger
for information.

As writers solve development problems, they often have to consider
questions of *dimension*. There must be a pleasing and effective proportion among all the parts of the piece of writing. There is a continual
process of subtracting and adding to keep the piece of writing in balance.

Finally, writers have to listen to their own voices. *Voice* is the force 20
which drives a piece of writing forward. It is an expression of the writer's
authority and concern. It is what is between the words on the page, what
glues the piece of writing together. A good piece of writing is always
marked by a consistent, individual voice.

As writers read and reread, write and rewrite, they move closer and
closer to the page until they are doing line-by-line editing. Writers read
their own pages with infinite care. Each sentence, each line, each clause,
each phrase, each word, each mark of punctuation, each section of
white space between the type has to contribute to the clarification of
meaning.

Slowly the writer moves from word to word, looking through language
to see the subject. As a word is changed, cut, or added, as a construction
is rearranged, all the words used before that moment and all those that
follow that moment must be considered and reconsidered.

Writers often read aloud at this stage of the editing process, muttering
or whispering to themselves, calling on the ear's experience with language. Does this sound right—or that? Writers edit, shifting back and
forth from eye to page to ear to page. I find I must do this careful editing
in short runs, no more than fifteen or twenty minutes at a stretch, or I
become too kind with myself. I begin to see what I hope is on the page,
not what actually is on the page.

This sounds tedious if you haven't done it, but actually it is fun. Making something right is immensely satisfying, for writers begin to learn
what they are writing about by writing. Language leads them to meaning, and there is the joy of discovery, of understanding, of making meaning clear as the writer employs the technical skills of language.

Words have double meanings, even triple and quadruple meanings. 25
Each word has its own potential of connotation and denotation. And
when writers rub one word against the other, they are often rewarded
with a sudden insight, an unexpected clarification.

The maker's eye moves back and forth from word to phrase to sentence
to paragraph to sentence to phrase to word. The maker's eye sees the need
for variety and balance, for a firmer structure, for a more appropriate

form. It peers into the interior of the paragraph, looking for coherence, unity, and emphasis, which make meaning clear.

I learned something about this process when my first bifocals were prescribed. I had ordered a larger section of the reading portion of the glass because of my work, but even so, I could not contain my eyes within this new limit of vision. And I still find myself taking off my glasses and bending my nose toward the page, for my eyes unconsciously flick back and forth across the page, back to another page, forward to still another, as I try to see each evolving line in relation to every other line.

When does this process end? Most writers agree with the great Russian writer Tolstoy, who said, "I scarcely ever reread my published writings, if by chance I come across a page, it always strikes me: all this must be rewritten; this is how I should have written it."

The maker's eye is never satisfied, for each word has the potential to ignite new meaning. This article has been twice written all the way through the writing process. . . . Now it is to be republished in a book. The editors made a few small suggestions, and then I read it with my maker's eye. Now it has been re-edited, re-revised, re-read, and re-re-edited, for each piece of writing to the writer is full of potential and alternatives.

A piece of writing is never finished. It is delivered to a deadline, torn out of the typewriter on demand, sent off with a sense of accomplishment and shame and pride and frustration. If only there were a couple more days, time for just another run at it, perhaps then. . . .

[1973]

105

ADRIENNE RICH   [b. 1929]

When We Dead Awaken: Writing as Re-Vision

Adrienne Rich was born in Baltimore, Maryland. Her father encouraged her to read and write from a young age; ultimately, her first poetry was composed under his tutelage. She graduated from Radcliffe in 1951, having won the Yale Younger Poets Prize for *A Change of World*, her first book. W. H. Auden, an early influence on Rich's writing, composed the book's preface, commenting on her polished technique and emotional restraint. Rich married Alfred Conrad, a Harvard economist, in 1953. The couple moved to Cambridge, Massachusetts, where they raised three sons. Rich struggled with her roles as wife and mother and became frustrated while trying to balance her family and her art. Her third book, *Snapshots of a Daughter-in-Law* (1963), was a turning point in Rich's poetry, both thematically and stylistically. When the reaction to *Snapshots* proved negative however, Rich followed up with *Necessities of Life* (1966), a reflective book examining death in relation to the rejection of her previous book. In 1966, Rich, like her husband, began her teaching career. She taught remedial English to college-aged, immigrant students. Rich continued to publish poetry volumes that addressed issues of women's rights and roles, lesbian identity, and the idea of privilege; her most recent collection is *An Atlas of the Difficult World* (1991). She has taught at institutions including Swarthmore, Brandeis, Cornell, and Columbia, and has been active in the fight for gay and lesbian rights, for which she received the Fund for Human Dignity Award of the National Gay Task Force in 1981.

In her essay "When the Dead Awaken: Writing as Re-Vision," Rich argues that not enough action has been taken to liberate female writers from traditional constraints. The presupposed definition of an "ideal" female prohibits them from adequately expressing themselves in a patriarchal society. To create examples of this, Rich draws from the works of acclaimed female writers such as Virginia Woolf, and analyzes their tones in order to translate their frustration. The essay shares both its title and theme with a play by Henrik Ibsen. Rich, like

Ibsen, explores the social possibilities that would be revealed by a woman's realization of her creative capabilities, and urgently calls feminists to action.

The Modern Language Association is both marketplace and funeral parlor for the professional study of Western literature in North America. Like all gatherings of the professions, it has been and remains a "procession of the sons of educated men" (Virginia Woolf): a congeries of old-boys' networks, academicians rehearsing their numb canons in sessions dedicated to the literature of white males, junior scholars under the lash of "publish or perish" delivering papers in the bizarrely lit drawing-rooms of immense hotels: a ritual competition veering between cynicism and desperation.

However, in the interstices of these gentlemanly rites (or, in Mary Daly's words, on the boundaries of this patriarchal space),[1] some feminist scholars, teachers, and graduate students, joined by feminist writers, editors, and publishers, have for a decade been creating more subversive occasions, challenging the sacredness of the gentlemanly canon, sharing the rediscovery of buried works by women, asking women's questions, bringing literary history and criticism back to life in both senses. The Commission of the Status of Women in the Profession was formed in 1969, and held its first public event in 1970. In 1971 the Commission asked Ellen Peck Killoh, Tillie Olsen, Elaine Reuben, and myself, with Elaine Hedges as moderator, to talk on "The Woman Writer in the Twentieth Century." The essay that follows was written for that forum, and later published, along with the other papers from the forum and workshops, in an issue of College English *edited by Elaine Hedges ("Women Writing and Teaching," vol. 34, no. 1, October 1972). With a few revisions, mainly updating, it was reprinted in* American Poets *in 1976, edited by William Heyen (New York: Bobbs-Merrill, 1976). That later text is the one published here.°*

The challenge flung by feminists at the accepted literary canon, at the methods of teaching it, and at the biased and astigmatic view of male "literary scholarship," has not diminished in the decade since the first Women's Forum; it has become broadened and intensified more recently by the challenges of black and lesbian feminists pointing out that feminist literary criticism itself has overlooked or held back from examining

---

°As Rich explains, this essay—written in 1971—was first published in 1972 and then included in her volume *On Lies, Secrets, and Silence* (1979). At that time she added the introductory note reprinted here, as well as some notes, identified as *"A.R., 1978."* [Editor's note in the Norton edition.]

the work of black women and lesbians. The dynamic between a political vision and the demand for a fresh vision of literature is clear: without a growing feminist movement, the first inroads of feminist scholarship could not have been made; without the sharpening of a black feminist consciousness, black women's writing would have been left in limbo between misogynist black male critics and white feminists still struggling to unearth a white women's tradition; without an articulate lesbian/feminist movement, lesbian writing would still be lying in that closet where many of us used to sit reading forbidden books "in a bad light."

Much, much more is yet to be done; and university curricula have of course changed very little as a result of all this. What *is* changing is the availability of knowledge, of vital texts, the visible effects on women's lives of seeing, hearing our wordless or negated experience affirmed and pursued further in language.

Ibsen's *When We Dead Awaken* is a play about the use that the male artist and thinker — in the process of creating culture as we know it — has made of women, in his life and in his work; and about a woman's slow struggling awakening to the use to which her life has been put. Bernard Shaw wrote in 1900 of this play:

> [Ibsen] shows us that no degradation ever devised or permitted is as disastrous as this degradation; that through it women can die into luxuries for men and yet can kill them; that men and women are becoming conscious of this; and that what remains to be seen as perhaps the most interesting of all imminent social developments is what will happen "when we dead awaken."[2]

It's exhilarating to be alive in a time of awakening consciousness; it can also be confusing, disorienting, and painful. The awakening of dead or sleeping consciousness has already affected the lives of millions of women, even those who don't know it yet. It is also affecting the lives of men, even those who deny its claims upon them. The argument will go on whether an oppressive economic class system is responsible for the oppressive nature of male/female relations, or whether, in fact, patriarchy—the domination of males—is the original model of oppression on which all others are based. But in the last few years the women's movement has drawn inescapable and illuminating connections between our sexual lives and our political institutions. The sleepwalkers are coming awake, and for the first time this awakening has a collective reality; it is no longer such a lonely thing to open one's eyes.

Re-vision—the act of looking back, of seeing with fresh eyes, of entering an old text from a new critical direction—is for women more than a   5

108

chapter in cultural history: it is an act of survival. Until we can understand the assumptions in which we are drenched we cannot know ourselves. And this drive to self-knowledge, for women, is more than a search for identity: it is part of our refusal of the self-destructiveness of male-dominated society. A radical critique of literature, feminist in its impulse, would take the work first of all as a clue to how we live, how we have been living, how we have been led to imagine ourselves, how our language has trapped as well as liberated us, how the very act of naming has been till now a male prerogative, and how we can begin to see and name—and therefore live—afresh. A change in the concept of sexual identity is essential if we are not going to see the old political order reassert itself in every new revolution. We need to know the writing of the past, and know it differently than we have ever known it; not to pass on a tradition but to break its hold over us.

For writers, and at this moment for women writers in particular, there is the challenge and promise of a whole new psychic geography to be explored. But there is also a difficult and dangerous walking on the ice, as we try to find language and images for the consciousness we are just coming into, and with little in the past to support us. I want to talk about some aspect of this difficulty and this danger.

Jane Harrison, the great classical anthropologist, wrote in 1914 in a letter to her friend Gilbert Murray:

> By and by, about "Women," it has bothered me often—why do women never want to write poetry about Man as a sex—why is Woman a dream and a terror to man and not the other way around? . . . Is it mere convention and propriety, or something deeper?[3]

I think Jane Harrison's question cuts deep into the myth-making tradition, the romantic tradition; deep into what women and men have been to each other; and deep into the psyche of the woman writer. Thinking about that question, I began thinking of the work of two twentieth-century women poets, Sylvia Plath and Diane Wakoski. It strikes me that in the work of both Man appears as, if not a dream, a fascination and a terror; and that the source of the fascination and the terror is, simply, Man's power—to dominate, tyrannize, choose, or reject the woman. The charisma of Man seems to come purely from his power over her and his control of the world by force, not from anything fertile or life-giving in him. And, in the work of both these poets, it is finally the woman's sense of *herself*—embattled, possessed—that gives the poetry its dynamic charge, its rhythms of struggle, need, will, and female energy. Until recently this female anger and this furious awareness of the Man's power over her were not available materials to the female poet, who tended to write of Love as the source of her suffering, and to view that victimization by Love as an almost inevitable fate. Or, like Marianne Moore and Elizabeth Bishop, she kept sexuality at a measured and chiseled distance in her poems.

One answer to Jane Harrison's question has to be that historically men and women have played very different parts in each others' lives. Where woman has been a luxury for man, and has served as the painter's model and the poet's muse, but also as comforter, nurse, cook, bearer of his seed, secretarial assistant, and copyist of manuscripts, man has played a quite different role for the female artist. Henry James repeats an incident which the writer Prosper Mérimée described, of how, while he was living with George Sand,

> he once opened his eyes, in the raw winter dawn, to see his companion, in a dressing-gown, on her knees before the domestic hearth, a candle-stick beside her and a red *madras* round her head, making bravely, with her own hands the fire that was to enable her to sit down betimes to urgent pen and paper. The story represents him as having felt that the spectacle chilled his ardor and tried his taste; her appearance was unfortunate, her occupation an inconsequence, and her industry a reproof—the result of all which was a lively irritation and an early rupture.[4]

The specter of this kind of male judgment, along with the misnaming and thwarting of her needs by a culture controlled by males, has created problems for the woman writer: problems of contact with herself, problems of language and style, problems of energy and survival.

In rereading Virginia Woolf's *A Room of One's Own* (1929) for the first time in some years, I was astonished at the sense of effort, of pains taken, of dogged tentativeness, in the tone of that essay. And I recognized that tone. I had heard it often enough, in myself and in other women. It is the tone of a woman almost in touch with her anger, who is determined not to appear angry, who is *willing* herself to be calm, detached, and even charming in a roomful of men where things have been said which are attacks on her very integrity. Virginia Woolf is addressing an audience of women, but she is acutely conscious—as she always was—of being overheard by men: by Morgan and Lytton and Maynard Keynes and for that matter by her father, Leslie Stephen.[5] She drew the language out into an exacerbated thread in her determination to have her own sensibility yet protect it from those masculine presences. Only at rare moments in that essay do you hear the passion in her voice; she was trying to sound as cool as Jane Austen, as Olympian as Shakespeare, because that is the way the men of the culture thought a writer should sound.

No male writer has written primarily or even largely for women, or with the sense of women's criticism as a consideration when he chooses his materials, his theme, his language. But to a lesser or greater extent, every woman writer has written for men even when, like Virginia Woolf, she was supposed to be addressing women. If we have come to the point when this balance might begin to change, when women can stop being haunted, not only by "convention and propriety" but by internalized fears of being and saying themselves, then it is an extraordinary moment for the woman writer—and reader.

I have hesitated to do what I am going to do now, which is to use myself as an illustration. For one thing, it's a lot easier and less danger-ous to talk about other women writers. But there is something else. Like Virginia Woolf, I am aware of the women who are not with us here because they are washing the dishes and looking after the children. Nearly fifty years after she spoke, that fact remains largely unchanged. And I am thinking also of women whom she left out of the picture altogether—women who are washing other people's dishes and caring for other people's children, not to mention women who went on the streets last night in order to feed their children. We seem to be special women here, we have liked to think of ourselves as special, and we have known that men would tolerate, even romanticize us as special, as long as our words and actions didn't threaten their privilege of tolerating or rejecting us and our work according to *their* ideas of what a special woman ought to be. An important insight of the radical women's move-ment has been how divisive and how ultimately destructive is this myth of the special woman, who is also the token woman. Every one of us here in this room has had great luck—we are teachers, writers, acade-micians; our own gifts could not have been enough, for we all know women whose gifts are buried or aborted. Our struggles can have mean-ing and our privileges—however precarious under patriarchy—can be justified only if they can help to change the lives of women whose gifts— and whose very being—continue to be thwarted and silenced.

My own luck was being born white and middle-class into a house full of books, with a father who encouraged me to read and write. So for about twenty years I wrote for a particular man, who criticized and praised me and made me feel I was indeed "special." The obverse side of this, of course, was that I tried for a long time to please him, or rather, not to displease him. And then of course there were other men—writers, teachers—the Man, who was not a terror or a dream but a literary mas-ter and a master in other ways less easy to acknowledge. And there were all those poems about women, written by men: it seemed to be a given that men wrote poems and women frequently inhabited them. These women were almost always beautiful, but threatened with the loss of

111

beauty, the loss of youth—the fate worse than death. Or, they were beautiful and died young, like Lucy and Lenore. Or, the woman was like Maud Gonne, cruel and disastrously mistaken, and the poem reproached her because she had refused to become a luxury for the poet.

A lot is being said today about the influence that the myths and images of women have on all of us who are products of culture. I think it has been a peculiar confusion to the girl or woman who tries to write because she is peculiarly susceptible to language. She goes to poetry or fiction looking for *her* way of being in the world, since she too has been putting words and images together; she is looking eagerly for guides, maps, possibilities; and over and over in the "words' masculine persuasive force" of literature she comes up against something that negates everything she is about: she meets the image of Woman in books written by men. She finds a terror and a dream, she finds a beautiful pale face, she finds La Belle Dame Sans Merci, she finds Juliet or Tess or Salomé, but precisely what she does not find is that absorbed, drudging, puzzled, sometimes inspired creature, herself, who sits at a desk trying to put words together.

So what does she do? What did I do? I read the older women poets with their peculiar keenness and ambivalence: Sappho, Christina Rossetti, Emily Dickinson, Elinor Wylie, Edna Millay, H. D. I discovered that the woman poet most admired at the time (by men) was Marianne Moore, who was maidenly, elegant, intellectual, discreet. But even in reading these women I was looking in them for the same things I had found in the poetry of men, because I wanted women poets to be the equals of men, and to be equal was still confused with sounding the same.

I know that my style was formed first by male poets: by the men I was   15 reading as an undergraduate—Frost, Dylan Thomas, Donne, Auden, MacNeice, Stevens, Yeats. What I chiefly learned from them was craft.[6] But poems are like dreams: in them you put what you don't know you know. Looking back at poems I wrote before I was twenty-one, I'm startled because beneath the conscious craft are glimpses of the split I even then experienced between the girl who wrote poems, who defined herself in writing poems, and the girl who was to define herself by her relationships with men. "Aunt Jennifer's Tigers" (1951), written while I was a student, looks with deliberate detachment at this split.

Aunt Jennifer's tigers stride across a screen,
Bright topaz denizens of a world of green.
They do not fear the men beneath the tree;
They pace in sleek chivalric certainty.

Aunt Jennifer's fingers fluttering through her wool
Find even the ivory needle hard to pull.

The massive weight of Uncle's wedding band
Sits heavily upon Aunt Jennifer's hand.

When Aunt is dead, her terrified hands will lie
Still ringed with ordeals she was mastered by.
The tigers in the panel that she made
Will go on striding, proud and unafraid.

In writing this poem, composed and apparently cool as it is, I thought I was creating a portrait of an imaginary woman. But this woman suffers from the opposition of her imagination, worked out in tapestry, and her lifestyle, "ringed with ordeals she was mastered by." It was important to me that Aunt Jennifer was a person as distinct from myself as possible — distanced by the formalism of the poem, by its objective, observant tone — even by putting the woman in a different generation.

In those years formalism was part of the strategy — like asbestos gloves, it allowed me to handle materials I couldn't pick up barehanded. A later strategy was to use the persona of a man, as I did in "The Loser" (1958):

A man thinks of the woman he once loved:
first, after her wedding, and then nearly a
decade later.

I
I kissed you, bride and lost, and went
home from that bourgeois sacrament,
your cheek still tasting cold upon
my lips that gave you benison
with all the swagger that they knew —
as losers somehow learn to do.

Your wedding made my eyes ache; soon
the world would be worse off for one
more golden apple dropped to ground
without the least protesting sound,
and you would windfall lie, and we
forget your shimmer on the tree.

Beauty is always wasted: if
not Mignon's song sung to the deaf,
at all events to the unmoved.
A face like yours cannot be loved
long or seriously enough.
Almost, we seem to hold it off.

II
Well, you are tougher than I thought.
Now when the wash with ice hangs taut
this morning of St. Valentine,
I see you strip the squeaking line,
your body weighed against the load,
and all my groans can do no good.

Because you still are beautiful,
though squared and stiffened by the pull
of what nine windy years have done.
You have three daughters, lost a son.
I see all your intelligence
flung into that unwearied stance.

My envy is of no avail.
I turn my head and wish him well
who chafed your beauty into use
and lives forever in a house
lit by the friction of your mind.
You stagger in against the wind.

I finished college, published my first book by a fluke, as it seemed to me, and broke off a love affair. I took a job, lived alone, went on writing, fell in love. I was young, full of energy, and the book seemed to mean that others agreed I was a poet. Because I was also determined to prove that as a woman poet I could also have what was then defined as a "full" woman's life, I plunged in my early twenties into marriage and had three children before I was thirty. There was nothing overt in the environment to warn me: these were the fifties, and in reaction to the earlier wave of feminism, middle-class women were making careers of domestic perfection, working to send their husbands through professional schools, then retiring to raise large families. People were moving out to the suburbs, technology was going to be the answer to everything, even sex; the family was in its glory. Life was extremely private; women were isolated from each other by the loyalties of marriage. I have a sense that women didn't talk to each other much in the fifties—not about their secret emptinesses, their frustrations. I went on trying to write; my second book and first child appeared in the same month. But by the time that book came out I was already dissatisfied with those poems, which seemed to me mere exercises for poems I hadn't written. The book was praised, however, for its "gracefulness"; I had a marriage and a child. If there were doubts, if there were periods of null depression or active despairing, these could only mean that I was ungrateful, insatiable, perhaps a monster.

About the time my third child was born, I felt that I had either to consider myself a failed woman and a failed poet, or to try to find some synthesis by which to understand what was happening to me. What frightened me most was the sense of drift, of being pulled along a current which called itself my destiny, but in which I seemed to be losing touch with whoever I had been, with the girl who had experienced her own will and energy almost ecstatically at times, walking around a city or riding a train at night or typing in a student room. In a poem about my grandmother I wrote (of myself): "A young girl, thought sleeping, is certified dead" ("Halfway"). I was writing very little, partly from fatigue, that female fatigue of suppressed anger and loss of contact with my own being; partly from the discontinuity of female life with its attention to small chores, errands, work that others constantly undo, small children's constant needs. What I did write was unconvincing to me; my anger and frustration were hard to acknowledge in or out of poems because in fact I cared a great deal about my husband and my children. Trying to look back and understand that time I have tried to analyze the real nature of the conflict. Most, if not all, human lives are full of fantasy—passive day-dreaming which need not be acted on. But to write poetry or fiction, or even to think well, is not to fantasize, or to put fantasies on paper. For a poem to coalesce, for a character or an action to take shape, there has to be an imaginative transformation of reality which is in no way passive. And a certain freedom of the mind is needed—freedom to press on, to enter the currents of your thought like a glider pilot, knowing that your motion can be sustained, that the buoyancy of your attention will not be suddenly snatched away. Moreover, if the imagination is to transcend and transform experience it has to question, to challenge, to conceive of alternatives, perhaps to the very life you are living at that moment. You have to be free to play around with the notion that day might be night, love might be hate; nothing can be too sacred for the imagination to turn into its opposite or to call experimentally by another name. For writing is renaming. Now, to be maternally with small children all day in the old way, to be with a man in the old way of marriage, requires a holding-back, a putting-aside of that imaginative activity, and demands instead a kind of conservatism. I want to make it clear that I am *not* saying that in order to write well, or think well, it is necessary to become unavailable to others, or to become a devouring ego. This has been the myth of the masculine artist and thinker; and I do not accept it. But to be a female human being trying to fulfill traditional female functions in a traditional way *is* in direct conflict with the subversive function of the imagination. The word traditional is important here. There must be ways, and we will be finding out more and more about them, in which the energy of creation and the energy of relation can be united. But in those years I always felt

115

the conflict as a failure of love in myself. I had thought I was choosing a full life; the life available to most men, in which sexuality, work, and parenthood could coexist. But I felt, at twenty-nine, guilt toward the people closest to me, and guilty toward my own being.

I wanted, then, more than anything, the one thing of which there was never enough: time to think, time to write. The fifties and early sixties were years of rapid revelations: the sit-ins and marches in the South, the Bay of Pigs, the early antiwar movement, raised large questions—questions for which the masculine world of the academy around me seemed to have expert and fluent answers. But I needed to think for myself—about pacifism and dissent and violence, about poetry and society, and about my own relationship to all these things. For about ten years I was reading in fierce snatches, scribbling in notebooks, writing poetry in fragments; I was looking desperately for clues, because if there were no clues then I thought I might be insane. I wrote in a notebook about this time:

> Paralyzed by the sense that there exists a mesh of relationships—e.g., between my anger at the children, my sensual life, pacifism, sex (I mean sex in its broadest significance, not merely sexual desire)—an interconnectedness which, if I could see it, make it valid, would give me back myself, make it possible to function lucidly and passionately. Yet I grope in and out among these dark webs.

I think I began at this point to feel that politics was not something "out there" but something "in here" and of the essence of my condition.

In the late fifties I was able to write, for the first time, directly about experiencing myself as a woman. The poem was jotted in fragments during children's naps, brief hours in a library, or at 3:00 A.M. after rising with a wakeful child. I despaired of doing any continuous work at this time. Yet I began to feel that my fragments and scraps had a common consciousness and a common theme, one which I would have been very unwilling to put on paper at an earlier time because I had been taught that poetry should be "universal," which meant, of course, nonfemale. Until then I had tried very much *not* to identify myself as a female poet. Over two years I wrote a ten-part poem called "Snapshots of a Daughter-in-Law" (1958–1960), in a longer looser mode than I'd ever trusted myself with before. It was an extraordinary relief to write that poem. It strikes me now as too literary, too dependent on allusion; I hadn't found the courage yet to do without authorities, or even to use the pronoun "I"— the woman in the poem is always "she." One section of it, No. 2, concerns a woman who thinks she is going mad; she is haunted by voices telling her to resist and rebel, voices which she can hear but not obey.

2.
Banging the coffee-pot into the sink
she hears the angels chiding, and looks out
past the raked gardens to the sloppy sky.
Only a week since They said: *Have no patience.*

The next time it was: *Be insatiable.*
Then: *Save yourself; others you cannot save.*
Sometimes she's let the tapstream scald her arm,
a match burn to her thumbnail,

or held her hand above the kettle's snout
right in the woolly steam. They are probably angels,
since nothing hurts her anymore, except
each morning's grit blowing into her eyes.

The poem "Orion," written five years later, is a poem of reconnection with a part of myself I had felt I was losing — the active principle, the energetic imagination, the "half-brother" whom I projected, as I had for many years, into the constellation Orion. It's no accident that the words "cold and egotistical" appear in this poem, and are applied to myself.

Far back when I went zig-zagging
through tamarack pastures
you were my genius, you
my cast-iron Viking, my helmed
lion-heart king in prison.
Years later now you're young

my fierce half-brother, staring
down from that simplified west
your breast open, your belt dragged down
by an oldfashioned thing, a sword
the last bravado you won't give over
though it weighs you down as you stride

and the stars in it are dim
and maybe have stopped burning.
But you burn, and I know it;
as I throw back my head to take you in
an old transfusion happens again:
divine astronomy is nothing to it.

Indoors I bruise and blunder,
break faith, leave ill enough
alone, a dead child born in the dark.

Night cracks up over the chimney,
pieces of time, frozen geodes
come showering down in the grate.

A man reaches behind my eyes
and finds them empty
a woman's head turns away
from my head in the mirror
children are dying my death
and eating crumbs of my life.

Pity is not your forte.
Calmly you ache up there
pinned aloft in your crow's nest,
my speechless pirate!
You take it all for granted
and when I look you back

it's with a starlike eye
shooting its cold and egotistical spear
where it can do least damage.
Breathe deep! No hurt, no pardon
out here in the cold with you
you with your back to the wall.

The choice still seemed to be between "love" — womanly, maternal love, altruistic love — a love defined and ruled by the weight of an entire culture; and egotism — a force directed by men into creation, achievement, ambition, often at the expense of others, but justifiably so. For weren't they men, and wasn't that their destiny as womanly, selfless love was ours? We know now that the alternatives are false ones — that the word "love" is itself in need of re-vision.

There is a companion poem to "Orion," written three years later, in which at last the woman in the poem and the woman writing the poem become the same person. It is called "Planetarium," and it was written after a visit to a real planetarium, where I read an account of the work of Caroline Herschel, the astronomer, who worked with her brother William, but whose name remained obscure, as his did not.

Thinking of Caroline Herschel, 1750–1848,
astronomer, sister of William; and others

A woman in the shape of a monster
a monster in the shape of a woman
the skies are full of them

118 -

a woman   'in the snow
among the Clocks and instruments
or measuring the ground with poles'

in her 98 years to discover
8 comets

she whom the moon ruled
like us
levitating into the night sky
riding the polished lenses

Galaxies of women, there
doing penance for impetuousness
ribs chilled
in those spaces   of the mind

An eye,

    'virile, precise and absolutely certain'
from the mad webs of Uranusborg

                    encountering the NOVA

every impulse of light exploding
from the core
as life flies out of us

        Tycho whispering at last
        'Let me not seem to have lived in vain'

What we see, we see
and seeing is changing

the light that shrivels a mountain
and leaves a man alive

Heartbeat of the pulsar
heart sweating through my body

The radio impulse
pouring in from Taurus

    I am bombarded yet I stand

I have been standing all my life in the
direct path of a battery of signals
the most accurately transmitted most
untranslateable language in the universe

I am a galactic cloud so deep   so invo-
luted that a light wave could take 15
years to travel through me   And has
taken   I am an instrument in the shape
of a woman trying to translate pulsations
into images   for the relief of the body
and the reconstruction of the mind.

In closing I want to tell you about a dream I had last summer. I
dreamed I was asked to read my poetry at a mass women's meeting, but
when I began to read, what came out were the lyrics of a blues song. I
share this dream with you because it seemed to me to say something
about the problems and the future of the woman writer, and probably of
women in general. The awakening of consciousness is not like the crossing of a frontier—one step and you are in another country. Much of
woman's poetry has been of the nature of the blues song: a cry of pain, of
victimization, or a lyric of seduction.[7] And today, much poetry by
women—and prose for that matter—is charged with anger. I think we
need to go through that anger, and we will betray our own reality if we
try, as Virginia Woolf was trying, for an objectivity, a detachment, that
would make us sound more like Jane Austen or Shakespeare. We know
more than Jane Austen or Shakespeare knew: more than Jane Austen
because our lives are more complex, more than Shakespeare because we
know more about the lives of women—Jane Austen and Virginia Woolf
included.

Both the victimization and the anger experienced by women are real,
and have real sources, everywhere in the environment, built into society,
language, the structures of thought. They will go on being trapped and
explored by poets, among others. We can neither deny them, nor will we
rest there. A new generation of women poets is already working out of
the psychic energy released when women begin to move out towards
what the feminist philosopher Mary Daly has described as the "new
space" on the boundaries of patriarchy.[8] Women are speaking to and of
women in these poems, out of a newly released courage to name, to love
each other, to share risk and grief and celebration.

To the eye of a feminist, the work of Western male poets now writing 25
reveals a deep, fatalistic pessimism as to the possibilities of change,
whether societal or personal, along with a familiar and threadbare use of
women (and nature) as redemptive on the one hand, threatening on the
other; and a new tide of phallocentric sadism and overt woman-hating
which matches the sexual brutality of recent films. "Political" poetry by
men remains stranded amid the struggles for power among male groups;
in condemning U.S. imperialism or the Chilean junta the poet can claim

to speak for the oppressed while remaining, as male, part of a system of sexual oppression. The enemy is always outside the self, the struggle somewhere else. The mood of isolation, self-pity, and self-imitation that pervades "nonpolitical" poetry suggests that a profound change in masculine consciousness will have to precede any new male poetic—or other—inspiration. The creative energy of patriarchy is fast running out; what remains is its self-generating energy for destruction. As women, we have our work cut out for us.

[1971]

Notes

1. Mary Daly, *Beyond God the Father* (Boston: Beacon, 1973), pp. 40–41.
2. G. B. Shaw, *The Quintessence of Ibsenism* (New York: Hill & Wang, 1922), p. 139.
3. J. G. Stewart, *Jane Ellen Harrison: A Portrait from Letters* (London: Merlin, 1959), p. 140.
4. Henry James, "Notes on Novelists," in *Selected Literary Criticism of Henry James*, Morris Shapira, ed. (London: Heinemann, 1963), pp. 157–58.
5. *A. R., 1978*: This intuition of mine was corroborated when, early in 1978, I read the correspondence between Woolf and Dame Ethel Smyth (Henry W. and Albert A. Berg Collection, The New York Public Library, Astor, Lenox and Tilden Foundations); in a letter dated June 8, 1933, Woolf speaks of having kept her own personality out of *A Room of One's Own* lest she not be taken seriously: " . . . how personal, so will they say, rubbing their hands with glee, women always are; *I even hear them as I write.*" (Italics mine.)
6. *A. R., 1978*: Yet I spent months, at sixteen, memorizing and writing imitations of Millay's sonnets; and in notebooks of that period I find what are obviously attempts to imitate Dickinson's metrics and verbal compression. I knew H. D. only through anthologized lyrics; her epic poetry was not then available to me.
7. *A. R., 1978*: When I dreamed that dream, was I wholly ignorant of the tradition of Bessie Smith and other women's blues lyrics which transcended victimization to sing of resistance and independence?
8. Mary Daly, *Beyond God the Father: Towards a Philosophy of Women's Liberation* (Boston: Beacon, 1973).

RICHARD RODRIGUEZ   [b. 1944]

Aria: Memoir of a
Bilingual Childhood

Born in 1944 in San Francisco and raised in Sacramento, California, to Mexican immigrants, **Richard Rodriguez** is a foremost and sometimes controversial Chicano voice. Best known for his memoir *Hunger of Memory: The Education of Richard Rodriguez* (1982), Rodriguez was a literary scholar and teacher until leaving the profession and becoming a full-time essayist. He is now a columnist and editor for the Pacific News Service and a contributor to numerous magazines and newspapers. His latest book, *Brown: The Last Discovery of America* (2002), continues his questioning of orthodoxy about race, identity, and politics in America.

"Aria: Memoir of a Bilingual Childhood" is taken from *Hunger of Memory.* That book cemented Rodriguez's controversial reputation because of its stands against bilingual education and affirmative action. Knowing these stands might be controversial, he takes them firmly: Of bilingual voters' ballots, Rodriguez writes, "It is not enough to say that these schemes are foolish and certainly doomed" (par. 61). As you read "Aria," note other moments in which Rodriguez takes on ideas with which he disagrees.

1

I remember to start with that day in Sacramento—a California now nearly thirty years past—when I first entered a classroom, able to understand some fifty stray English words.

The third of four children, I had been preceded to a neighborhood Roman Catholic school by an older brother and sister. But neither of them had revealed very much about their classroom experiences. Each afternoon they returned, as they left in the morning, always together, speaking in Spanish as they climbed the five steps of the porch. And their mysterious books, wrapped in shopping-bag paper, remained on the table next to the door, closed firmly behind them.

An accident of geography sent me to a school where all my classmates were white, many the children of doctors and lawyers and business executives. All my classmates certainly must have been uneasy on that first day of school—as most children are uneasy—to find themselves apart from their families in the first institution of their lives. But I was astonished.

The nun said, in a friendly but oddly impersonal voice, "Boys and girls, this is Richard Rodriguez." (I heard her sound out: *Rich-heard Road-ree-guess.*) It was the first time I had heard anyone name me in English. "Richard," the nun repeated more slowly, writing my name down in her black leather book. Quickly I turned to see my mother's face dissolve in a watery blur behind the pebbled glass door.

Many years later there is something called bilingual education—a 5
scheme proposed in the late 1960s by Hispanic-American social activists, later endorsed by a congressional vote. It is a program that seeks to permit non-English-speaking children, many from lower-class homes, to use their family language as the language of school. (Such is the goal its supporters announce.) I hear them and am forced to say no: It is not possible for a child—any child—ever to use his family's language in school. Not to understand this is to misunderstand the public uses of schooling and to trivialize the nature of intimate life—a family's "language."

Memory teaches me what I know of these matters; the boy reminds the adult. I was a bilingual child, a certain kind—socially disadvantaged—the son of working-class parents, both Mexican immigrants.

In the early years of my boyhood, my parents coped very well in America. My father had steady work. My mother managed at home. They were nobody's victims. Optimism and ambition led them to a house (our home) many blocks from the Mexican south side of town. We lived among *gringos* and only a block from the biggest, whitest houses. It never occurred to my parents that they couldn't live wherever they chose. Nor was the Sacramento of the fifties bent on teaching them a contrary lesson. My mother and father were more annoyed than intimidated by those two or three neighbors who tried initially to make us unwelcome. ("Keep your brats away from my sidewalk!") But despite all they achieved, perhaps because they had so much to achieve, any deep feeling of ease, the confidence of "belonging" in public was withheld from them both. They regarded the people at work, the faces in crowds, as very distant from us. They were the others, *los gringos*. That term was interchangeable in their speech with another, even more telling, *los americanos*.

123

I grew up in a house where the only regular guests were my relations. For one day, enormous families of relatives would visit and there would be so many people that the noise and the bodies would spill out to the backyard and front porch. Then, for weeks, no one came by. (It was usually a salesman who rang the doorbell.) Our house stood apart. A gaudy yellow in a row of white bungalows. We were the people with the noisy dog. The people who raised pigeons and chickens. We were the foreigners on the block. A few neighbors smiled and waved. We waved back. But no one in the family knew the names of the old couple who lived next door; until I was seven years old, I did not know the names of the kids who lived across the street.

In public, my father and mother spoke a hesitant, accented, not always grammatical English. And they would have to strain—their bodies tense—to catch the sense of what was rapidly said by *los gringos*. At home they spoke Spanish. The language of their Mexican past sounded in counterpoint to the English of public society. The words would come quickly, with ease. Conveyed through those sounds was the pleasing, soothing, consoling reminder of being at home.

During those years when I was first conscious of hearing, my mother 10 and father addressed me only in Spanish; in Spanish I learned to reply. By contrast, English (*inglés*), rarely heard in the house, was the language I came to associate with *gringos*. I learned my first words of English overhearing my parents speak to strangers. At five years of age, I knew just enough English for my mother to trust me on errands to stores one block away. No more.

I was a listening child, careful to hear the very different sounds of Spanish and English. Wide-eyed with hearing, I'd listen to sounds more than words. First, there were English (*gringo*) sounds. So many words were still unknown that when the butcher or the lady at the drugstore said something to me, exotic polysyllabic sounds would bloom in the midst of their sentences. Often, the speech of people in public seemed to me very loud, booming with confidence. The man behind the counter would literally ask, "What can I do for you?" But by being so firm and so clear, the sound of his voice said that he was a *gringo*; he belonged in public society.

I would also hear then the high nasal notes of middle-class American speech. The air stirred with sound. Sometimes, even now, when I have been traveling abroad for several weeks, I will hear what I heard as a boy. In hotel lobbies or airports, in Turkey or Brazil, some Americans will pass, and suddenly I will hear it again—the high sound of American voices. For a few seconds I will hear it with pleasure, for it is now the sound of *my* society—a reminder of home. But inevitably—already on the flight headed for home—the sound fades with repetition. I will be unable to hear it anymore.

When I was a boy, things were different. The accent of *los gringos* was never pleasing nor was it hard to hear. Crowds at Safeway or at bus stops would be noisy with sound. And I would be forced to edge away from the chirping chatter above me.

I was unable to hear my own sounds, but I knew very well that I spoke English poorly. My words could not stretch far enough to form complete thoughts. And the words I did speak I didn't know well enough to make into distinct sounds. (Listeners would usually lower their heads, better to hear what I was trying to say.) But it was one thing for *me* to speak English with difficulty. It was more troubling for me to hear my parents speak in public: their high-whining vowels and guttural consonants; their sentences that got stuck with "eh" and "ah" sounds; the confused syntax; the hesitant rhythm of sounds so different from the way *gringos* spoke. I'd notice, moreover, that my parents' voices were softer than those of *gringos* we'd meet.

I am tempted now to say that none of this mattered. In adulthood I am embarrassed by childhood fears. And, in a way, it didn't matter very much that my parents could not speak English with ease. Their linguistic difficulties had no serious consequences. My mother and father made themselves understood at the county hospital clinic and at government offices. And yet, in another way, it mattered very much—it was unsettling to hear my parents struggle with English. Hearing them, I'd grow nervous, my clutching trust in their protection and power weakened. 15

There were many times like the night at a brightly lit gasoline station (a blaring white memory) when I stood uneasily, hearing my father. He was talking to a teenaged attendant. I do not recall what they were saying, but I cannot forget the sounds my father made as he spoke. At one point his words slid together to form one word—sounds as confused as the threads of blue and green oil in the puddle next to my shoes. His voice rushed through what he had left to say. And, toward the end, reached falsetto notes, appealing to his listener's understanding. I looked away to the lights of passing automobiles. I tried not to hear anymore. But I heard only too well the calm, easy tones in the attendant's reply. Shortly afterward, walking toward home with my father, I shivered when he put his hand on my shoulder. The very first chance that I got, I evaded his grasp and ran on ahead into the dark, skipping with feigned boyish exuberance.

But then there was Spanish. *Español:* my family's language. *Español:* the language that seemed to me a private language. I'd hear strangers on the radio and in the Mexican Catholic church across town speaking in Spanish, but I couldn't really believe that Spanish was a public language, like English. Spanish speakers, rather, seemed related to me, for I sensed that we shared—through our language—the experience of feeling apart from *los gringos*. It was thus a ghetto Spanish that I heard and I spoke. Like those whose lives are bound by a barrio, I was reminded by Spanish of my separateness from *los otros, los gringos* in power. But more intensely than for most barrio children—because I did not live in a barrio—Spanish seemed to me the language of home. (Most days it was only at home that I'd hear it.) It became the language of joyful return.

A family member would say something to me and I would feel myself specially recognized. My parents would say something to me and I would feel embraced by the sounds of their words. Those sounds said: *I am speaking with ease in Spanish. I am addressing you in words I never use with* los gringos. *I recognize you as someone special, close, like no one outside. You belong with us. In the family.*

(*Ricardo.*)

At the age of five, six, well past the time when most other children no 20 longer easily notice the difference between sounds uttered at home and words spoken in public, I had a different experience. I lived in a world magically compounded of sounds. I remained a child longer than most; I lingered too long, poised at the edge of language—often frightened by the sounds of *los gringos*, delighted by the sounds of Spanish at home. I shared with my family a language that was startlingly different from that used in the great city around us.

For me there were none of the gradations between public and private society so normal to a maturing child. Outside the house was public society; inside the house was private. Just opening or closing the screen door behind me was an important experience. I'd rarely leave home all alone or without reluctance. Walking down the sidewalk, under the canopy of tall trees, I'd warily notice the—suddenly—silent neighborhood kids who stood warily watching me. Nervously, I'd arrive at the grocery store to hear there the sounds of the *gringo*—foreign to me—reminding me that in this world so big, I was a foreigner. But then I'd return. Walking back toward our house, climbing the steps from the sidewalk, when the front door was open in summer, I'd hear voices beyond the screen door talking in Spanish. For a second or two, I'd stay, linger there, listening. Smiling, I'd hear my mother call out, saying in Spanish (words): "Is that you, Richard?" All the while her sounds would assure me: *You are home now; come closer; inside. With us.*

"*Sí,*" I'd reply.

Once more inside the house I would resume (assume) my place in the family. The sounds would dim, grow harder to hear. Once more at home, I would grow less aware of that fact. It required, however, no more than the blurt of the doorbell to alert me to listen to sounds all over again. The house would turn instantly still while my mother went to the door. I'd hear her hard English sounds. I'd wait to hear her voice return to soft-sounding Spanish, which assured me, as surely as did the clicking tongue of the lock on the door, that the stranger was gone.

Plainly, it is not healthy to hear such sounds so often. It is not healthy to distinguish public words from private sounds so easily. I remained cloistered by sounds, timid and shy in public, too dependent on voices at home. And yet it needs to be emphasized: I was an extremely happy child at home. I remember many nights when my father would come back from work, and I'd hear him call out to my mother in Spanish, sounding relieved. In Spanish, he'd sound light and free notes he never could manage in English. Some nights I'd jump up just at hearing his voice. With *mis hermanos* I would come running into the room where he was with my mother. Our laughing (so deep was the pleasure!) became screaming. Like others who know the pain of public alienation, we transformed the knowledge of our public separateness and made it consoling—the reminder of intimacy. Excited, we joined our voices in a celebration of sounds. *We are speaking now the way we never speak out in public. We are alone—together*, voices sounded, surrounded to tell me. Some nights, no one seemed willing to loosen the hold sounds had on us. At dinner, we invented new words. (Ours sounded Spanish, but made sense only to us.) We pieced together new words by taking, say, an English verb and giving it Spanish endings. My mother's instructions at bedtime would be lacquered with mock-urgent tones. Or a word like *sí* would become, in several notes, able to convey added measures of feeling. Tongues explored the edges of words, especially the fat vowels. And we happily sounded that military drum roll, the twirling roar of the Spanish *r*. Family language: my family's sounds. The voices of my parents and sisters and brother. Their voices insisting: *You belong here. We are family members. Related. Special to one another. Listen!* Voices singing and sighing, rising, straining, then surging, teeming with pleasure that burst syllables into fragments of laughter. At times it seemed there was steady quiet only when, from another room, the rustling whispers of my parents faded and I moved closer to sleep.

2

Supporters of bilingual education today imply that students like me miss a great deal by not being taught in their family's language. What they seem not to recognize is that, as a socially disadvantaged child, I considered Spanish to be a private language. What I needed to learn in school was that I had the right—and the obligation—to speak the public language of *los gringos*. The odd truth is that my first-grade classmates could have become bilingual, in the conventional sense of that word, more easily than I. Had they been taught (as upper-middle-class children are often taught early) a second language like Spanish or French, they could have regarded it simply as that: another public language. In my case such bilingualism could not have been so quickly achieved. What I did not believe was that I could speak a single public language.

Without question, it would have pleased me to hear my teachers address me in Spanish when I entered the classroom. I would have felt much less afraid. I would have trusted them and responded with ease. But I would have delayed—for how long postponed?—having to learn the language of public society. I would have evaded—and for how long could I have afforded to delay?—learning the great lesson of school, that I had a public identity.

Fortunately, my teachers were unsentimental about their responsibility. What they understood was that I needed to speak a public language. So their voices would search me out, asking me questions. Each time I'd hear them, I'd look up in surprise to see a nun's face frowning at me. I'd mumble, not really meaning to answer. The nun would persist, "Richard, stand up. Don't look at the floor. Speak up. Speak to the entire class, not just to me!" But I couldn't believe that the English language was mine to use. (In part, I did not want to believe it.) I continued to mumble. I resisted the teacher's demands. (Did I somehow suspect that once I learned public language my pleasing family life would be changed?) Silent, waiting for the bell to sound, I remained dazed, diffident, afraid.

Because I wrongly imagined that English was intrinsically a public language and Spanish an intrinsically private one, I easily noted the difference between classroom language and the language of home. At school, words were directed to a general audience of listeners. ("Boys and girls.") Words were meaningfully ordered. And the point was not self-expression alone but to make oneself understood by many others. The teacher quizzed: "Boys and girls, why do we use that word in this sentence? Could we think of a better word to use there? Would the sentence change its meaning if the words were differently arranged? And wasn't there a better way of saying much the same thing?" (I couldn't say. I wouldn't try to say.)

Three months. Five. Half a year passed. Unsmiling, ever watchful, my teachers noted my silence. They began to connect my behavior with the difficult progress my older sister and brother were making. Until one Saturday morning three nuns arrived at the house to talk to our parents. Stiffly, they sat on the blue living room sofa. From the doorway of another room, spying the visitors, I noted the incongruity—the clash of two worlds, the faces and voices of school intruding upon the familiar setting of home. I overheard one voice gently wondering, "Do your children speak only Spanish at home, Mrs. Rodriguez?" While another voice added, "That Richard especially seems so timid and shy."

That Rich-heard!   30

With great tact the visitors continued, "Is it possible for you and your husband to encourage your children to practice their English when they are home?" Of course, my parents complied. What would they not do for their children's well-being? And how could they have questioned the Church's authority which those women represented? In an instant, they agreed to give up the language (the sounds) that had revealed and accentuated our family's closeness. The moment after the visitors left, the change was observed. "*Ahora,* speak to us *en inglés,*" my father and mother united to tell us.

At first, it seemed a kind of game. After dinner each night, the family gathered to practice "our" English. (It was still then *inglés,* a language foreign to us, so we felt drawn as strangers to it.) Laughing, we would try to define words we could not pronounce. We played with strange English sounds, often over-anglicizing our pronunciations. And we filled the smiling gaps of our sentences with familiar Spanish sounds. But that was cheating, somebody shouted. Everyone laughed. In school, meanwhile, like my brother and sister, I was required to attend a daily tutoring session. I needed a full year of special attention. I also needed my teachers to keep my attention from straying in class by calling out, *Rich-heard*—their English voices slowly prying loose my ties to my other name, its three notes, *Ri-car-do.* Most of all I needed to hear my mother and father speak to me in a moment of seriousness in broken—suddenly heartbreaking—English. The scene was inevitable: One Saturday morning I entered the kitchen where my parents were talking in Spanish. I did not realize that they were talking in Spanish however until, at the moment they saw me, I heard their voices change to speak English. Those *gringo* sounds they uttered startled me. Pushed me away. In that moment of trivial misunderstanding and profound insight, I felt my throat twisted by unsounded grief. I turned quickly and left the room. But I had no place to escape to with Spanish. (The spell was broken.) My brother and sisters were speaking English in another part of the house.

Again and again in the days following, increasingly angry, I was obliged to hear my mother and father: "Speak to us *en inglés.*" (*Speak.*) Only then did I determine to learn classroom English. Weeks after, it happened: One day in school I raised my hand to volunteer an answer. I spoke out in a loud voice. And I did not think it remarkable when the entire class understood. That day, I moved very far from the disadvantaged child I had been only days earlier. The belief, the calming assurance that I belonged in public, had at last taken hold.

Shortly after, I stopped hearing the high and loud sounds of *los grin-gos*. A more and more confident speaker of English, I didn't trouble to listen to *how* strangers sounded, speaking to me. And there simply were too many English-speaking people in my day for me to hear American accents anymore. Conversations quickened. Listening to persons who sounded eccentrically pitched voices, I usually noted their sounds for an initial few seconds before I concentrated on *what* they were saying. Conversations became content-full. Transparent. Hearing someone's *tone* of voice—angry or questioning or sarcastic or happy or sad—I didn't distinguish it from the words it expressed. Sound and word were thus tightly wedded. At the end of a day, I was often bemused, always re-lieved, to realize how "silent," though crowded with words, my day in public had been. (This public silence measured and quickened the change in my life.)

At last, seven years old, I came to believe what had been technically 35 true since my birth: I was an American citizen.

But the special feeling of closeness at home was diminished by then. Gone was the desperate, urgent, intense feeling of being at home; rare was the experience of feeling myself individualized by family intimates. We remained a loving family, but one greatly changed. No longer so close; no longer bound tight by the pleasing and troubling knowledge of our public separateness. Neither my older brother nor sister rushed home after school anymore. Nor did I. When I arrived home there would often be neighborhood kids in the house. Or the house would be empty of sounds.

Following the dramatic Americanization of their children, even my parents grew more publicly confident. Especially my mother. She learned the names of all the people on our block. And she decided we needed to have a telephone installed in the house. My father continued to use the word *gringo*. But it was no longer charged with the old bitter-ness or distrust. (Stripped of any emotional content, the word simply be-came a name for those Americans not of Hispanic descent.) Hearing him, sometimes, I wasn't sure if he was pronouncing the Spanish word *gringo* or saying gringo in English.

Matching the silence I started hearing in public was a new quiet at home. The family's quiet was partly due to the fact that, as we children learned more and more English, we shared fewer and fewer words with our parents. Sentences needed to be spoken slowly when a child ad-dressed his mother or father. (Often the parent wouldn't understand.) The child would need to repeat himself. (Still the parent misunder-stood.) The young voice, frustrated, would end up saying, "Never mind"—the subject was closed. Dinners would be noisy with the clink-ing of knives and forks against dishes. My mother would smile softly between her remarks; my father at the other end of the table would chew and chew at his food, while he stared over the heads of his children.

My *mother!* My *father!* After English became my primary language, I no longer knew what words to use in addressing my parents. The old Spanish words (those tender accents of sound) I had used earlier— *mamá* and *papá*—I couldn't use anymore. They would have been too painful reminders of how much had changed in my life. On the other hand, the words I heard neighborhood kids call *their* parents seemed equally unsatisfactory. *Mother* and *Father; Ma, Papa, Pa, Dad, Pop* (how I hated the all-American sound of that last word especially)—all these terms I felt were unsuitable, not really terms of address for *my* parents. As a result, I never used them at home. Whenever I'd speak to my parents, I would try to get their attention with eye contact alone. In public conversations, I'd refer to "my parents" or "my mother and father."

My mother and father, for their part, responded differently, as their   40 children spoke to them less. She grew restless, seemed troubled and anxious at the scarcity of words exchanged in the house. It was she who would question me about my day when I came home from school. She smiled at small talk. She pried at the edges of my sentences to get me to say something more. (What?) She'd join conversations she overheard, but her intrusions often stopped her children's talking. By contrast, my father seemed reconciled to the new quiet. Though his English improved somewhat, he retired into silence. At dinner he spoke very little. One night his children and even his wife helplessly giggled at his garbled English pronunciation of the Catholic Grace before Meals. Thereafter he made his wife recite the prayer at the start of each meal, even on formal occasions, when there were guests in the house. Hers became the public voice of the family. On official business, it was she, not my father, one would usually hear on the phone or in stores, talking to strangers. His children grew so accustomed to his silence that, years later, they would speak routinely of his shyness. (My mother would often try to explain: Both his parents died when he was eight. He was raised by an uncle who treated him like little more than a menial servant. He was never encouraged to speak. He grew up alone. A man of few words.) But my father was not shy, I realized, when I'd watch him speaking Spanish with relatives. Using Spanish, he was quickly effusive. Especially when talking with other men, his voice would spark, flicker, flare alive with sounds. In Spanish, he expressed ideas and feelings he rarely revealed in English. With firm Spanish sounds, he conveyed confidence and authority English would never allow him.

The silence at home, however, was finally more than a literal silence. Fewer words passed between parent and child, but more profound was the silence that resulted from my inattention to sounds. At about the time I no longer bothered to listen with care to the sounds of English in public, I grew careless about listening to the sounds family members made when they spoke. Most of the time I heard someone speaking at home and didn't distinguish his sounds from the words people uttered in public. I didn't even pay much attention to my parents' accented and un-grammatical speech. At least not at home. Only when I was with them in public would I grow alert to their accents. Though, even then, their sounds caused me less and less concern. For I was increasingly confident of my own public identity.

I would have been happier about my public success had I not some-times recalled what it had been like earlier, when my family had conveyed its intimacy through a set of conveniently private sounds. Sometimes in public, hearing a stranger, I'd hark back to my past. A Mexican farmworker approached me downtown to ask directions to somewhere. "¿Hijito . . . ?" he said. And his voice summoned deep longing. Another time, standing beside my mother in the visiting room of a Carmelite convent, before the dense screen which rendered the nuns shadowy figures, I heard sev-eral Spanish-speaking nuns — their busy, singsong overlapping voices — assure us that yes, yes, we were remembered, all our family was remem-bered in their prayers. (Their voices echoed faraway family sounds.) Another day, a dark-faced old woman — her hand light on my shoulder — steadied herself against me as she boarded a bus. She murmured some-thing I couldn't quite comprehend. Her Spanish voice came near, like the face of a never-before-seen relative in the instant before I was kissed. Her voice, like so many of the Spanish voices I'd hear in public, recalled the golden age of my youth. Hearing Spanish then, I continued to be a care-ful, if sad, listener to sounds. Hearing a Spanish-speaking family walking behind me, I turned to look. I smiled for an instant, before my glance found the Hispanic-looking faces of strangers in the crowd going by.

Today I hear bilingual educators say that children lose a degree of "in-dividuality" by becoming assimilated into public society. (Bilingual schooling was popularized in the seventies, that decade when middle-class ethnics began to resist the process of assimilation — the American melting pot.) But the bilingualists simplistically scorn the value and ne-cessity of assimilation. They do not seem to realize that there are *two* ways a person is individualized. So they do not realize that while one suffers a diminished sense of *private* individuality by becoming assimi-lated into public society, such assimilation makes possible the achieve-ment of *public* individuality.

The bilingualists insist that a student should be reminded of his differ-ence from others in mass society, his heritage. But they equate mere sep-arateness with individuality. The fact is that only in private — with

132

intimates—is separateness from the crowd a prerequisite for individuality. (An intimate draws me apart, tells me that I am unique, unlike all others.) In public, by contrast, full individuality is achieved, paradoxically, by those who are able to consider themselves members of the crowd. Thus it happened for me: Only when I was able to think of myself as an American, no longer an alien in *gringo* society, could I seek the rights and opportunities necessary for full public individuality. The social and political advantages I enjoy as a man result from the day that I came to believe that my name, indeed, is *Rich-heard Road-ree-guess*. It is true that my public society today is often impersonal. (My public society is usually mass society.) Yet despite the anonymity of the crowd and despite the fact that the individuality I achieve in public is often tenuous—because it depends on my being one in a crowd—I celebrate the day I acquired my new name. Those middle-class ethnics who scorn assimilation seem to me filled with decadent self-pity, obsessed by the burden of public life. Dangerously, they romanticize public separateness and they trivialize the dilemma of the socially disadvantaged.

My awkward childhood does not prove the necessity of bilingual edu- 45 cation. My story discloses instead an essential myth of childhood—inevitable pain. If I rehearse here the changes in my private life after my Americanization, it is finally to emphasize the public gain. The loss implies the gain: The house I returned to each afternoon was quiet. Intimate sounds no longer rushed to the door to greet me. There were other noises inside. The telephone rang. Neighborhood kids ran past the door of the bedroom where I was reading my schoolbooks—covered with shopping-bag paper. Once I learned public language, it would never again be easy for me to hear intimate family voices. More and more of my day was spent hearing words. But that may only be a way of saying that the day I raised my hand in class and spoke loudly to an entire roomful of faces, my childhood started to end.

3

I grew up victim to a disabling confusion. As I grew fluent in English, I no longer could speak Spanish with confidence. I continued to understand spoken Spanish. And in high school, I learned how to read and write Spanish. But for many years I could not pronounce it. A powerful guilt blocked my spoken words; an essential glue was missing whenever I'd try to connect words to form sentences. I would be unable to break a barrier of sound, to speak freely. I would speak, or try to speak, Spanish, and I would manage to utter halting, hiccuping sounds that betrayed my unease.

When relatives and Spanish-speaking friends of my parents came to the house, my brother and sisters seemed reticent to use Spanish, but at least they managed to say a few necessary words before being excused. I never managed so gracefully. I was cursed with guilt. Each time I'd hear myself addressed in Spanish, I would be unable to respond with any success. I'd know the words I wanted to say, but I couldn't manage to say them. I would try to speak, but everything I said seemed to me horribly anglicized. My mouth would not form the words right. My jaw would tremble. After a phrase or two, I'd cough up a warm, silvery sound. And stop.

It surprised my listeners to hear me. They'd lower their heads, better to grasp what I was trying to say. They would repeat their questions in gentle, affectionate voices. But by then I would answer in English. No, no, they would say, we want you to speak to us in Spanish. (". . . en español.") But I couldn't do it. Pocho then they called me. Sometimes playfully, teasingly, using the tender diminutive—mi pochito. Sometimes not so playfully, mockingly, Pocho. (A Spanish dictionary defines that word as an adjective meaning "colorless" or "bland." But I heard it as a noun, naming the Mexican-American who, in becoming an American, forgets his native society.) "¡Pocho!" the lady in the Mexican food store muttered, shaking her head. I looked up to the counter where red and green peppers were strung like Christmas tree lights and saw the frowning face of the stranger. My mother laughed somewhere behind me. (She said that her children didn't want to practice "our Spanish" after they started going to school.) My mother's smiling voice made me suspect that the lady who faced me was not really angry at me. But, searching her face, I couldn't find the hint of a smile.

Embarrassed, my parents would regularly need to explain their children's inability to speak flowing Spanish during those years. My mother met the wrath of her brother, her only brother, when he came up from Mexico one summer with his family. He saw his nieces and nephews for the very first time. After listening to me, he looked away and said what a disgrace it was that I couldn't speak Spanish, "su proprio idioma." He made that remark to my mother; I noticed, however, that he stared at my father.

I clearly remember one other visitor from those years. A long-time 50 friend of my father from San Francisco would come to stay with us for several days in late August. He took great interest in me after he realized that I couldn't answer his questions in Spanish. He would grab me as I started to leave the kitchen. He would ask me something. Usually he wouldn't bother to wait for my mumbled response. Knowingly, he'd murmur: "¿Ay Pocho, Pocho, adónde vas?" And he would press his thumbs into the upper part of my arms, making me squirm with currents of pain. Dumbly, I'd stand there, waiting for his wife to notice us, for her to call him off with a benign smile. I'd giggle, hoping to deflate the tension between us, pretending that I hadn't seen the glittering scorn in his glance.

I remember that man now, but seek no revenge in this telling. I recount such incidents only because they suggest the fierce power Spanish had for many people I met at home; the way Spanish was associated with closeness. Most of those people who called me a *pocho* could have spoken English to me. But they would not. They seemed to think that Spanish was the only language we could use, that Spanish alone permitted our close association. (Such persons are vulnerable always to the ghetto merchant and the politician who have learned the value of speaking their clients' family language to gain immediate trust.) For my part, I felt that I had somehow committed a sin of betrayal by learning English. But betrayal against whom? Not against visitors to the house exactly. No, I felt that I had betrayed my immediate family. I *knew* that my parents had encouraged me to learn English. I *knew* that I had turned to English only with angry reluctance. But once I spoke English with ease, I came to *feel* guilty. (This guilt defied logic.) I felt that I had shattered the intimate bond that had once held the family close. This original sin against my family told whenever anyone addressed me in Spanish and I responded, confounded.

But even during those years of guilt, I was coming to sense certain consoling truths about language and intimacy. I remember playing with a friend in the backyard one day, when my grandmother appeared at the window. Her face was stern with suspicion when she saw the boy (the *gringo*) I was with. In Spanish she called out to me, sounding the whistle of her ancient breath. My companion looked up and watched her intently as she lowered the window and moved, still visible, behind the light curtain, watching us both. He wanted to know what she had said. I started to tell him, to say — to translate her Spanish words into English. The problem was, however, that though I knew how to translate exactly *what* she had told me, I realized that any translation would distort the deepest meaning of her message: It had been directed only to me. This message of intimacy could never be translated because it was not *in* the words she had used but passed *through* them. So any translation would have seemed wrong; her words would have been stripped of an essential meaning. Finally, I decided not to tell my friend anything. I told him that I didn't hear all she had said.

This insight unfolded in time. Making more and more friends outside my house, I began to distinguish intimate voices speaking through *English*. I'd listen at times to a close friend's confidential tone or secretive whisper. Even more remarkable were those instances when, for no special reason apparently, I'd become conscious of the fact that my companion was speaking only to me. I'd marvel just hearing his voice. It was a stunning event: to be able to break through his words, to be able to hear this voice of the other, to realize that it was directed only to me. After such moments of intimacy outside the house, I began to trust hearing intimacy conveyed through my family's English. Voices at home at last punctured sad confusion. I'd hear myself addressed as an intimate at home once again. Such moments were never as raucous with sound as past times had been when we had had "private" Spanish to use. (Our English-sounding house was never to be as noisy as our Spanish-speaking house had been.) Intimate moments were usually soft moments of sound. My mother was in the dining room while I did my homework nearby. And she looked over at me. Smiled. Said something—her words said nothing very important. But her voice sounded to tell me (*We are together*) I was her son.

(*Richard!*)

Intimacy thus continued at home; intimacy was not stilled by English. 55 It is true that I would never forget the great change of my life, the diminished occasions of intimacy. But there would also be times when I sensed the deepest truth about language and intimacy: *Intimacy is not created by a particular language; it is created by intimates.* The great change in my life was not linguistic but social. If, after becoming a successful student, I no longer heard intimate voices as often as I had earlier, it was not because I spoke English rather than Spanish. It was because I used public language for most of the day. I moved easily at last, a citizen in a crowded city of words.

4

This boy became a man. In private now, alone, I brood over language and intimacy—the great themes of my past. In public I expect most of the faces I meet to be the faces of strangers. (How do you do?) If meetings are quick and impersonal, they have been efficiently managed. I rush past the sounds of voices attending only to the words addressed to me. Voices seem planed to an even surface of sound, soundless. A business associate speaks in a deep baritone, but I pass through the timbre to attend to his words. The crazy man who sells me a newspaper every night mumbles something crazy, but I have time only to pretend that I have heard him say hello. Accented versions of English make little impression on me. In the rush-hour crowd a Japanese tourist asks me a question, and I inch past his accent to concentrate on what he is saying. The Eastern European immigrant in a neighborhood delicatessen

136

speaks to me through a marinade of sounds, but I respond to his words. I note for only a second the Texas accent of the telephone operator or the Mississippi accent of the man who lives in the apartment below me.

My city seems silent until some ghetto black teenagers board the bus I am on. Because I do not take their presence for granted, I listen to the sounds of their voices. Of all the accented versions of English I hear in a day, I hear theirs most intently. They are *the* sounds of the outsider. They annoy me for being loud—so self-sufficient and unconcerned by my presence. Yet for the same reason they seem to me glamorous. (A romantic gesture against public acceptance.) Listening to their shouted laughter, I realize my own quiet. Their voices enclose my isolation. I feel envious, envious of their brazen intimacy.

I warn myself away from such envy, however. I remember the black political activists who have argued in favor of using black English in schools. (Their argument varies only slightly from that made by foreign-language bilingualists.) I have heard "radical" linguists make the point that black English is a complex and intricate version of English. And I do not doubt it. But neither do I think that black English should be a language of public instruction. What makes black English inappropriate in classrooms is not something *in* the language. It is rather what lower-class speakers make of it. Just as Spanish would have been a dangerous language for me to have used at the start of my education, so black English would be a dangerous language to use in the schooling of teenagers for whom it reinforces feelings of public separateness.

This seems to me an obvious point. But one that needs to be made. In recent years there have been attempts to make the language of the alien public language. "Bilingual education, two ways to understand . . . ," television and radio commercials glibly announce. Proponents of bilingual education are careful to say that they want students to acquire good schooling. Their argument goes something like this: Children permitted to use their family language in school will not be so alienated and will be better able to match the progress of English-speaking children in the crucial first months of instruction. (Increasingly confident of their abilities, such children will be more inclined to apply themselves to their studies in the future.) But then the bilingualists claim another, very different goal. They say that children who use their family language in school will retain a sense of their individuality—their ethnic heritage and cultural ties. Supporters of bilingual education thus want it both ways. They propose bilingual schooling as a way of helping students acquire the skills of the classroom crucial for public success. But they likewise insist that bilingual instruction will give students a sense of their identity apart from the public.

Behind this screen there gleams an astonishing promise: One can be- 60

137

come a public person while still remaining a private person. At the very same time one can be both! There need be no tension between the self in the crowd and the self apart from the crowd! Who would not want to believe such an idea? Who can be surprised that the scheme has won the support of many middle-class Americans? If the barrio or ghetto child can retain his separateness even while being publicly educated, then it is almost possible to believe that there is no private cost to be paid for public success. Such is the consolation offered by any of the current bilingual schemes. Consider, for example, the bilingual voters' ballot. In some American cities one can cast a ballot printed in several languages. Such a document implies that a person can exercise that most public of rights—the right to vote—while still keeping apart, unassimilated from public life.

It is not enough to say that these schemes are foolish and certainly doomed. Middle-class supporters of public bilingualism toy with the confusion of those Americans who cannot speak standard English as well as they can. Bilingual enthusiasts, moreover, sin against intimacy. An Hispanic-American writer tells me, "I will never give up my family language; I would as soon give up my soul." Thus he holds to his chest a skein of words, as though it were the source of his family ties. He credits to language what he should credit to family members. A convenient mistake. For as long as he holds on to words, he can ignore how much else has changed in his life.

It has happened before. In earlier decades, persons newly successful and ambitious for social mobility similarly seized upon certain "family words." Working-class men attempting political power took to calling one another "brother." By so doing they escaped oppressive public isolation and were able to unite with many others like themselves. But they paid a price for this union. It was a public union they forged. The word they coined to address one another could never be the sound (*brother*) exchanged by two in intimate greeting. In the union hall the word "brother" became a vague metaphor; with repetition a weak echo of the intimate sound. Context forced the change. Context could not be overruled. Context will always guard the realm of the intimate from public misuse.

Today nonwhite Americans call "brother" to strangers. And white feminists refer to their mass union of "sisters." And white middle-class teenagers continue to prove the importance of context as they try to ignore it. They seize upon the idioms of the black ghetto. But their attempt to appropriate such expressions invariably changes the words. As it becomes a public expression, the ghetto idiom loses its sound—its message of public separateness and strident intimacy. It becomes with public repetition a series of words, increasingly lifeless.

The mystery remains: intimate utterance. The communication of intimacy passes through the word to enliven its sound. But it cannot be held by the word. Cannot be clutched or ever quoted. It is too fluid. It depends not on word but on person.

My grandmother!   65

She stood among my other relations mocking me when I no longer spoke Spanish. *"Pocho,"* she said. But then it made no difference. (She'd laugh.) Our relationship continued. Language was never its source. She was a woman in her eighties during the first decade of my life. A mysterious woman to me, my only living grandparent. A woman of Mexico. The woman in long black dresses that reached down to her shoes. My one relative who spoke no word of English. She had no interest in *gringo* society. She remained completely aloof from the public. Protected by her daughters. Protected even by me when we went to Safeway together and I acted as her translator. Eccentric woman. Soft. Hard.

When my family visited my aunt's house in San Francisco, my grandmother searched for me among my many cousins. She'd chase them away. Pinching her granddaughters, she'd warn them all away from me. Then she'd take me to her room, where she had prepared for my coming. There would be a chair next to the bed. A dusty jellied candy nearby. And a copy of *Life en Español* for me to examine. "There," she'd say. I'd sit there content. A boy of eight. *Pocho.* Her favorite. I'd sift through the pictures of earthquake-destroyed Latin American cities and blond-wigged Mexican movie stars. And all the while I'd listen to the sound of my grandmother's voice. She'd pace round the room, searching through closets and drawers, telling me stories of her life. Her past. They were stories so familiar to me that I couldn't remember the first time I'd heard them. I'd look up sometimes to listen. Other times she'd look over at me. But she never seemed to expect a response. Sometimes I'd smile or nod. (I understood exactly what she was saying.) But it never seemed to matter to her one way or another. It was enough I was there. The words she spoke were almost irrelevant to that fact—the sounds she made. Content.

The mystery remained: intimate utterance.

I learn little about language and intimacy listening to those social activists who propose using one's family language in public life. Listening to songs on the radio, or hearing a great voice at the opera, or overhearing the woman downstairs singing to herself at an open window, I learn much more. Singers celebrate the human voice. Their lyrics are words. But animated by voice those words are subsumed into sounds. I listen with excitement as the words yield their enormous power to sound— though the words are never totally obliterated. In most songs the drama or tension results from the fact that the singer moves between word (sense) and note (song). At one moment the song simply "says" something. At another moment the voice stretches out the words—the heart cannot contain!—and the voice moves toward pure sound. Words take flight.

Singing out words, the singer suggests an experience of sound most 70 intensely mine at intimate moments. Literally, most songs are about love. (Lost love; celebrations of loving; pleas.) By simply being occasions when sound escapes word, however, songs put me in mind of the most intimate moments of my life.

Finally, among all types of song, it is the song created by lyric poets that I find most compelling. There is no other public occasion of sound so important for me. Written poems exist on a page, at first glance, as a mere collection of words. And yet, despite this, without musical accompaniment, the poet leads me to hear the sounds of the words that I read. As song, the poem passes between sound and sense, never belonging for long to one realm or the other. As public artifact, the poem can never duplicate intimate sound. But by imitating such sound, the poem helps me recall the intimate times of my life. I read in my room—alone—and grow conscious of being alone, sounding my voice, in search of another. The poem serves then as a memory device. It forces remembrance. And refreshes. It reminds me of the possibility of escaping public words, the possibility that awaits me in meeting the intimate.

The poems I read are not nonsense poems. But I read them for reasons which, I imagine, are similar to those that make children play with meaningless rhyme. I have watched them before: I have noticed the way children create private languages to keep away the adult; I have heard their chanting riddles that go nowhere in logic but harken back to some kingdom of sound; I have watched them listen to intricate nonsense rhymes, and I have noted their wonder. I was never such a child. Until I was six years old, I remained in a magical realm of sound. I didn't need to remember that realm because it was present to me. But then the screen door shut behind me as I left home for school. At last I began my movement toward words. On the other side of initial sadness would come the realization that intimacy cannot be held. With time would come the knowledge that intimacy must finally pass.

I would dishonor those I have loved and those I love now to claim anything else. I would dishonor our closeness by holding on to a particular language and calling it my family language. Intimacy is not trapped within words. It passes through words. It passes. The truth is that intimates leave the room. Doors close. Faces move away from the window. Time passes. Voices recede into the dark. Death finally quiets the voice.

And there is no way to deny it. No way to stand in the crowd, uttering one's family language.

The last time I saw my grandmother I was nine years old. I can tell you some of the things she said to me as I stood by her bed. I cannot, however, quote the message of intimacy she conveyed with her voice. She laughed, holding my hand. Her voice illumined disjointed memories as it passed them again. She remembered her husband, his green eyes, the magic name of Narciso. His early death. She remembered the farm in Mexico. The eucalyptus nearby. (Its scent, she remembered, like incense.) She remembered the family cow, the bell round its neck heard miles away. A dog. She remembered working as a seamstress. How she'd leave her daughters and son for long hours to go into Guadalajara to work. And how my mother would come running toward her in the sun—her bright yellow dress—to see her return. *"Mmmaaammmmáááá,"* the old lady mimicked her daughter (my mother) to her son. She laughed. There was the snap of a cough. An aunt came into the room and told me it was time I should leave. "You can see her tomorrow," she promised. And so I kissed my grandmother's cracked face. And the last thing I saw was her thin, oddly youthful thigh, as my aunt rearranged the sheet on the bed.

At the funeral parlor a few days after, I knelt with my relatives during the rosary. Among their voices but silent, I traced, then lost, the sounds of individual aunts in the surge of the common prayer. And I heard at that moment what I have since heard often again—the sounds the women in my family make when they are praying in sadness. When I went up to look at my grandmother, I saw her through the haze of a veil draped over the open lid of the casket. Her face appeared calm—but distant and unyielding to love. It was not the face I remembered seeing most often. It was the face she made in public when the clerk at Safeway asked her some question and I would have to respond. It was her public face the mortician had designed with his dubious art.

[1982]

FAN SHEN

The Classroom and the Wider Culture: Identity as a Key to Learning English Composition

Fan Shen was born in the People's Republic of China, graduating with a B.A. from Lanzhou University, and then continuing his education in the United States with an M.A. from the University of Nebraska and a Ph.D. from Marquette University. He is a professor of English at Rochester Community and Technical College in Minnesota. His memoir about growing up during the Cultural Revolution in China, *Gang of One: Memoirs of a Red Guard*, has been met with wide acclaim and was picked Editor's Choice for 2004 by the American Library Association's Booklist. Shen has also translated three books from English into Chinese and writes for both English and Chinese periodicals.

Fan Shen's essay "The Classroom and the Wider Culture: Identity as a Key to Learning English Composition," originally published in *College Composition and Communication* in 1989, takes issue with the customary approach of American composition teachers to their Asian students. For Fan Shen, a native of China, composing a praiseworthy essay in English required he adapt his Chinese identity, ideologies, and artistic sensibilities to those of the West. Shen hopes to make American writing teachers cognizant of the unnerving necessity for Asian students to give birth to a new, westernized identity in order to conceive their English compositions.

One day in June 1975, when I walked into the aircraft factory where I was working as an electrician, I saw many large-letter posters on the walls and many people parading around the workshops shouting slogans like

"Down with the word 'I'!" and "Trust in masses and the Party!" I then remembered that a new political campaign called "Against Individualism" was scheduled to begin that day. Ten years later, I got back my first English composition paper at the University of Nebraska–Lincoln. The professor's first comments were: "Why did you always use 'we' instead of 'I'?" and "Your paper would be stronger if you eliminated some sentences in the passive voice." The clashes between my Chinese background and the requirements of English composition had begun. At the center of this mental struggle, which has lasted several years and is still not completely over, is the prolonged, uphill battle to recapture "myself."

In this paper I will try to describe and explore this experience of reconciling my Chinese identity with an English identity dictated by the rules of English composition. I want to show how my cultural background shaped—and shapes—my approaches to my writing in English and how writing in English redefined—and redefines—my *ideological* and *logical* identities. By "ideological identity" I mean the system of values that I acquired (consciously and unconsciously) from my social and cultural background. And by "logical identity" I mean the natural (or Oriental) way I organize and express my thoughts in writing. Both had to be modified or redefined in learning English composition. Becoming aware of the process of redefinition of these different identities is a mode of learning that has helped me in my efforts to write in English, and, I hope, will be of help to teachers of English composition in this country. In presenting my case for this view, I will use examples from both my composition courses and literature courses, for I believe that writing papers for both kinds of courses contributed to the development of my "English identity." Although what I will describe is based on personal experience, many Chinese students whom I talked to said that they had had the same or similar experiences in their initial stages of learning to write in English.

IDENTITY OF THE SELF: IDEOLOGICAL AND CULTURAL

Starting with the first English paper I wrote, I found that learning to compose in English is not an isolated classroom activity, but a social and cultural experience. The rules of English composition encapsulate values that are absent in, or sometimes contradictory to, the values of other societies (in my case, China). Therefore, learning the rules of English composition is, to a certain extent, learning the values of Anglo-American society. In writing classes in the United States I found that I had to reprogram my mind, to redefine some of the basic concepts and values that I had about myself, about society, and about the universe, values that had been imprinted and reinforced in my mind by my cultural background, and that had been part of me all my life.

Rule number one in English composition is: Be yourself. (More than one composition instructor has told me, "Just write what *you* think.") The values behind this rule, it seems to me, are based on the principle of protecting and promoting individuality (and private property) in this country. The instruction was probably crystal clear to students raised on these values, but, as a guideline of composition, it was not very clear or useful to me when I first heard it. First of all, the image or meaning that I attached to the word "I" or "myself" was, as I found out, different from that of my English teacher. In China, "I" is always subordinated to "We"—be it the working class, the Party, the country, or some other collective body. Both political pressure and literary tradition require that "I" be somewhat hidden or buried in writings and speeches; presenting the "self" too obviously would give people the impression of being disrespectful of the Communist Party in political writings and boastful in scholarly writings. The word "I" has often been identified with another "bad" word, "individualism," which has become a synonym for selfishness in China. For a long time the words "self" and "individualism" have had negative connotations in my mind, and the negative force of the words naturally extended to the field of literary studies. As a result, even if I had brilliant ideas, the "I" in my papers always had to show some modesty by not competing with or trying to stand above the names of ancient and modern authoritative figures. Appealing to Mao or other Marxist authorities became the required way (as well as the most "forceful" or "persuasive" way) to prove one's point in written discourse. I remember that in China I had even committed what I can call "reversed plagiarism"—here, I suppose it would be called "forgery"—when I was in middle school: willfully attributing some of my thoughts to "experts" when I needed some arguments but could not find a suitable quotation from a literary or political "giant."

Now, in America, I had to learn to accept the words "I" and "self" as 5 something glorious (as Whitman did), or at least something not to be ashamed of or embarrassed about. It was the first and probably biggest step I took into English composition and critical writing. Acting upon my professor's suggestion, I intentionally tried to show my "individuality" and to "glorify" "I" in my papers by using as many "I's" as possible— "I think," "I believe," "I see"—and deliberately cut out quotations from authorities. It was rather painful to hand in such "pompous" (I mean immodest) papers to my instructors. But to an extent it worked. After a while I became more comfortable with only "the shadow of myself." I felt more at ease to put down *my* thoughts without looking over my shoulder to worry about the attitudes of my teachers or the reactions of the Party secretaries, and to speak out as "bluntly" and "immodestly" as my American instructors demanded.

But writing many "I's" was only the beginning of the process of redefining myself. Speaking of redefining myself is, in an important sense, speaking of redefining the word "I." By such a redefinition I mean not only the change in how I envisioned myself, but also the change in how *I* perceived the world. The old "I" used to embody only one set of values, but now it had to embody multiple sets of values. To be truly "myself," which I knew was a key to my success in learning English composition, meant *not to be my Chinese self* at all. That is to say, when I write in English I have to wrestle with and abandon (at least temporarily) the whole system of ideology which previously defined me in myself. I had to forget Marxist doctrines (even though I do not see myself as a Marxist by choice) and the Party lines imprinted in my mind and familiarize myself with a system of capitalist/bourgeois values. I had to put aside an ideology of collectivism and adopt the values of individualism. In composition as well as in literature classes, I had to make a fundamental adjustment: If I used to examine society and literary materials through the microscopes of Marxist dialectical materialism and historical materialism, I now had to learn to look through the microscopes the other way around, i.e., to learn to look at and understand the world from the point of view of "idealism." (I must add here that there are American professors who use a Marxist approach in their teaching.)

The word "idealism," which affects my view of both myself and the universe, is loaded with social connotations, and can serve as a good example of how redefining a key word can be a pivotal part of redefining my ideological identity as a whole.

To me, idealism is the philosophical foundation of the dictum of English composition: "Be yourself." In order to write good English, I knew that I had to be myself, which actually meant not to be my Chinese self. It meant that I had to create an English self and be *that* self. And to be that English self, I felt, I had to understand and accept idealism the way a Westerner does. That is to say, I had to accept the way a Westerner sees himself in relation to the universe and society. On the one hand, I knew a lot about idealism. But on the other hand, I knew nothing about it. I mean I knew a lot about idealism through the propaganda and objections of its opponent, Marxism, but I knew little about it from its own point of view. When I thought of the word "materialism"—which is a major part of Marxism and in China has repeatedly been "shown" to be the absolute truth—there were always positive connotations, and words like "right," "true," etc., flashed in my mind. On the other hand, the word "idealism" always came to me with the dark connotations that surround

145

words like "absurd," "illogical," "wrong," etc. In China "idealism" is depicted as a ferocious and ridiculous enemy of Marxist philosophy. Idealism, as the simplified definition imprinted in my mind had it, is the view that the material world does not exist; that all that exists is the mind and its ideas. It is just the opposite of Marxist dialectical materialism which sees the mind as a product of the material world. It is not too difficult to see that idealism, with its idea that mind is of primary importance, provides a philosophical foundation for the Western emphasis on the value of individual human minds, and hence individual human beings. Therefore, my final acceptance of myself as of primary importance—an importance that overshadowed that of authority figures in English composition—was, I decided, dependent on an acceptance of idealism.

My struggle with idealism came mainly from my efforts to understand and to write about works such as Coleridge's *Biographia Literaria* and Emerson's "Over-Soul." For a long time I was frustrated and puzzled by the idealism expressed by Coleridge and Emerson—given their ideas, such as "I think, therefore I am" (Coleridge obviously borrowed from Descartes) and "the transparent eyeball" (Emerson's view of himself)— because in my mind, drenched as it was in dialectical materialism, there was always a little voice whispering in my ear "You are, therefore you think." I could not see how human consciousness, which is not material, could create apples and trees. My intellectual conscience refused to let me believe that the human mind is the primary world and the material world secondary. Finally, I had to imagine that I was looking at a world with my head upside down. When I imagined that I was in a new body (born with the head upside down) it was easier to forget biases imprinted in my subconsciousness about idealism, the mind, and my former self. Starting from scratch, the new inverted self—which I called my "English Self" and into which I have transformed myself—could understand and *accept*, with ease, idealism as "the truth" and "himself" (i.e., my English Self) as the "creator" of the world.

Here is how I created my new "English Self." I played a "game" similar 10
to ones played by mental therapists. First I made a list of (simplified) features about writing associated with my old identity (the Chinese Self), both ideological and logical, and then beside the first list I added a column of features about writing associated with my new identity (the English Self). After that I pictured myself getting out of my old identity, the timid, humble, modest Chinese "I," and creeping into my new identity (often in the form of a new skin or a mask), the confident, assertive, and aggressive English "I." The new "Self" helped me to remember and accept the different rules of Chinese and English composition and the values that underpin these rules. In a sense, creating an English Self is a

146

way of reconciling my old cultural values with the new values required by English writing, without losing the former.

An interesting structural but not material parallel to my experiences in this regard has been well described by Min-zhan Lu in her important article, "From Silence to Words: Writing as Struggle" (*College English* 49 [April 1987]: 437–48). Min-zhan Lu talks about struggles between two selves, an open self and a secret self, and between two discourses, a mainstream Marxist discourse and a bourgeois discourse her parents wanted her to learn. But her struggle was different from mine. Her Chinese self was severely constrained and suppressed by mainstream cultural discourse, but never interfused with it. Her experiences, then, were not representative of those of the majority of the younger generation who, like me, were brought up on only one discourse. I came to English composition as a Chinese person, in the fullest sense of the term, with a Chinese identity already fully formed.

IDENTITY OF THE MIND: ILLOGICAL AND ALOGICAL

In learning to write in English, besides wrestling with a different ideological system, I found that I had to wrestle with a logical system very different from the blueprint of logic at the back of my mind. By "logical system" I mean two things: the Chinese way of thinking I used to approach my theme or topic in written discourse, and the Chinese critical/logical way to develop a theme or topic. By English rules, the first is illogical, for it is the opposite of the English way of approaching a topic; the second is alogical (nonlogical), for it mainly uses mental pictures instead of words as a critical vehicle.

The Illogical Pattern

In English composition, an essential rule for the logical organization of a piece of writing is the use of a "topic sentence." In Chinese composition, "from surface to core" is an essential rule, a rule which means that one ought to reach a topic gradually and "systematically" instead of "abruptly."

The concept of a topic sentence, it seems to me, is symbolic of the values of a busy people in an industrialized society, rushing to get things done, hoping to attract and satisfy the busy reader very quickly. Thinking back, I realized that I did not fully understand the virtue of the concept until my life began to rush at the speed of everyone else's in this

147

country. Chinese composition, on the other hand, seems to embody the values of a leisurely paced rural society whose inhabitants have the time to chew and taste a topic slowly. In Chinese composition, an introduction explaining how and why one chooses this topic is not only acceptable, but often regarded as necessary. It arouses the reader's interest in the topic little by little (and this is seen as a virtue of composition) and gives him/her a sense of refinement. The famous Robert B. Kaplan "noodles" contrasting a spiral Oriental thought process with a straight-line Western approach ("Cultural Thought Patterns in Inter-Cultural Education," *Readings on English as a Second Language*, Ed. Kenneth Croft, 2nd ed., Winthrop, 1980, 403–10) may be too simplistic to capture the preferred pattern of writing in English, but I think they still express some truth about Oriental writing. A Chinese writer often clears the surrounding bushes before attacking the real target. This bush-clearing pattern in Chinese writing goes back two thousand years to Kong Fuzi (Confucius). Before doing anything, Kong says in his *Luen Yu (Analects)*, one first needs to call things by their proper names (expressed by his phrase "Zheng Ming" 正名). In other words, before touching one's main thesis, one should first state the "conditions" of composition: how, why, and when the piece is being composed. All of this will serve as a proper foundation on which to build the "house" of the piece. In the two thousand years after Kong, this principle of composition was gradually formalized (especially through the formal essays required by imperial examinations) and became known as "Ba Gu," or the eight-legged essay. The logic of Chinese composition, exemplified by the eight-legged essay, is like the peeling of an onion: Layer after layer is removed until the reader finally arrives at the central point, the core.

Ba Gu still influences modern Chinese writing. Carolyn Matalene has 15 an excellent discussion of this logical (or illogical) structure and its influence on her Chinese students' efforts to write in English ("Contrastive Rhetoric: An American Writing Teacher in China," *College English* 47 [November 1985]: 789–808). A recent Chinese textbook for composition lists six essential steps (factors) for writing a narrative essay, steps to be taken in this order: time, place, character, event, cause, and consequence (*Yuwen Jichu Zhishi Liushi Jiang* [*Sixty Lessons on the Basics of the Chinese Language*], Ed. Beijing Research Institute of Education, Beijing Publishing House, 1981, 525–609). Most Chinese students (including me) are taught to follow this sequence in composition.

The straightforward approach to composition in English seemed to me, at first, illogical. One could not jump to the topic. One had to walk step by step to reach the topic. In several of my early papers I found that the Chinese approach — the bush-clearing approach — persisted, and

I had considerable difficulty writing (and in fact understanding) topic sentences. In what I deemed to be topic sentences, I grudgingly gave out themes. Today, those papers look to me like Chinese papers with forced or false English openings. For example, in a narrative paper on a trip to New York, I wrote the forced/false topic sentence, "A trip to New York in winter is boring." In the next few paragraphs, I talked about the weather, the people who went with me, and so on, before I talked about what I learned from the trip. My real thesis was that one could always learn something even on a boring trip.

The Alogical Pattern

In learning English composition, I found that there was yet another cultural blueprint affecting my logical thinking. I found from my early papers that very often I was unconsciously under the influence of a Chinese critical approach called the creation of "yijing," which is totally non-Western. The direct translation of the word "yijing" is: yi, "mind or consciousness," and jing, "environment." An ancient approach which has existed in China for many centuries and is still the subject of much discussion, yijing is a complicated concept that defies a universal definition. But most critics in China nowadays seem to agree on one point, that yijing is the critical approach that separates Chinese literature and criticism from Western literature and criticism. Roughly speaking, yijing is the process of creating a pictorial environment while reading a piece of literature. Many critics in China believe that yijing is a creative process of inducing oneself, while reading a piece of literature or looking at a piece of art, to create mental pictures, in order to reach a unity of nature, the author, and the reader. Therefore, it is by its very nature both creative and critical. According to the theory, this nonverbal, pictorial process leads directly to a higher ground of beauty and morality. Almost all critics in China agree that yijing is not a process of logical thinking — it is not a process of moving from the premises of an argument to its conclusion, which is the foundation of Western criticism. According to yijing, the process of criticizing a piece of art or literary work has to involve the process of creation on the reader's part. In yijing, verbal thoughts and pictorial thoughts are one. Thinking is conducted largely in pictures and then "transcribed" into words. (Ezra Pound once tried to capture the creative aspect of yijing in poems such as "In a Station of the Metro." He also tried to capture the critical aspect of it in his theory of imagism and vorticism, even though he did not know the term "yijing.") One characteristic of the yijing approach to criticism, therefore, is that it often includes a description of the created mental pictures on the part of the reader/critic and his/her mental attempt to bridge (unite) the literary work, the pictures, with ultimate beauty and peace.

In looking back at my critical papers for various classes, I discovered that I unconsciously used the approach of yijing, especially in some of my earlier papers when I seemed not yet to have been in the grip of Western logical critical approaches. I wrote, for instance, an essay entitled "Wordsworth's Sound and Imagination: The Snowdon Episode." In the major part of the essay I described the pictures that flashed in my mind while I was reading passages in Wordsworth's long poem, *The Prelude*.

I saw three climbers (myself among them) winding up the mountain in silence "at the dead of night," absorbed in their "private thoughts." The sky was full of blocks of clouds of different colors, freely changing their shapes, like oily pigments disturbed in a bucket of water. All of a sudden, the moonlight broke the darkness "like a flash," lighting up the mountain tops. Under the "naked moon," the band saw a vast sea of mist and vapor, a silent ocean. Then the silence was abruptly broken, and we heard the "roaring of waters, torrents, streams/Innumerable, roaring with one voice" from a "blue chasm," a fracture in the vapor of the sea. It was a joyful revelation of divine truth to the human mind: the bright, "naked" moon sheds the light of "higher reasons" and "spiritual love" upon us; the vast ocean of mist looked like a thin curtain through which we vaguely saw the infinity of nature beyond; and the sounds of roaring waters coming out of the chasm of vapor cast us into the boundless spring of imagination from the depth of the human heart. Evoked by the divine light from above, the human spring of imagination is joined by the natural spring and becomes a sustaining source of energy, feeding "upon infinity" while transcending infinity at the same time. . . .

Here I was describing my own experience more than Wordsworth's. The picture described by the poet is taken over and developed by the reader. The imagination of the author and the imagination of the reader are thus joined together. There was no "because" or "therefore" in the paper. There was little *logic*. And I thought it was (and it is) criticism. This seems to me a typical (but simplified) example of the yijing approach. (Incidentally, the instructor, a kind professor, found the paper interesting, though a bit "strange.")

I am not saying that such a pattern of "alogical" thinking is wrong—in fact some English instructors find it interesting and acceptable—but it is very non-Western. Since I was in this country to learn the English language and English literature, I had to abandon Chinese "pictorial logic," and to learn Western "verbal logic."

IF I HAD TO START AGAIN

The change is profound: Through my understanding of new meanings 20
of words like "individualism," "idealism," and "I," I began to accept the
underlying concepts and values of American writing, and by learning to
use "topic sentences" I began to accept a new logic. Thus, when I write
papers in English, I am able to obey all the general rules of English composition. In doing this I feel that I am writing through, with, and
because of a new identity. I welcome the change, for it has added a new
dimension to me and to my view of the world. I am not saying that I have
entirely lost my Chinese identity. In fact I feel that I will never lose it.
Any time I write in Chinese, I resume my old identity, and obey the rules
of Chinese composition such as "Make the 'I' modest," and "Beat around
the bush before attacking the central topic." It is necessary for me to
have such a Chinese identity in order to write authentic Chinese. (I have
seen people who, after learning to write in English, use English logic and
sentence patterning to write Chinese. They produce very awkward Chinese texts.) But when I write in English, I imagine myself slipping into a
new "skin," and I let the "I" behave much more aggressively and knock
the topic right on the head. Being conscious of these different identities
has helped me to reconcile different systems of values and logic, and has
played a pivotal role in my learning to compose in English.

Looking back, I realize that the process of learning to write in English is
in fact a process of creating and defining a new identity and balancing it
with the old identity. The process of learning English composition would
have been easier if I had realized this earlier and consciously sought to
compare the two different identities required by the two writing systems
from two different cultures. It is fine and perhaps even necessary for
American composition teachers to teach about topic sentences, paragraphs, the use of punctuation, documentation, and so on, but can anyone
design exercises sensitive to the ideological and logical differences that
students like me experience—and design them so they can be introduced
at an early stage of an English composition class? As I pointed out earlier,
the traditional advice "Just be yourself" is not clear and helpful to students
from Korea, China, Vietnam, or India. From "Be yourself" we are likely to
hear either "Forget your cultural habit of writing" or "Write as you would
write in your own language." But neither of the two is what the instructor
meant or what we want to do. It would be helpful if he or she pointed out
the different cultural/ideological connotations of the word "I," the connotations that exist in a group-centered culture and an individual-centered
culture. To sharpen the contrast, it might be useful to design papers on
topics like "The Individual vs. The Group: China vs. America" or "Different
'I's' in Different Cultures."

Carolyn Matalene mentioned in her article (789) an incident concerning American businessmen who presented their Chinese hosts with gifts of cheddar cheese, not knowing that the Chinese generally do not like cheese. Liking cheddar cheese may not be essential to writing English prose, but being truly accustomed to the social norms that stand behind ideas such as the English "I" and the logical pattern of English composition—call it "compositional cheddar cheese"—is essential to writing in English. Matalene does not provide an "elixir" to help her Chinese students like English "compositional cheese," but rather recommends, as do I, that composition teachers not be afraid to give foreign students English "cheese," but to make sure to hand it out slowly, sympathetically, and fully realizing that it tastes very peculiar in the mouths of those used to a very different cuisine.

LESLIE MARMON SILKO [b. 1948]

Language and Literature from a Pueblo Indian Perspective

Born in 1948 and raised in the Laguna Pueblo near Albuquerque, New Mexico, **Leslie Marmon Silko** is a poet, fiction writer, and essayist whose work focuses on Native American culture and its relationship to white American culture. Her fiction and poetry draw on the oral traditions of the Laguna. She is best known for her first novel, *Ceremony* (1977), and for her novel about the impact of the European conquest on Native Americans, *Almanac of the Dead* (1991). Her latest novel is *Gardens in the Dunes* (1999).

"Language and Literature from a Pueblo Indian Perspective" is not fiction, but it is about storytelling. Although Silko doesn't address this question explicitly, think about what it might mean to a working novelist to come from a culture with this kind of storytelling tradition.

Where I come from, the words that are most highly valued are those which are spoken from the heart, unpremeditated and unrehearsed. Among the Pueblo people, a written speech or statement is highly suspect because the true feelings of the speaker remain hidden as he reads words that are detached from the occasion and the audience. I have intentionally not written a formal paper to read to this session because of this and because I want you to hear and to experience English in a nontraditional structure, a structure that follows patterns from the oral tradition. For those of you accustomed to a structure that moves from point A to point B to point C, this presentation may be somewhat diffi-

This "essay" is an edited transcript of an oral presentation. The "author" deliberately did not read from a prepared paper so that the audience could experience firsthand one dimension of the oral tradition — nonlinear structure. Her remarks were intended to be heard, not read. [Silko's note.]

"Language and Literature from a Pueblo Indian Perspective" from *English Literature: Opening Up the Canon*. Leslie A. Fiedler and Houston A. Baker Jr., eds. Selected Papers from the English Institute, 1979. pp. 54–72. Copyright © 1981. Reprinted by permission of The Johns Hopkins University Press.

cult to follow because the structure of Pueblo expression resembles something like a spider's web—with many little threads radiating from a center, criss-crossing each other. As with the web, the structure will emerge as it is made and you must simply listen and trust, as the Pueblo people do, that meaning will be made.

I suppose the task that I have today is a formidable one because basically I come here to ask you, at least for a while, to set aside a number of basic approaches that you have been using and probably will continue to use in approaching the study of English or the study of language; first of all, I come to ask you to see language from the Pueblo perspective, which is a perspective that is very much concerned with including the whole of creation and the whole of history and time. And so we very seldom talk about breaking language down into words. As I will continue to relate to you, even the use of a specific language is less important than the one thing—which is the "telling," or the storytelling. And so, as Simon Ortiz has written, if you approach a Pueblo person and want to talk words or, worse than that, to break down an individual word into its components, ofttimes you will just get a blank stare, because we don't think of words as being isolated from the speaker, which, of course, is one element of the oral tradition. Moreover, we don't think of words as being alone: words are always with other words, and the other words are almost always in a story of some sort.

Today I have brought a number of examples of stories in English because I would like to get around to the question that has been raised, or the topic that has come along here, which is what changes we Pueblo writers might make with English as a language for literature. But at the same time I would like to explain the importance of storytelling and how it relates to a Pueblo theory of language.

So first I would like to go back to the Pueblo Creation story. The reason I go back to that story is because it is an all-inclusive story of creation and how life began. Tséitsínako, Thought Woman, by thinking of her sisters, and together with her sisters, thought of everything which is, and this world was created. And the belief was that everything in this world was a part of the original creation, and that the people at home realized that far away there were others—other human beings. There is even a section of the story which is a prophesy—which describes the origin of the European race, the African, and also remembers the Asian origins.

Starting out with this story, with this attitude which includes all 5 things, I would like to point out that the reason the people are more concerned with story and communication and less with a particular language is in part an outgrowth of the area [pointing to a map] where we find ourselves. Among the twenty Pueblos there are at least six distinct languages, and possibly seven. Some of the linguists argue—and I don't set myself up to be a linguist at all—about the number of distinct languages. But certainly Zuni is all alone, and Hopi is all alone, and from mesa to mesa there are subtle differences in language—very great differences. I think that this might be the reason that what particular language was being used wasn't as important as what a speaker was trying to say. And this, I think, is reflected and stems or grows out of a particular view of the story—that is, that language *is* story. At Laguna many words have stories which make them. So when one is telling a story, and one is using words to tell the story, each word that one is speaking has a story of its own too. Often the speakers or tellers go into the stories of the words they are using to tell one story so that you get stories within stories, so to speak. This structure becomes very apparent in the storytelling, and what I would like to show you later on by reading some pieces that I brought is that this structure also informs the writing and the stories which are currently coming from Pueblo people. I think what is essential is this sense of story, and story within story, and the idea that one story is only the beginning of many stories, and the sense that stories never truly end. I would like to propose that these views of structure and the dynamics of storytelling are some of the contributions which Native American cultures bring to the English language or at least to literature in the English language.

First of all, a lot of people think of storytelling as something that is done at bedtime—that it is something that is done for small children. When I use the term storytelling, I include a far wider range of telling activity. I also do not limit storytelling to simply old stories, but to again go back to the original view of creation, which sees that it is all part of a whole; we do not differentiate or fragment stories and experiences. In the beginning, Tséitsínako, Thought Woman, thought of all these things, and all of these things are held together as one holds many things together in a single thought.

So in the telling (and today you will hear a few of the dimensions of this telling) first of all, as was pointed out earlier, the storytelling always includes the audience and the listeners, and, in fact, a great deal of the story is believed to be inside the listener, and the storyteller's role is to draw the story out of the listeners. This kind of shared experience grows out of a strong community base. The storytelling goes on and continues from generation to generation.

The Origin story functions basically as a maker of our identity—with the story we know who we are. We are the Lagunas. This is where we came from. We came this way. We came by this place. And so from the time you are very young, you hear these stories, so that when you go out into the wider world, when one asks who you are, or where are you from, you immediately know: we are the people who came down from the north. We are the people of these stories. It continues down into clans so that you are not just talking about Laguna Pueblo people, you are talking about your own clan. Within the clans there are stories which identify the clan.

In the Creation story, Antelope says that he will help knock a hole in the earth so that the people can come up, out into the next world. Antelope tries and tries, and he uses his hooves and is unable to break through; and it is then that Badger says, "Let me help you." And Badger very patiently uses his claws and digs a way through, bringing the people into the world. When the Badger clan people think of themselves, or when the Antelope people think of themselves, it is as people who are of *this* story, and this is *our* place, and we fit into the very beginning when the people first came, before we began our journey south.

So you can move, then, from the idea of one's identity as a tribal per- 10 son into clan identity. Then we begin to get to the extended family, and this is where we begin to get a kind of story coming into play which some people might see as a different kind of story, though Pueblo people do not. Anthropologists and ethnologists have, for a long time, differentiated the types of oral language they find in the Pueblos. They tended to rule out all but the old and sacred and traditional stories and were not interested in family stories and the family's account of itself. But these family stories are just as important as the other stories—the older stories. These family stories are given equal recognition. There is no definite, pre-set pattern for the way one will hear the stories of one's own family, but it is a very critical part of one's childhood, and it continues on throughout one's life. You will hear stories of importance to the family— sometimes wonderful stories—stories about the time a maternal uncle got the biggest deer that was ever seen and brought back from the mountains. And so one's sense of who the family is, and who you are, will then extend from that—"I am from the family of my uncle who brought in this wonderful deer, and it was a wonderful hunt"—so you have this sort of building or sense of identity.

There are also other stories, stories about the time when another uncle, perhaps, did something that wasn't really acceptable. In other words, this process of keeping track, of telling, is an all-inclusive process which begins to create a total picture. So it is very important that you know all of the stories—both positive and not so positive—about one's own family. The reason that it is very important to keep track of all the stories in one's own family is because you are liable to hear a story from somebody else who is perhaps an enemy of the family, and you are liable to hear a version which has been changed, a version which makes your family sound disreputable—something that will taint the honor of the family. But if you have already heard the story, you know your family's version of what *really* happened that night, so when somebody else is mentioning it, you will have a version of the story to counterbalance it. Even when there is no way around it—old Uncle Pete did a terrible thing—by knowing the stories that come out of other families, by keeping very close watch, listening constantly to learn the stories about other families, one is in a sense able to deal with terrible sorts of things that might happen within one's own family. When a member of one's own family does something that cannot be excused, one always knows stories about similar things which happened in other families. And it is not done maliciously. I think it is very important to realize this. Keeping track of all the stories within the community gives a certain distance, a useful perspective which brings incidents down to a level we can deal with. If others have done it before, it cannot be so terrible. If others have endured, so can we.

The stories are always bringing us together, keeping this whole together, keeping this family together, keeping this clan together. "Don't go away, don't isolate yourself, but come here, because we have all had these kinds of experiences"—this is what the people are saying to you when they tell you these other stories. And so there is this constant pulling together to resist what seems to me to be a basic part of human nature: when some violent emotional experience takes place, people get the urge to run off and hide or separate themselves from others. And of course, if we do that, we are not only talking about endangering the group, we are also talking about the individual or the individual family never being able to recover or to survive. Inherent in this belief is the feeling that one does not recover or get well by one's self, but it is together that we look after each other and take care of each other.

In the storytelling, then, we see this process of bringing people together, and it works not only on the family level, but also on the level of the individual. Of course, the whole Pueblo concept of the individual is a little bit different from the usual Western concept of the individual. But one of the beauties of the storytelling is that when something happens to an individual, many people will come to you and take you aside, or maybe a couple of people will come and talk to you. These are occasions of storytelling. These occasions of storytelling are continuous; they are a way of life.

Storytelling lies at the heart of the Pueblo people, and so when someone comes in and says, "When did they tell the stories, or what time of day does the storytelling take place?" that is a ridiculous question. The storytelling goes on constantly—as some old grandmother puts on the shoes of a little child and tells the child the story of a little girl who didn't wear her shoes. At the same time somebody comes into the house for coffee to talk with an adolescent boy who has just been into a lot of trouble, to reassure him that *he* got into that kind of trouble, or somebody else's son got into that kind of trouble too. You have this constant ongoing process, working on many different levels.

One of the stories I like to bring up about helping the individual in cri- 15 sis is a recent story, and I want to remind you that we make no distinctions between the stories—whether they are history, whether they are fact, whether they are gossip—these distinctions are not useful when we are talking about this particular experience with language. Anyway, there was a young man who, when he came back from the war in Vietnam, had saved up his Army pay and bought a beautiful red Volkswagen Beetle. He was very proud of it, and one night drove up to a place right across the reservation line. It is a very notorious place for many reasons, but one of the more notorious things about the place is a deep arroyo behind the place. This is the King's Bar. So he ran in to pick up a cold six-pack to take home, but he didn't put on his emergency brake. And his little red Volkswagen rolled back into the arroyo and was all smashed up. He felt very bad about it, but within a few days everybody had come to him and told him stories about other people who had lost cars to that arroyo. And probably the story that made him feel the best was about the time that George Day's station wagon, with his mother-in-law and kids in the back, rolled into that arroyo. So everybody was saying, "Well, at least your mother-in-law and kids weren't in the car when it rolled in," and you can't argue with that kind of story. He felt better then because he wasn't alone anymore. He and his smashed-up Volkswagen were now joined with all the other stories of cars that fell into that arroyo.

Again there is a very beautiful little story. It comes from far out of the past. It is a story that is sometimes told to people who suffer great family or personal loss. I would like to read that story to you now, and while I am reading it to you, try to listen on a couple of levels at once. I want you to listen to the usage of English. I came from a family which has been doing something that isn't exactly standard English for a while. I come from a family which, basically, is intent on getting the stories told; and we *will* get those stories told, and language *will* work for us. It is imperative to tell and not to worry over a specific language. The imperative is the telling. This is an old story from Aunt Suzie. She is one of the first generations of persons at Laguna who began experimenting with our notion of English—who began working to make English speak for us—that is, to speak from the heart. As I read the story to you, you will hear some words that came from Carlisle. She was taken from Laguna, New Mexico, on a train when she was a little girl, and she spent six years at Carlisle, Pennsylvania, in an Indian school, which was like being sent to prison. But listen and you will hear the Carlisle influence.

This is a story that is sometimes given to you when there has been a great loss.

This took place partly in old Acoma and Laguna. Waithia was a little girl living in Acoma. One day she said, "Mother, I would like to have some yastoah to eat." Yastoah is the hardened crust of corn meal mush that curls up. The very name *yastoah* means sort of "curled up," you know, dried, just as mush dries on top. She said, "I would like to have some yastoah," and her mother said, "My dear little girl, I can't make you any yastoah because we haven't any wood, but if you will go down off the mesa, down below, and pick up some pieces of wood, bring them home and I will make you some yastoah." So Waithia was glad and ran down the precipitous cliff of the mesa. Down below, just as her mother told her, there were pieces of wood, some curled, some crooked in shape, that she was to pick up and take home. She found just such wood as these.

She went home and she had them in a little wickerlike bag. First she called to her mother as she got home and said, "Mother, upstairs." The Pueblo people always called "upstairs" because long ago their homes were two or three stories, and that was their entrance, from the top. She said, "*Naya, deeni!* Mother, upstairs!" And her mother came. The little girl said, "I have brought the wood you wanted me to bring." She opened her little wicker basket and laid them out and they were snakes. They were snakes instead of the crooked pieces of wood, and her mother said, "Oh, my dear child. You have brought snakes instead." She says, "Go take them back and put them back just where you got them." The little girl ran down the mesa again. Down below to the flats. And she put those snakes back just where she got them. They were snakes instead, and she was very much hurt about this, and she said, "I am not going home. I am going away to the beautiful lake place and drown myself in that lake, Kawaik *bunyanah*, to the west. I will go there and drown myself."

So she started off, and as she came by the Enchanted Mesa, Kátsima, she met an old man, very aged, and he saw her running, and he said, "My dear child, where are you going?" She said, "I am going to Kawaik and jump into the lake there." "Why?" "Well, because," she says, "my mother didn't want to make any yastoah." And the old man said, "Oh, no, you must not go my child. Come with me and I will take you home." He tried to catch her, but she was very light and skipped along, and every time he would try to grab her she would skip faster away from him.

So he was coming home with some wood on his back, strapped to his back and tied with yucca. He just let that strap go and let the wood fall. He went as fast as he could up the cliff to the little girl's home. When he got to the place where she lived, he called to her mother, "*Deeni!* Upstairs!" "Come on up." And he says, "I can't. I just came to bring you a message. Your little daughter is running away. She is going to Kawaik to drown herself in the lake there." "Oh, my dear little girl!" the mother said.

So she busied herself around and made her the yastoah she loved so much. Corn mush, curled at the top. She must have found enough wood to boil the corn meal and make the yastoah.

And while the mush was cooling, she got the little girl's clothing, she got the little dress and all her other garments, little buckskin moccasins that she had, and put them in a bundle, too—probably a yucca bag. And she started down as fast as she could on the east side of Acoma. There used to be a trail there, you know. It's gone now. But it was accessible in those days. And she followed, and she saw her way at a distance—saw the daughter—she kept calling: "Tsumatusu, my daughter, come back. I have got your yastoah for you." But the little girl did not turn. She kept on ahead, and she cried. And what she cried is the song: "My mother, my mother, she didn't want me to have any yastoah. So now I am going to go away and drown myself." Her mother heard her cry and said, "My little daughter, come back here." "No," and she kept a distance away from her.

And they came nearer and nearer to the lake that was here. And she could see her daughter now, very plain. "Come back, my daughter, I have your yastoah." And no, she kept on, and finally she reached the lake, and she stood on the edge. She tied a little feather in her hair, which is traditional: in death they tie this little feather on the head. She carried a little feather, the girl did, and she tied it in her hair with a little piece of string, right on top of her head she put the feather. Just about as her mother was to reach her, she jumped into the lake. The little feather was whirling around and around in the depths below.

Of course the mother was very sad. She went, grieved, back to Acoma and climbed her mesa home, and the little clothing, the little moccasins she brought, and the yastoah. She stood on the edge of the mesa and scattered them out. She scattered them to the east and west, to the north and to the south—in all directions and where every one of the little clothing and the little moccasins and shawls and yastoah [fell], all of them turned into butterflies, all colors of butterflies! And today they say that Acoma has more beautiful butterflies: red ones, white ones, blue ones, yellow ones. They came from this little girl's clothing. [Copyright © 1981 by L. M. Silko in *Storyteller*, a Richard Seaver Book.]

Now that is a story that anthropologists would consider to be a very old story. The version I have given you is just as Aunt Suzie tells it. You can occasionally hear some English she picked up at Carlisle—words like "precipitous." You will also notice that there is a great deal of repetition, and a little reminder about yastoah and how it was made. There is a remark about the cliff trail at Acoma—that it was once there, but is there no longer. This story may be told at a time of sadness or loss, but within this story many other elements are brought together. Things are not separated out and put into separate categories; all things are brought together. So that the reminder about the yastoah is valuable information that is repeated, a recipe, if you will. The information about the old trail at Acoma reveals that stories are, in a sense, maps, since even to this day there is little information or material about trails that is passed around with writing. In the structure of this story the repetitions are, of course, designed to help you be able to remember. It is repeated again and again, and then it moves on. There is a very definite pattern that you will hear in these pieces. . . .

As the old people say, "If you can remember the stories, you will be all right. Just remember the stories." And, of course, usually when they say that to you, when you are young, you wonder what in the world they mean. But when I returned—I had been away from Laguna Pueblo for a couple of years, well more than a couple of years after college and so forth—I returned to Laguna and I went to Laguna-Acoma high school to visit an English class, and I was wondering how the telling was continuing, because Laguna Pueblo, as the anthropologists have said, is one of the more acculturated pueblos. So I walked into this high school English class and there they were sitting, these very beautiful Laguna and Acoma kids. But I knew that out in their lockers they had cassette tape recorders, and I knew that at home they had stereos, and they were listening to Kiss and Led Zeppelin and all those other things. I was almost afraid, but I had to ask—I had with me a book of short fiction (it's called *The Man to Send Rain Clouds* [New York: Viking Press, 1974]), and among the stories of other Native American writers, it has stories that I have written and Simon Ortiz has written. And there is one particular story in the book about the killing of a state policeman in New Mexico by three Acoma Pueblo men. It was an act that was committed in the early fifties. I was afraid to ask, but I had to. I looked at the class and I said, "How many of you heard this story before you read it in the book?" And I was prepared to hear this crushing truth that indeed the anthropologists were right about the old traditions dying out. But it was amazing, you know, almost all but one or two students raised their hands. They had heard that story, just as Simon and I had heard it, when we were young. That was my first indication that storytelling continues on. About half of them had heard it in English, about half of them had heard it in Laguna. I think again, getting back to one of the original statements, that if you begin to look at the core of the importance of the language and how it fits in with the culture, it is the *story* and the feeling of the story which matters more than what language it's told in.

One of the other advantages that we have enjoyed is that we have always been able to stay with the land. The stories cannot be separated from geographical locations, from actual physical places within the land. We were not relocated like so many Native American groups who were torn away from our ancestral land. And the stories are so much a part of these places that it is almost impossible for future generations to lose the stories because there are so many imposing geological elements. Just as Houston Baker was speaking about the mesas—there are such gigantic boulders—you cannot *live* in that land without asking or looking or noticing a boulder or rock. And there's always a story. There's always at least one story connected with those places. . . .

Dennis Brutus talked about the "yet unborn" as well as "those from the past," and how we are still *all* in *this* place, and language—the storytelling—is our entryway of passing or being with them, of being together again. When Aunt Suzie told her stories, she would tell a younger child to go open the door so that our esteemed predecessors may bring in their gifts to us. "They are out there," Aunt Suzie would say. "Let them come in. They're here, they're here with us *within* the stories." 20

I last visited her about four months ago. She is 106, and so if you walk into the room and try to ask her how many years she was at Carlisle Indian School—a direct question—she says she doesn't remember. But if you just let her speak her mind, everything that she says is very clear. And while I was there, she said, "Well, I'll be leaving here soon. I think I'll be leaving here, next week, and I will be going over to the Cliff House." She said, "It's going to be real good to get back over there." I was listening, and I was thinking of her house at Paguate, at Paguate village, which is north of Laguna. And she continued on, "Well" (and she gave her Indian name) "my mother's sister will be there. She has been living there. She will be there and we will be over there, and I will get a chance to write down these stories I've been telling you." And it wasn't until she said it was her mother's sister who would be there that I realized she wasn't talking about dying or death at all. She was talking about "going over there," and she meant it as a journey, a journey that perhaps we can only begin to understand through an appreciation for the boundless capacity of language which, through storytelling, brings us together, despite great distances between cultures, despite great distances in time.

[1979]

LINDA SIMON   [b. 1946]

The Naked Source

Educated at Queens College and Brandeis University, where she received her Ph.D. in English and American literature, writer **Linda Simon** has written several books, including *The Biography of Alice B. Toklas* (1977), *Thornton Wilder: His World* (1979), and *Genuine Reality: A Life of William James* (1999). Her study of William James led her to her most recent book, *Dark Light: Electricity and Anxiety from the Telegraph to the X-Ray* (2004). Currently a professor of English at Skidmore College, Simon specializes in nonfiction creative writing and the genre and craft of biography, among other subjects.

In her essay "The Naked Source," Simon argues that memorizing facts and summarizing what other people have said is not what history is all about. Rather, students should be encouraged to locate, interrogate, and construct narratives from primary sources so that they might themselves be doing the work of historians.

It is true that my students do not know history. That annals of the American past, as students tell it, are compressed into a compact chronicle: John Kennedy and Martin Luther King flourish just a breath away from FDR and Woodrow Wilson, who themselves come right on the heels of Jefferson and Lincoln. The far and distant past is more obscure still.

Some, because they are bright and inquisitive, have learned names, dates, and the titles of major events. But even these masters of Trivial Pursuit often betray their ignorance of a real sense of the past. Teachers all have favorite oneliners that point to an abyss in historical knowledge. Mine is: Sputnik *who*?

There is no debate here. Students do not know history. Students should learn history. There is less agreement about what they should know, why they should know it, and far less agreement about how they should pursue this study of the past.

When I ask my students why they need to know history, they reply earnestly: We need to learn history because those who do not know history are doomed to repeat the mistakes of the past. They have heard this somewhere, although no one can attribute the remark. And if they are

"The Naked Source," *Michigan Quarterly Review*, Vol. XXVII, No. 3, Summer 1988. Copyright © 1988 by Linda Simon. Reprinted by permission of the author.

told that George Santayana said it, they know not who Santayana was, although if you care to inform them they will dutifully record his name, dates (1863–1952), and the title of the work (*The Life of Reason*) in which the remark was made.

Is that so? I ask. What will not be repeated?   5

Inevitably they respond emotionally with the example of the Holocaust. Some have watched an episode of a PBS series. Some have seen the film *The Diary of Anne Frank*. Such genocide, they reply, will not be repeated because we know about it. Undaunted by examples of contemporary genocide, they remain firm in their conviction. Genocide, they maintain. And the Great Depression.

The Great Depression has made a big impact on the adolescent imagination. Given any work of literature written at any time during the 1930s, some students will explain it as a direct response to the Great Depression. Wasn't everyone depressed, after all? And aren't most serious works of literature grim, glum, dark, and deep. There you have it.

But now we know about the Great Depression. And so it will not, cannot, happen again.

I am not persuaded that requiring students to read Tacitus or Thucydides, Carl Becker or Francis Parkman, Samuel Eliot Morison or Arnold Toynbee will remedy this situation, although I believe that students, and we, might well benefit from these writers' illumination. What students lack, after all, is a sense of historical-mindedness, a sense that lives were lived in a context, a sense that events (the Battle of Barnet, for example) had consequences (if men were slain on the battlefield, they could not return to the farm), a sense that answers must generate questions, more questions, and still more subtle questions.

As it is, students learning history, especially in the early grades, are 10 asked prescribed questions and are given little opportunity to pursue their own inquiry or satisfy their own curiosity. The following questions are from current high school texts:

Has the role of the present United Nations proved that the hopes and dreams of Woodrow Wilson were achievable? If so, how? If not, why?

What were the advantages of an isolationist policy for the United States in the nineteenth century? Were there disadvantages?

Questions such as these perpetuate the idea that history is a body of knowledge on which students will be tested. The first question, in other words, asks students: Did you read the section in the text on the role of the United Nations? Did you read the section on Wilson's aims in proposing the League of Nations? Can you put these two sections together?

The second question asks students: Did you understand the term *isolationist*? Did you read the section on U.S. foreign relations in the nineteenth century? Can you summarize the debate that the authors of the textbook recount?

Questions such as these perpetuate the idea that history can uncover "facts" and "truth," that history is objective, and that students, if only they are diligent, can recover "right answers" about the past. Questions such as these ignore the role of historians. Even those bright students who can recall dates and events rarely can recall the name of a historian, much less any feeling about who this particular man or woman was. For many students, historical facts are things out there, like sea shells or autumn leaves, and it hardly matters who fetches them. The sea shell will look the same whether it is gathered in Charles Beard's pocket or Henri Pirenne's.

What students really need to learn, more than "history," is a sense of the historical method of inquiry. They need to know what it is that historians do and how they do it. They need to understand the role of imagination and intuition in the telling of histories, they need to practice, themselves, confronting sources, making judgments, and defending conclusions.

When I ask my freshmen what they think historians do, they usually 15 offer me some lofty phrases about "influencing the course of future events." But what I mean is: what do historians do after breakfast? That is a question few of my students can answer. And they are surprised when I read them the following passage by British historian A. L. Rowse from his book *The Use of History*.

You might think that in order to learn history you need a library of books to begin with. Not at all: that only comes at the end. What you need at the beginning is a pair of stout walking shoes, a pencil and a notebook; perhaps I should add a good county guide covering the area you mean to explore...and a map of the country...that gives you field footpaths and a wealth of things of interest, marks churches and historic buildings and ruins, wayside crosses and holy wells, prehistoric camps and dykes, the sites of battles. When you can't go for a walk, it is a quite a good thing to study the map and plan where you would like to go. I am all in favour of the open-air approach to history; the most delightful and enjoyable, the most imaginative and informative, and—what not everybody understands—the best training.

It is the best training because it gives the would-be historian an encounter with the things that all historians look at and puzzle over: primary sources about the past. Historians look at battlefields and old buildings, read letters and diaries and documents, interview eyewitnesses or participants in events. And they ask questions of these sources. Gradually, after asking increasingly sophisticated questions, they make some sense, for themselves, of what once happened.

What professional historians do, however, is not what most students do when they set out to learn history within the confines of a course. Instead of putting students face to face with primary sources, instructors are more likely to send them to read what other people say about the past. Students begin with a library of books of secondary sources, or they may begin with a text. But that, cautions Rowse, should come "at the end." Instead of allowing students to gain experience in weighing evidence and making inferences, the structures of many courses encourage them to amass information. "I found it!" exclaim enthusiastic students. They need to ask, "But what does it mean?"

They need to ask that question of the kinds of sources that historians actually use. Instead of reading Morison's rendering of Columbus's voyages, for example, students might read Columbus himself: his journal, his letters to the Spanish monarchs. Then they can begin to decide for themselves what sort of man this was and what sort of experience he had. Morison—as excellent a historian as he is—comes later. With some sense of the sources that Morison used, students can begin to evaluate his contribution to history, to understand how he drew conclusions from the material available to him, to see how "facts" are augmented by historical intuition. They can begin to understand, too, that the reconstruction of the past is slow and painstaking work.

Courses that cover several decades or even millennia may give students a false impression of historical inquiry. Historians, like archaeologists or epidemiologists, move slowly through bumpy and perilous terrain. They are used to travelling for miles only to find themselves stranded at a dead end. Once, in the archives of Westminster Abbey, I eagerly awaited reading a fragment of a letter from King Henry VI (after all, that is how it was described in the card catalog), only to lift out of an envelope the corner of a page, about an inch across, with the faintest ink-mark the only evidence that it had, five hundred years before, been a letter at all.

Slowly the historian assembles pieces of the past. A household 20 expense record might be the only artifact proving that a certain medieval woman existed. How much can be known about her? How much can be known by examining someone's checkbook today? Yet historians must make do with just such odd legacies: wills and land deeds, maps and drawings, family portraits or photographs. Can you imagine the excitement over the discovery of a diary or a cache of letters? At last, a text. But the diary may prove a disappointment, a frustration. William James recorded the title of a book he may have been reading or the name of a visitor. Didn't he understand that a historian or biographer would need the deep, reflective ruminations of which we know he was more than capable?

Students have not had these experiences. When they are asked to write, they write *about* history. The research paper or the term paper seems to many of them another form of test—this time a take-home drawn out over weeks. Even if they have learned that "voice" and "audience" are important for a writer, they see history papers as different. They must be objective; they must learn proper footnoting and documentation. They must compile an impressive bibliography. Most important, they must find something out. The research paper produces nothing so much as anxiety, and the student often feels overwhelmed by the project.

They might, instead, be asked to write history as historians do it. They might be introduced to archives—in their college, in their community, in their state capital. They might be encouraged to interview people, and to interview them again and again until they begin to get the kind of information that will enlighten them about a particular time or event. They might be encouraged to read newspapers on microfilm or the bound volumes of old magazines that are yellowing in the basement of their local library. And then they might be asked to write in that most challenging form: the historical narrative.

"I can recall experiencing upon the completing of my first work of history," George Kennan wrote once, "... a moment of panic when the question suddenly presented itself to me: What is it that I have done here? Perhaps what I have written is not really history but rather some sort of novel, the product of my own imagination,—an imagination stimulated, inspired and informed, let us hope, by the documents I have been reading, but imagination nevertheless." Most historians share Kennan's reaction.

Students, of course, can never discover the boundary between "fact" and imaginative construction unless they have contact with primary sources. They cannot know where the historian has intervened to analyze the information he or she has discovered. "Most of the facts that you excavate," Morison wrote in "History as a Literary Art," "are dumb things; it is for you to make them speak by proper selection, arrangement, and emphasis." Morison suggested that beginning historians look to such writers as Sherwood Anderson and Henry James for examples of the kind of palpable description and intense characterization that can make literature—historical or fictional—come alive.

Students need to be persuaded that they are writing literature, not taking a test, when they set out to be historians. Their writing needs to be 25

167

read and evaluated not only for the facts that they have managed to compile, but for the sense of the past that they have conveyed. They need to discover that the past was not only battles and elections, Major Forces and Charismatic Leaders, but ordinary people, growing up, courting, dancing to a different beat, camping by a river that has long since dried up, lighting out for a territory that no longer exists. Except in the imagination of historians, as they confront the naked source, unaided.

WILLIAM STAFFORD [1914–1995]

A Way of Writing

Born in Hutchinson, Kansas, **William Stafford** (1914–1995) studied at
the University of Kansas and then at the University of Iowa Writers'
Workshop. In between, he was a conscientious objector during World
War II and worked in labor camps. In 1948 Stafford moved to Oregon,
where he taught at Lewis and Clark College until he retired in 1980.
His first major collection of poems, *Traveling through the Dark*, was
published when Stafford was forty-eight. It won the National Book
Award in 1963. He went on to publish more than sixty-five volumes of
poetry and prose and came to be known as a very influential teacher of
poetry. From 1970 to 1971 he was Consultant in Poetry at the Library
of Congress.

   In "A Way of Writing," first published in *Field*, the Oberlin College
literary magazine (1970), Stafford revels in the richness of the writing
process, describing his delight at spontaneous connections and the
trust he places in his own craft. Fearless and undirected at the outset
of a writing session, Stafford waits for ideas to wash through him, for
thoughts to attract his attention, and remains astounded by that "precious interval" between not knowing what to write and that moment
when "stray impulses" are guiding his "confident forward progress." "A
writer," he says, "is one who has become accustomed to trusting that
grace, or luck, or—skill."

A writer is not so much someone who has something to say as he is
someone who has found a process that will bring about new things he
would not have thought of if he had not started to say them. That is, he
does not draw on a reservoir; instead, he engages in an activity that
brings to him a whole succession of unforeseen stories, poems, essays,
plays, laws, philosophies, religions, or—but wait!

   Back in school, from the first when I began to try to write things, I felt
this richness. One thing would lead to another; the world would give and
give. Now, after twenty years or so of trying, I live by that certain richness,

William Stafford, Excerpt from "A Way of Writing," *Field: Contemporary Poetry and
Poetics*, no. 2, Spring 1970. Reprinted by permission of Oberlin College Press.

an idea hard to pin, difficult to say, and perhaps offensive to some. For there are strange implications in it.

One implication is the importance of just plain receptivity. When I write, I like to have an interval before me when I am not likely to be interrupted. For me, this means usually the early morning, before others are awake. I get pen and paper, take a glance out the window (often it is dark out there), and wait. It is like fishing. But I do not wait very long, for there is always a nibble—and this is where receptivity comes in. To get started I will accept anything that occurs to me. Something always occurs, of course, to any of us. We can't keep from thinking. Maybe I have to settle for an immediate impression: It's cold, or hot, or dark, or bright, or in between! Or—well, the possibilities are endless. If I put down something, that thing will help the next thing come, and I'm off. If I let the process go on, things will occur to me that were not at all in my mind when I started. These things, odd or trivial as they may be, are somehow connected. And if I let them string out, surprising things will happen.

If I let them string out.... Along with initial receptivity, then, there is another readiness: I must be willing to fail. If I am to keep on writing, I cannot bother to insist on high standards. I must get into action and not let anything stop me, or even slow me much. By "standards" I do not mean "correctness"—spelling, punctuation, and so on. These details become mechanical for anyone who writes for a while. I am thinking about what many people would consider "important" standards, such matters as social significance, positive values, consistency, etc. I resolutely disregard these. Something better, greater, is happening! I am following a process that leads so wildly and originally into new territory that no judgment can at the moment be made about values, significance, and so on. I am making something new, something that has not been judged before. Later others—and maybe I myself—will make judgments. Now, I am headlong to discover. Any distraction may harm the creating.

So, receptive, careless of failure, I spin out things on the page. And a wonderful freedom comes. If something occurs to me, it is all right to accept it. It has one justification: It occurs to me. No one else can guide me. I must follow my own weak, wandering, diffident impulses.

A strange bonus happens. At times, without my insisting on it, my writings become coherent; the successive elements that occur to me are clearly related. They lead by themselves to new connections. Sometimes the language, even the syllables that happen along, may start a trend. Sometimes the materials alert me to something waiting in my mind, ready for sustained attention. At such times, I allow myself to be eloquent, or intentional, or for great swoops (treacherous! not to be trusted!) reasonable. But I do not insist on any of that; for I know that back of my activity there will be the coherence of my self, and that indulgence of my impulses will bring recurrent patterns and meanings again.

This attitude toward the process of writing creatively suggests a problem for me, in terms of what others say. They talk about "skills" in writing. Without denying that I do have experience, wide reading, automatic orthodoxies, and maneuvers of various kinds, I still must insist that I am often baffled about what "skill" has to do with the precious little area of confusion when I do not know what I am going to say and then I find out what I am going to say. That precious interval I am unable to bridge by skill. What can I witness about it? It remains mysterious, just as all of us must feel puzzled about how we are so inventive as to be able to talk along through complexities with our friends, not needing to plan what we are going to say, but never stalled for long in our confident forward progress. Skill? If so, it is the skill we all have, something we must have learned before the age of three or four.

A writer is one who has become accustomed to trusting that grace, or luck, or—skill.

Yet another attitude I find necessary: Most of what I write, like most of what I say in casual conversation, will not amount to much. Even I will realize, and even at the time, that it is not negotiable. It will be like practice. In conversation I allow myself random remarks—in fact, as I recall, that is the way I learned to talk—, so in writing I launch many expendable efforts. A result of this free way of writing is that I am not writing for others, mostly; they will not see the product at all unless the activity eventuates in something that later appears to be worthy. My guide is the self, and its adventuring in the language brings about communication.

This process-rather-than-substance view of writing invites a final, dual reflection: 10

1. Writers may not be special—sensitive or talented in any usual sense. They are simply engaged in sustained use of a language skill we all have. Their "creations" come about through confident reliance on stray impulses that will, with trust, find occasional patterns that are satisfying.

2. But writing itself is one of the great, free human activities. There is scope for individuality, and elation, and discovery, in writing. For the person who follows with trust and forgiveness what occurs to him, the world remains always ready and deep, an inexhaustible environment, with the combined vividness of an actuality and flexibility of a dream. Working back and forth between experience and thought, writers have more than space and time can offer. They have the whole unexplored realm of human vision.

A sample daily-writing sheet and the poem as revised

15 December 1969

At the fountain on Main Street I saw
our shadows. It did not drink but
waited on cement and water while I drank.
There were two people and but one shadow.
Two people in love have but one shadow.
I looked at ferns, noticing that a bird
flying past made a shadow on the sky.
There is a place in the air where our house
used to be. Once I crawled through
grassblades to hear the sounds of their shadows.
One of the shadows moved, and it was
the earth where a mole was passing.
I could hear little paws in the dirt,
and fur brush along the tunnel, and even,
somehow, the mole shadow.
Out in places like Wyoming some of the shadows
are cut out and pasted on fossils.
There are mountains that erode when
clouds drag across them. ~~[illegible]~~ You can hear
the tick of the light breaking edges off white stones.
In my prayers I let yesterday begin
and then go behind this hour now. Every heart
pumps from a well full of shadows.
In churches their hearts pump from wells
full of shadows. sermons
In churches they pump sermons from
wells full of shadows.

Shadows

I

Out in places like Wyoming some of the shadows

are cut out and pasted on fossils.

There are mountains that erode when
clouds drag across them. You can hear the tick

~~the tick~~ of the light breaking edges off white stones.

At a fountain on Main Street I saw

our shadow. It did not drink but

waited on cement and water while I drank.

There were two people and but one shadow.

I looked up so hard outward that a bird

flying past made a shadow on the sky.

There is a place in the air where our house
used to be.

Once I crawled through grassblades to hear

the sounds of their shadows. One of the shadows

moved, and it was the earth where a mole

was passing. I could hear little

paws in the dirt, and fur brush along

the tunnel, and even, somehow, the mole shadow.

In churches when hearts pump sermons

from wells full of shadows.

In my prayers I let yesterday begin

and then go behind this hour now.

173

Shadows

Out in places like Wyoming some of the shadows
are cut out and pasted on fossils.
There are mountains that erode when
clouds drag across them. You hear the tick
of sunlight breaking edges off white stones.

At a fountain on Main Street I saw
our shadow. It did not drink but
waited on cement and water while I drank.
There were two people and but one shadow.

I looked up so hard outward that a bird
flying past made a shadow on the sky.
There is a place in the air where
our old house used to be.

Once I crawled through grassblades to hear
the sounds of their shadows. One shadow
moved, and it was the earth where a mole
was passing. I could hear little
paws in the dirt, and fur brush along
the tunnel, and even, somehow, the mole shadow.

In my prayers I let yesterday begin
and then go behind this hour now,
in churches where hearts pump sermons
from wells full of shadows.

174

AMY TAN   [b. 1952]

Mother Tongue

Amy Tan, born in 1952, was raised in northern California. Formerly a
business writer, Tan is now a novelist. She is best known for her first
book, *The Joy Luck Club* (1989), but has also written *The Kitchen God's
Wife* (1991), *The Hundred Secret Senses* (1995), and *The Bonesetter's
Daughter* (2001). Her fiction grows out of her experiences as the child
of Chinese immigrants growing up and living in American culture.

In "Mother Tongue," Tan describes the variety of Englishes she
uses. In doing so, she addresses the connections between languages
and cultures, but in her writing she also demonstrates what she says
about herself in the essay: "I am a writer. And by that definition, I am
someone who has always loved language" (par. 2).

I am not a scholar of English or literature. I cannot give you much more
than personal opinions on the English language and its variations in this
country or others.

I am a writer. And by that definition, I am someone who has always
loved language. I am fascinated by language in daily life. I spend a great
deal of my time thinking about the power of language—the way it can
evoke an emotion, a visual image, a complex idea, or a simple truth.
Language is the tool of my trade. And I use them all—all the Englishes I
grew up with.

Recently, I was made keenly aware of the different Englishes I do use.
I was giving a talk to a large group of people, the same talk I had already
given to half a dozen other groups. The nature of the talk was about my
writing, my life, and my book, *The Joy Luck Club*. The talk was going
along well enough, until I remembered one major difference that made
the whole talk sound wrong. My mother was in the room. And it was perhaps the first time she had heard me give a lengthy speech, using the
kind of English I have never used with her. I was saying things like "The
intersection of memory upon imagination" and "There is an aspect of
my fiction that relates to thus-and-thus"—a speech filled with carefully
wrought grammatical phrases, burdened, it suddenly seemed to me,

with nominalized forms, past perfect tenses, conditional phrases, all the forms of standard English that I had learned in school and through books, the forms of English I did not use at home with my mother.

Just last week, I was walking down the street with my mother, and I again found myself conscious of the English I was using, the English I do use with her. We were talking about the price of new and used furniture and I heard myself saying this: "Not waste money that way." My husband was with us as well, and he didn't notice any switch in my English. And then I realized why. It's because over the twenty years we've been together I've often used that same kind of English with him, and sometimes he even uses it with me. It has become our language of intimacy, a different sort of English that relates to family talk, the language I grew up with.

So you'll have some idea of what this family talk I heard sounds like, 5 I'll quote what my mother said during a recent conversation which I videotaped and then transcribed. During this conversation, my mother was talking about a political gangster in Shanghai who had the same last name as her family's, Du, and how the gangster in his early years wanted to be adopted by her family, which was rich by comparison. Later, the gangster became more powerful, far richer than my mother's family, and one day showed up at my mother's wedding to pay his respects. Here's what she said in part:

"Du Yusong having business like fruit stand. Like off the street kind. He is Du like Du Zong—but not Tsung-ming Island people. The local people call putong, the river east side, he belong to that side local people. That man want to ask Du Zong father take him in like become own family. Du Zong father wasn't look down on him, but didn't take seriously, until that man big like become a mafia. Now important person, very hard to inviting him. Chinese way, came only to show respect, don't stay for dinner. Respect for making big celebration, he shows up. Mean gives lots of respect. Chinese custom. Chinese social life that way. If too important won't have to stay too long. He come to my wedding. I didn't see, I heard it. I gone to boy's side, they have YMCA dinner. Chinese age I was nineteen."

You should know that my mother's expressive command of English belies how much she actually understands. She reads the *Forbes* report, listens to *Wall Street Week*, converses daily with her stockbroker, reads all of Shirley MacLaine's books with ease—all kinds of things I can't begin to understand. Yet some of my friends tell me they understand 50 percent of what my mother says. Some say they understand 80 to 90 percent. Some say they understand none of it, as if she were speaking pure Chinese. But to me, my mother's English is perfectly clear, perfectly natural. It's my mother tongue. Her language, as I hear it, is vivid, direct, full of observation and imagery. That was the language that helped shape the way I saw things, expressed things, made sense of the world.

Lately, I've been giving more thought to the kind of English my mother speaks. Like others, I have described it to people as "broken" or "fractured" English. But I wince when I say that. It has always bothered me that I can think of no other way to describe it other than "broken," as if it were damaged and needed to be fixed, as if it lacked a certain wholeness and soundness. I've heard other terms used, "limited English," for example. But they seem just as bad, as if everything is limited, including people's perceptions of the limited English speaker.

I know this for a fact, because when I was growing up, my mother's "limited" English limited *my* perception of her. I was ashamed of her English. I believed that her English reflected the quality of what she had to say. That is, because she expressed them imperfectly her thoughts were imperfect. And I had plenty of empirical evidence to support me: the fact that people in department stores, at banks, and at restaurants did not take her seriously, did not give her good service, pretended not to understand her, or even acted as if they did not hear her.

My mother has long realized the limitations of her English as well. 10 When I was fifteen, she used to have me call people on the phone to pretend I was she. In this guise, I was forced to ask for information or even to complain and yell at people who had been rude to her. One time it was a call to her stockbroker in New York. She had cashed out her small portfolio and it just so happened we were going to go to New York the next week, our very first trip outside California. I had to get on the phone and say in an adolescent voice that was not very convincing, "This is Mrs. Tan."

And my mother was standing in the back whispering loudly, "Why he don't send me check, already two weeks late. So mad he lie to me, losing me money."

And then I said in perfect English, "Yes, I'm getting rather concerned. You had agreed to send the check two weeks ago, but it hasn't arrived."

Then she began to talk more loudly. "What he want, I come to New York tell him front of his boss, you cheating me?" And I was trying to calm her down, make her be quiet, while telling the stockbroker, "I can't tolerate any more excuses. If I don't receive the check immediately, I am going to have to speak to your manager when I'm in New York next week." And sure enough, the following week there we were in front of this astonished stockbroker, and I was sitting there red-faced and quiet, and my mother, the real Mrs. Tan, was shouting at his boss in her impeccable broken English.

We used a similar routine just five days ago, for a situation that was far less humorous. My mother had gone to the hospital for an appointment, to find out about a benign brain tumor a CAT scan had revealed a month ago. She said she had spoken very good English, her best English, no mistakes. Still, she said, the hospital did not apologize when they said they had lost the CAT scan and she had come for nothing. She said they did not seem to have any sympathy when she told them she was anxious to know the exact diagnosis, since her husband and son had both died of brain tumors. She said they would not give her any more information until the next time and she would have to make another appointment for that. So she said she would not leave until the doctor called her daughter. She wouldn't budge. And when the doctor finally called her daughter, me, who spoke in perfect English—lo and behold—we had assurances the CAT scan would be found, promises that a conference call on Monday would be held, and apologies for any suffering my mother had gone through for a most regrettable mistake.

I think my mother's English almost had an effect on limiting my possibilities in life as well. Sociologists and linguists probably will tell you that a person's developing language skills are more influenced by peers. But I do think that the language spoken in the family, especially in immigrant families which are more insular, plays a large role in shaping the language of the child. And I believe that it affected my results on achievement tests, IQ tests, and the SAT. While my English skills were never judged as poor, compared to math, English could not be considered my strong suit. In grade school I did moderately well, getting perhaps B's, sometimes B-pluses, in English and scoring perhaps in the sixtieth or seventieth percentile on achievement tests. But those scores were not good enough to override the opinion that my true abilities lay in math and science, because in those areas I achieved A's and scored in the ninetieth percentile or higher.

This was understandable. Math is precise; there is only one correct answer. Whereas, for me at least, the answers on English tests were always a judgment call, a matter of opinion and personal experience. Those tests were constructed around items like fill-in-the-blank sentence completion, such as "Even though Tom was ____, Mary thought he was ____." And the correct answer always seemed to be the most bland combinations of thoughts, for example, "Even though Tom was shy, Mary thought he was charming," with the grammatical structure "even though" limiting the correct answer to some sort of semantic opposites, so you wouldn't get answers like, "Even though Tom was foolish, Mary thought he was ridiculous." Well, according to my mother, there were very few limitations as to what Tom could have been and what Mary might have thought of him. So I never did well on tests like that.

15

The same was true with word analogies, pairs of words in which you were supposed to find some sort of logical, semantic relationship—for example, "*Sunset* is to *nightfall* as ____ is to ____." And here you would be presented with a list of four possible pairs, one of which showed the same kind of relationship: *red* is to *stoplight, bus* is to *arrival, chills* is to *fever, yawn* is to *boring*. Well, I could never think that way. I knew what the tests were asking, but I could not block out of my mind the images already created by the first pair, "*sunset* is to *nightfall*"—and I would see a burst of colors against a darkening sky, the moon rising, the lowering of a curtain of stars. And all the other pairs of words—red, bus, stoplight, boring—just threw up a mass of confusing images, making it impossible for me to sort out something as logical as saying: "A sunset precedes nightfall" is the same as "a chill precedes a fever." The only way I would have gotten that answer right would have been to imagine an associative situation, for example, my being disobedient and staying out past sunset, catching a chill at night, which turns into feverish pneumonia as punishment, which indeed did happen to me.

I have been thinking about all this lately, about my mother's English, about achievement tests. Because lately I've been asked, as a writer, why there are not more Asian Americans represented in American literature. Why are there few Asian Americans enrolled in creative writing programs? Why do so many Chinese students go into engineering? Well, these are broad sociological questions I can't begin to answer. But I have noticed in surveys—in fact, just last week—that Asian students, as a whole, always do significantly better on math achievement tests than in English. And this makes me think that there are other Asian-American students whose English spoken in the home might also be described as "broken" or "limited." And perhaps they also have teachers who are steering them away from writing and into math and science, which is what happened to me.

Fortunately, I happen to be rebellious in nature and enjoy the challenge of disproving assumptions made about me. I became an English major my first year in college, after being enrolled as pre-med. I started writing nonfiction as a freelancer the week after I was told by my former boss that writing was my worst skill and I should hone my talents toward account management.

But it wasn't until 1985 that I finally began to write fiction. And at first 20 I wrote using what I thought to be wittily crafted sentences, sentences that would finally prove I had mastery over the English language. Here's an example from the first draft of a story that later made its way into *The Joy Luck Club*, but without this line: "That was my mental quandary in its nascent state." A terrible line, which I can barely pronounce.

Fortunately, for reasons I won't get into today, I later decided I should envision a reader for the stories I would write. And the reader I decided upon was my mother, because these were stories about mothers. So with this reader in mind—and in fact she did read my early drafts—I began to write stories using all the Englishes I grew up with: the English I spoke to my mother, which for lack of a better term might be described as "simple"; the English she used with me, which for lack of a better term might be described as "broken"; my translation of her Chinese, which could certainly be described as "watered down"; and what I imagined to be her translation of her Chinese if she could speak in perfect English, her internal language, and for that I sought to preserve the essence, but neither an English nor a Chinese structure. I wanted to capture what language ability tests can never reveal: her intent, her passion, her imagery, the rhythms of her speech, and the nature of her thoughts.

Apart from what any critic had to say about my writing, I knew I had succeeded where it counted when my mother finished reading my book and gave me her verdict: "So easy to read."

[1991]

LEWIS THOMAS   [1913–1993]

Notes on Punctuation

Born in 1913, in Flushing, New York, to a family physician and his wife, **Lewis Thomas** achieved prominence in the areas of medical research and literature. At age 15, Thomas entered Princeton, developing an interest in poetry, literary humor, and writing. By the time he enrolled at Harvard Medical School in 1933, medicine had begun to evolve toward a clinical science. Thomas supported himself in part by selling blood and writing poetry, publishing his verse in *The Atlantic Monthly*, *Harper's Bazaar*, and the *Saturday Evening Post*. Later, as a medical researcher, Thomas utilized his imagination to generate inventive scientific hypotheses that achieved wide recognition. In 1971, Thomas began composing a series of essays, "Nature of a Biologist," that appeared monthly in *The New England Journal of Medicine*. Thomas's writing displayed a distinct style that combined natural description with personal meditation. His first published collection of essays, *The Lives of a Cell* (1974), received a National Book Award. Throughout his life, he refined his personal style, elaborating on central themes that related biological science to human nature and stressed the unity of all life. Thomas published a second collection of NEJM essays, titled *The Medusa and the Snail*, in 1979. His other books included *Listening to Mahler's Ninth Symphony* (1983) and *The Fragile Spaces* (1992). During his career, Thomas integrated writing with active medical practice and teaching. At the time of his death, he served as chief executive officer of New York City's Sloan-Kettering Institute.

There are no precise rules about punctuation (Fowler lays out some general advice (as best he can under the complex circumstances of English prose (he points out, for example, that we possess only four stops (the comma, the semicolon, the colon and the period (the question mark and exclamation point are not, strictly speaking, stops; they are indicators of tone (oddly enough, the Greeks employed the semicolon for their question mark (it produces a strange sensation to read a Greek sentence which is a straightforward question: Why weepest thou; (instead of Why weepest thou? (and, of course, there are parentheses (which are surely a kind of punctuation making this whole much more complicated by having to count up the left-handed parentheses in order to be sure of closing with the right number (but if the parentheses were left out, with nothing to work with but the stops, we would have considerably more flexibility in the deploying of layers of meaning than if we tried to separate all the clauses by physical barriers (and in the latter case, while we might have more precision and exactitude for our meaning, we would lose the essential flavor of language, which is its wonderful ambiguity))))))))))).

The commas are the most useful and usable of all the stops. It is highly important to put them in place as you go along. If you try to come back after doing a paragraph and stick them in the various spots that tempt you you will discover that they tend to swarm like minnows into all sorts of crevices whose existence you hadn't realized and before you know it the whole long sentence becomes immobilized and lashed up squirming in commas. Better to use them sparingly, and with affection, precisely when the need for each one arises, nicely, by itself.

I have grown fond of semicolons in recent years. The semicolon tells you that there is still some question about the preceding full sentence; something needs to be added; it reminds you sometimes of the Greek usage. It is almost always a greater pleasure to come across a semicolon than a period. The period tells you that that is that; if you didn't get all the meaning you wanted or expected, anyway you got all the writer intended to parcel out and now you have to move along. But with a semicolon there you get a pleasant little feeling of expectancy; there is more to come; read on; it will get clearer.

Colons are a lot less attractive, for several reasons: firstly, they give you the feeling of being rather ordered around, or at least having your nose pointed in a direction you might not be inclined to take if left to yourself, and, secondly, you suspect you're in for one of those sentences that will be labeling the points to be made: firstly, secondly and so forth, with the implication that you haven't sense enough to keep track of a sequence of notions without having them numbered. Also, many writers use this system loosely and incompletely, starting out with number one and number two as though counting off on their fingers but then going on and on without the succession of labels you've been led to expect, leaving you floundering about searching for the ninthly or seventeenthly that ought to be there but isn't.

Exclamation points are the most irritating of all. Look! they say, look at what I just said! How amazing is my thought! It is like being forced to watch someone else's small child jumping up and down crazily in the center of the living room shouting to attract attention. If a sentence really has something of importance to say, something quite remarkable, it doesn't need a mark to point it out. And if it is really, after all, a banal

5

182

sentence needing more zing, the exclamation point simply emphasizes its banality!

Quotation marks should be used honestly and sparingly, when there is a genuine quotation at hand, and it is necessary to be very rigorous about the words enclosed by the marks. If something is to be quoted, the *exact* words must be used. If part of it must be left out because of space limitations, it is good manners to insert three dots to indicate the omission, but it is unethical to do this if it means connecting two thoughts which the original author did not intend to have tied together. Above all, quotation marks should not be used for ideas that you'd like to disown, things in the air so to speak. Nor should they be put in place around clichés; if you want to use a cliché you must take full responsibility for it yourself and not try to job it off on anon., or on society. The most objectionable misuse of quotation marks, but one which illustrates the dangers of misuse in ordinary prose, is seen in advertising, especially in advertisements for small restaurants, for example "just around the corner," or "a good place to eat." No single, identifiable, citable person ever really said, for the record, "just around the corner," much less "a good place to eat," least likely of all for restaurants of the type that use this type of prose.

The dash is a handy device, informal and essentially playful, telling you that you're about to take off on a different tack but still in some way connected with the present course — only you have to remember that the dash is there, and either put a second dash at the end of the notion to let the reader know that he's back on course, or else end the sentence, as here, with a period.

The greatest danger in punctuation is for poetry. Here it is necessary to be as economical and parsimonious with commas and periods as with the words themselves, and any marks that seem to carry their own subtle meanings, like dashes and little rows of periods, even semicolons and question marks, should be left out altogether rather than inserted to clog up the thing with ambiguity. A single exclamation point in a poem, no matter what else the poem has to say, is enough to destroy the whole work.

The things I like best in T. S. Eliot's poetry, especially in the *Four Quartets*, are the semicolons. You cannot hear them, but they are there, laying out the connections between the images and the ideas. Sometimes you get a glimpse of a semicolon coming, a few lines farther on, and it is like climbing a steep path through woods and seeing a wooden bench just at a bend in the road ahead, a place where you can expect to sit for a moment, catching your breath.

Commas can't do this sort of thing; they can only tell you how the different parts of a complicated thought are to be fitted together, but you can't sit, not even take a breath, just because of a comma,

10

183

WILLIAM ZINSSER

Clutter

William Zinsser was born in New York City, graduated from Princeton
University in 1944, and subsequently began a long association with the
New York Herald Tribune as a writer, editor, and critic. Since, Zinsser
has contributed to *Life* and the *New Yorker,* among other magazines.
His experience teaching writing at Yale (1970–1979) led to the publication of *On Writing Well* in 1976, now a classic guide for nonfiction writers in its seventh edition. In *On Writing Well*, Zinsser recounts his own
struggles to both master and impart on his students the writer's
"craft." His other books include *Writing to Learn* (1988) and *Writing
about Your Life: A Journey into the Past* (2004), a guide to memoir
encouraging writers to focus on small, authentic moments and to be
themselves in their writing. Zinsser's most recent work includes *Writing Places: The Life and Journey of a Writer and Teacher* (2010).

 In "Clutter," excerpted from *On Writing Well*, Zinsser identifies how
linguistic flourishes can often interfere with a writer's clarity. Language, according to Zinsser, must serve a purpose: A writer cannot
hold onto words simply because he or she thinks they are "beautiful."

Fighting clutter is like fighting weeds—the writer is always slightly
behind. New varieties sprout overnight, and by noon they are part of
American speech. Consider what President Nixon's aide John Dean
accomplished in just one day of testimony on television during the
Watergate hearings. The next day everyone in America was saying "at
this point in time" instead of "now."

 Consider all the prepositions that are draped onto verbs that don't
need any help. We no longer head committees. We head them up. We
don't face problems anymore. We face up to them when we can free up a
few minutes. A small detail, you may say—not worth bothering about. It
is worth bothering about. Writing improves in direct ratio to the number
of things we can keep out of it that shouldn't be there. "Up" in "free up"

William Zinsser, "Clutter." Chapter 3 from *On Writing Well*, Thirtieth Anniversary Edition, by William Zinsser, published by HarperCollins. Copyright © 1976, 1980, 1985,
1988, 1990, 1994, 1998, 2001, 2006 by William Zinsser. Reprinted by permission of the
author.

shouldn't be there. Examine every word you put on paper. You'll find a surprising number that don't serve any purpose.

Take the adjective "personal," as in "a personal friend of mine," "his personal feeling" or "her personal physician." It's typical of hundreds of words that can be eliminated. The personal friend has come into the language to distinguish him or her from the business friend, thereby debasing both language and friendship. Someone's feeling *is* that person's personal feeling—that's what "his" means. As for the personal physician, that's the man or woman summoned to the dressing room of a stricken actress so she won't have to be treated by the impersonal physician assigned to the theater. Someday I'd like to see that person identified as "her doctor." Physicians are physicians, friends are friends. The rest is clutter.

Clutter is the laborious phrase that has pushed out the short word that means the same thing. Even before John Dean, people had stopped saying "now." They were saying "currently" ("all our operators are currently assisting other customers"), or "at the present time," or "presently" (which means "soon"). Yet the idea can always be expressed by "now" to mean the immediate moment ("Now I can see him"), or by "today" to mean the historical present ("Today prices are high"), or simply by a form of the verb "to be" ("It is raining"). There's no need to say, "At the present time we are experiencing precipitation."

"Experiencing" is one of the worst clutterers. Even your dentist will 5 ask if you are experiencing any pain. If he had his own kid in the chair he would say, "Does it hurt?" He would, in short, be himself. By using a more pompous phrase in his professional role, he not only sounds more important; he blunts the painful edge of truth. It's the language of the flight attendant demonstrating the oxygen mask that will drop down if the plane should run out of air. "In the unlikely possibility that the aircraft should experience such an eventuality," she begins—a phrase so oxygen-depriving in itself that we are prepared for any disaster.

Clutter is the ponderous euphemism that turns a slum into a depressed socioeconomic area, garbage collectors into waste-disposal personnel and the town dump into the volume reduction unit. I think of Bill Mauldin's cartoon of two hoboes riding a freight car. One of them says, "I started as a simple bum, but now I'm hard-core unemployed." Clutter is political correctness gone amok. I saw an ad for a boys' camp designed to provide "individual attention for the minimally exceptional."

Clutter is the official language used by corporations to hide their mistakes. When the Digital Equipment Corporation eliminated 3,000 jobs its statement didn't mention layoffs; those were "involuntary methodologies." When an Air Force missile crashed, it "impacted with the ground prematurely." When General Motors had a plant shutdown, that was a "volume-related production-schedule adjustment." Companies that go belly-up have "a negative cash-flow position."

Clutter is the language of the Pentagon calling an invasion a "reinforced protective reaction strike" and justifying its vast budgets on the need for "counterforce deterrence." As George Orwell pointed out in "Politics and the English Language," an essay written in 1946 but often cited during the wars in Cambodia, Vietnam and Iraq, "political speech and writing are largely the defense of the indefensible. . . . Thus political language has to consist largely of euphemism, question-begging and sheer cloudy vagueness." Orwell's warning that clutter is not just a nuisance but a deadly tool has come true in the recent decades of American military adventurism. It was during George W. Bush's presidency that "civilian casualties" in Iraq became "collateral damage."

Verbal camouflage reached new heights during General Alexander Haig's tenure as President Reagan's secretary of state. Before Haig, nobody had thought of saying "at this juncture of maturization" to mean "now." He told the American people that terrorism could be fought with "meaningful sanctionary teeth" and that intermediate nuclear missiles were "at the vortex of cruciality." As for any worries that the public might harbor, his message was "leave it to Al," though what he actually said was, "We must push this to a lower decibel of public fixation. I don't think there's much of a learning curve to be achieved in this area of content."

I could go on quoting examples from various fields—every profession 10 has its growing arsenal of jargon to throw dust in the eyes of the populace. But the list would be tedious. The point of raising it now is to serve notice that clutter is the enemy. Beware, then, of the long word that's no better than the short word: "assistance" (help), "numerous" (many), "facilitate" (ease), "individual" (man or woman), "remainder" (rest), "initial" (first), "implement" (do), "sufficient" (enough), "attempt" (try), "referred to as" (called) and hundreds more. Beware of all the slippery new fad words: paradigm and parameter, prioritize and potentialize. They are all weeds that will smother what you write. Don't dialogue with someone you can talk to. Don't interface with anybody.

Just as insidious are the word clusters with which we explain how we propose to go about our explaining: "I might add," "It should be pointed out," "It is interesting to note." If you might add, add it. If it should be pointed out, point it out. If it is interesting to note, *make* it interesting; are we not all stupefied by what follows when someone says, "This will interest you"? Don't inflate what needs no inflating: "with the possible exception of" (except), "due to the fact that" (because), "he totally lacked the ability to" (he couldn't), "until such time as" (until), "for the purpose of" (for).

Is there any way to recognize clutter at a glance? Here's a device my students at Yale found helpful. I would put brackets around every component in a piece of writing that wasn't doing useful work. Often just one word got bracketed: the unnecessary preposition appended to a verb ("order up"), or the adverb that carries the same meaning as the verb ("smile happily"), or the adjective that states a known fact ("tall skyscraper"). Often my brackets surrounded the little qualifiers that weaken any sentence they inhabit ("a bit," "sort of"), or phrases like "in a sense," which don't mean anything. Sometimes my brackets surrounded an entire sentence—the one that essentially repeats what the previous sentence said, or that says something readers don't need to know or can figure out for themselves. Most first drafts can be cut by 50 percent without losing any information or losing the author's voice.

My reason for bracketing the students' superfluous words, instead of crossing them out, was to avoid violating the students' sacred prose. I wanted to leave the sentence intact for them to analyze. I was saying, "I may be wrong, but I think this can be deleted and the meaning won't be affected. But *you* decide. Read the sentence without the bracketed material and see if it works." In the early weeks of the term I handed back papers that were festooned with brackets. Entire paragraphs were bracketed. But soon the students learned to put mental brackets around their own clutter, and by the end of the term their papers were almost clean. Today many of those students are professional writers, and they tell me, "I still see your brackets—they're following me through life."

You can develop the same eye. Look for the clutter in your writing and prune it ruthlessly. Be grateful for everything you can throw away. Reexamine each sentence you put on paper. Is every word doing new work? Can any thought be expressed with more economy? Is anything pompous or pretentious or faddish? Are you hanging on to something useless just because you think it's beautiful?

Simplify, simplify.   15

[1976]